Fixing Your Computer

ABSOLUTE
BEGINNER'S
GUIDE

Paul McFedries

800 E
Indian

Fixing Your Computer Absolute Beginner's Guide

ISBN-13: 978-0-7897-5122-5
ISBN-10: 0-7897-5122-4

Library of Congress Control Number: 2013940849

Printed in the United States of America

First Printing: July 2013

Trademarks

Warning and Disclaimer

Bulk Sales

Que Publishing offers excellent discounts on this book when ordered in quantity for bulk purchases or special sales. For more information, please contact

U.S. Corporate and Government Sales
1-800-382-3419
corpsales@pearsontechgroup.com

For sales outside the United States, please contact

International Sales
international@pearsoned.com

Editor-in-Chief
Greg Wiegand

Executive Editor
Rick Kughen

Managing Editor
Sandra Schroeder

Project Editor
Seth Kerney

Copy Editor
Chuck Hutchinson

Indexer
Heather McNeill

Proofreader
Jess DeGabriele

Technical Editor
Karen Weinstein

Publishing Coordinator
Kristen Watterson

Book Designer
Anne Jones

Compositor
TnT Design, Inc.

Contents at a Glance

Table of Contents

About the Author

Paul McFedries is full-time technical writer and passionate computer tinkerer. He is the author of more than 80 computer books that have sold more than four million copies worldwide. His recent titles include the Sams Publishing books *Windows 7 Unleashed* and *Windows Home Server 2011 Unleashed*, and the Que Publishing books *PCs for Grownups*, *Windows 8 In Depth* (coauthored with Brian Knittel), *Formulas and Functions with Microsoft Excel 2013*, and *My Office 2013 RT*. Paul is also the proprietor of Word Spy (www.wordspy.com), a website devoted to tracking new words and phrases as they enter the English language. Paul's web home is at www.mcfedries.com, and he can be followed on Twitter at twitter.com/paulmcf and twitter.com/wordspy.

Dedication

For Karen

Acknowledgments

In this book you learn that with a bit of know-how, a modicum of patience, and perhaps a screwdriver or two, you can repair a PC all by yourself. This makes repairing a computer a lot different from publishing a book. Oh, sure, I wrote this book all by myself, but the finished product you're reading now was a group effort, no doubt about it. For proof, go back a bit and read the credits page, which lists everyone who had a finger in this particular publishing pie, and I thank them all for doing such a good job on this book. Some of those people I worked with directly, so I'd like to take a second to thank them personally. Rick "Two Hats" Kughen was both the book's acquisitions editor and its development editor, and I'm mighty glad on both counts because this book was a hoot to write, and Rick's editorial direction and suggestions were right on the money and made this book many notches better than it would have been otherwise. Seth Kerney was the book's amazingly competent and organized project editor. Chuck Hutchinson was the book's copy editor, and besides dotting my i's and crossing my t's, Chuck gave the book a consistent style and tone, which requires concentration, confidence, and an eagle eye. Karen Weinstein was the book's technical editor, and I continue to be amazed at just how much Karen knows about almost all aspects of computing. Her experience and insights were very much welcome in this book. Finally, I'd be sorely remiss if I didn't also single out Karen Hammond, who took the wonderful photographs you see throughout this book.

We Want to Hear from You!

As the reader of this book, you are our most important critic and commentator. We value your opinion and want to know what we're doing right, what we could do better, what areas you'd like to see us publish in, and any other words of wisdom you're willing to pass our way.

We welcome your comments. You can email or write to let us know what you did or didn't like about this book—as well as what we can do to make our books better.

Please note that we cannot help you with technical problems related to the topic of this book.

When you write, please be sure to include this book's title and author as well as your name and email address. We will carefully review your comments and share them with the author and editors who worked on the book.

Email: feedback@quepublishing.com

Mail: Que Publishing
        ATTN: Reader Feedback
        800 East 96th Street
        Indianapolis, IN 46240 USA

Reader Services

Visit our website and register this book at quepublishing.com/register for convenient access to any updates, downloads, or errata that might be available for this book.

INTRODUCTION

One of the hallmarks of our age is the decline of the do-it-yourselfer in favor of the hire-an-expert-to-do-it-insteader. Toilet not flushing? Hire a plumber. Porch falling down? Hire a carpenter. Lights on the blink? Hire an electrician. You could argue, as many people have done, that a return to a DIY ethos would be good for society and good for the soul. The reality is that most of us don't have enough knowledge, skills, or time to repair a toilet, rebuild a porch, or replace a light switch without seriously electrocuting ourselves.

However, I would argue that one area where we almost always do *not* need to hire an expert is the digital domain of the PC. That statement might strike you as a tad crazy. After all, what could be more complicated, heck more *intimidating*, than a PC and all its mysterious electronics? Yes, it's certainly true that a typical PC is a head-scratchingly complex collection of transistors, chips, and diodes, a kind of Rube Goldberg machine for the digital age. But it's also true that when a PC fails in some way, it almost always fails in a relatively *simple* way. Most PC problems are solved just by tweaking a setting, updating some software, or by merely rebooting the computer! Other problems require replacing parts, but this is a task that's easily learned by any curious and motivated beginner.

I'm talking, of course, about *you*. Learning how to fix your PC is fun and nowhere as hard as you might think, for three reasons:

- All the parts you need—the power supply, memory, hard drive, expansion cards, and so on—are readily available online or from big-box retailers or electronics stores.
- All the tools you need—really not much more than a screwdriver or two—are part of most people's toolkits or can be easily obtained.
- All the techniques you need—inserting chips and cards, connecting cables, and tightening screws—are simple and straightforward.

Add to this the simple fact that repairing your own PC is better than hiring someone else to do it because it's cheaper, faster, and you get an empowering sense of ownership and accomplishment. Besides, repairing your own PC is both educational and just plain fun, so it's no wonder that so many people nowadays are going (or would like to go) the fix-it-yourself route.

FIY: Fix-It-Yourself

Welcome, then, to *Fixing Your Computer Absolute Beginner's Guide*, the book that will be your guide on this fix-it-yourself path. This book shows you everything you need to know to maintain, upgrade, and repair a PC. Even if you've never looked inside a computer and wouldn't know a motherboard from an expansion board or a CPU from a GPU, this book gives you the know-how and confidence to fix a PC with your bare hands.

To that end, the first part of the book shows you a few useful PC maintenance chores and techniques. You learn how to maintain the PC hardware (Chapter 1), maintain Windows (Chapter 2), and prepare your PC for any trouble that might come down the road (Chapter 3).

The second part of the book switches to troubleshooting and repair mode, where you learn some usefully universal troubleshooting techniques (Chapter 4), how to troubleshoot your PC's hardware (Chapter 5), how to recover from problems (Chapter 6), and how to get your network back up and running (Chapter 7).

Finally, the third part of the book lets you get your hands dirty (metaphorically speaking) by taking you through a number of PC upgrade and repair projects. After first showing you some basic repair skills (Chapter 8) and how to buy PC parts (Chapter 9), you learn how to upgrade or replace the power supply (Chapter 10), the hard drive (Chapter 11), the CD or DVD drive (Chapter 12), the memory (Chapter 13), the video card and monitor (Chapter 14), the sound system (Chapter 15), the processor (Chapter 16), the laptop battery (Chapter 17), and the network (Chapter 18).

Who Should Read This Book?

This book is aimed at budding PC fixer-uppers who want to try their hand at repairing a broken PC and at upgrading a PC to get more life or performance out of it. This book should also appeal to people who have tried other books in the same field, only to find them too intimidating, too simplistic, or too cutesy.

To that end, this book includes the following features:

- Buyer's guides that enable you to make smart and informed choices when purchasing hardware

- Easy-to-follow explanations of key concepts

- Extensive use of clear and detailed photos to illustrate hardware and all fixing and upgrading techniques

- Tips, tricks, and shortcuts to make fixing and upgrading a PC easier and faster

- A friendly and lightly humorous tone that I hope will help you feel at home with the subject and keep boredom at bay

Conventions Used in This Book

To make your life easier, this book includes various features and conventions that help you get the most out of this book and out of fixing a PC:

Steps	Throughout the book, I've broken many building, upgrading, and repairing tasks into easy-to-follow step-by-step procedures.
Things you type	Whenever I suggest that you type something, what you type appears in a `bold monospace` font.
Filenames, folder names, and code	These things appear in a `monospace` font.
Commands	Commands and their syntax use the **bold** font.
Pull-down menu commands	I use the following style for all application menu commands: *Menu, Command*, where *Menu* is the name of the menu you pull down and *Command* is the name of the command you select. Here's an example: File, Open. This means you pull down the File menu and select the Open command.

This book also uses the following boxes to draw your attention to important (or merely interesting) information:

 NOTE   The Note box presents asides that give you more information about the current topic. These tidbits provide extra insights that offer a better understanding of the task.

 TIP   The Tip box tells you about methods that are easier, faster, or more efficient than the standard methods.

 CAUTION   The all-important Caution box tells you about potential accidents waiting to happen. There are always ways to mess things up when you're working with computers. These boxes help you avoid those traps and pitfalls.

1

MAINTAINING YOUR PC

You might be tempted just to let your PC sit there whirring away day in and day out while you go about your digital business. However, this live-and-let-compute attitude can lead to big problems down the road. Why? Because a computer is a machine and, like any machine ever produced by the hand of man, it needs some occasional maintenance to keep it working smoothly and reliably. Happily, as you see in this chapter, these maintenance chores really are only "occasional," so keeping your PC healthy won't take up a big chunk of your precious time.

Cleaning the PC

One of the things I've noticed about working with PCs is that every new computer always strikes me as a beautiful piece of machinery. Objectively, I know that most PCs are just plain vanilla (or whatever) boxes, but there's something about a new machine that makes it look like a work of computing art. However, in the long run, a PC is only as good-looking as it is clean and, most unfortunately, computers never stay clean for very long. The screen gets fingerprints on it; the keyboard collects crumbs and other particles; the mouse gets grimy; and, unless you've got some kind of heavy-duty air purifier on the job, all computer parts are world-class dust magnets.

To keep your computer looking sharp, you should give it a thorough cleaning every so often. How often? That depends on your own cleanliness standards and outside factors such as how dusty your room is. On average, though, twice a year ought to be good enough in most cases.

Dust: Your PC's Worst Nightmare

Your PC has interior fans that serve to flow air through the system and keep it cool. It usually has at least one intake fan that brings in cool air from the outside of the case and at least one exhaust fan that blows out hot air from inside the case. Unfortunately, in most environments the intake fan brings in lots of junk along with the outside air: mostly dust, but also human hair, pet hair, carpet fibers, and whatever else might be hanging around at ground level. Most of this grime takes up residence inside the case, which can be very bad for your computer's health:

- Dust collects on electrical connections, which can make those connections unreliable.

- A component that's covered in dust will retain more heat, which could cause it to perform erratically or even to fail because of overheating.

- The excess heat that dusty components generate causes your overall system to run hotter. This can make your system louder (because the fans have to work harder to cool the system) and can shorten the life span of crucial components such as the processor.

Dust, clearly, is a bad thing, but how should you deal with it? There are two ways to tackle the dust problem:

- **Compressed gas or air**—This is a can of air or a gas such as carbon dioxide under pressure, and you use it to blow away dust and other debris. I'm not a huge fan of this method because all it tends to do is blow the dust back into the air where it will simply settle elsewhere. However, it's often useful for getting to dust in areas where a vacuum (discussed next) can't reach.

CAUTION If you use canned air, be sure to always keep the can upright to avoid spraying liquid over your components!

- **Vacuum**—Be sure to use an attachment that has soft bristles to avoid damaging any of the sensitive electronics inside your PC. If you want to take things up a notch, get a computer vacuum, which has attachments specifically designed for cleaning computers, as shown in Figure 1.1. If you want to go the whole hog, get an electronics vacuum that has an antistatic feature (and a hefty price tag, too).

 TIP Ideally, the vacuum's hose and attachments don't have any metal parts that could damage a PC's components. If you're looking to buy a vacuum, get one with all-plastic accessories.

FIGURE 1.1

A vacuum designed to work with computers and other electronic components.

Cleaning the Screen, Keyboard, and Mouse

The most frequent objects of your cleaning duties will be the screen (because you look at it all day) and the mouse and keyboard (because you handle them all day). Here are the basic cleaning steps for these components:

1. Turn off and unplug the PC and the monitor, and remove any other cables attached to the PC.

2. Use a soft, dry, clean cloth to wipe any excess dust from the screen, keyboard, and mouse. If these components are still dirty (fingerprints, smudges, and so on), continue with the remaining steps.

3. Take a soft, clean cloth and dampen it with water. Be sure to merely dampen the cloth because you don't want there to be any excess water that might drip off the cloth.

CAUTION   Never spray water or any other liquid onto an LCD screen. The liquid could seep into the monitor and damage the electronics.

TIP   If water seems too low-tech of a solution (pun intended), give Klear Screen a try. It comes in a kit form that contains iKlear, an anti-static screen polish, and a soft chamois cloth. See www.klearscreen.com for more information. Another good product is Monster iClean Screen Cleaner (see www.monstercable.com/productdisplay.asp?pin=2105).

4. Use the damp cloth to wipe the screen, keyboard, and mouse.

5. Using a soft brush attachment, vacuum your keyboard to suck up any dust or other particles that have settled in between (and even below) the keys. (If you can't get a particular piece of debris out from under a key, you can usually pop off the key, vacuum up the offending particle, and then reattach the key.)

Cleaning the Front and Back of the PC

The exterior of the PC collects a ton of dust over time, which not only looks ugly but also can harm your computer, as I described earlier. Here are the basic steps you should follow to clean the exterior (I cover the power supply separately in the next section):

1. If you haven't done so already, turn off and unplug the PC and the monitor, and remove any other cables attached to the PC.

2. On the front of the PC, check for and, if necessary, vacuum any dust accumulating around the DVD/CD drive. If your vacuum has a micro-crevice attachment (see Figure 1.2), use it to suck up the dust in the crevices around the drive.

FIGURE 1.2

Vacuum the dust around the DVD/CD drive, ideally with a micro-crevice attachment.

3. Vacuum any dust accumulating around the memory card reader, if your PC has one.

4. Dust always builds up around the case's front intake fan (see Figure 1.3), so give that area of the case a good vacuum.

FIGURE 1.3

Vacuum the dust around the opening to the case's front intake fan.

5. Use a soft brush attachment to vacuum any dust accumulating around the ports that are on the front of the PC.

6. On the back of the PC, use a soft brush attachment to vacuum any dust accumulating around the device connectors (see Figure 1.4).

FIGURE 1.4

In the back of the PC, vacuum the dust around the connectors using a soft brush attachment.

7. The case grill that covers the exhaust fan is a prime spot for dust to collect (see Figure 1.5), so give that area a thorough vacuuming.

FIGURE 1.5

Vacuum the dust collecting on the exhaust fan grill.

8. Vacuum any other stray dust that you see on rear of the computer.

Cleaning the Power Supply

In Chapter 10, "Replacing the Power Supply," I introduce you to the power supply and make the case that it is one of the most important components in any PC because your machine needs a strong and steady supply of power to operate efficiently and steadily. The importance of the power supply also means you should take extra care to keep it clean, so I'll cover the cleaning of this component separately.

→ For more on the power supply, **see** "Getting to Know the Power Supply," **p. 156**.

Cleaning the power supply requires both external and internal steps, as follows:

1. If you haven't done so already, turn off and unplug the PC and the monitor and remove any other cables attached to the PC.

2. Use a soft brush attachment to vacuum any dust on the grill that covers the power supply, as shown in Figure 1.6.

TIP   How can you tell which grill on the back of the PC belongs to the power supply? Almost all power supply units come with two features that can help you locate the correct grill: the connector for the PC's power cable and an on/off switch for the power supply itself, both of which are pointed out in Figure 1.6.

Power supply on/off switch

PC power cable connector

FIGURE 1.6

Vacuum the dust from the power supply grill.

3. If the back of the power supply (the part you see when you look at the back of the computer case) has a removable grill, detach the grill. (The grill is usually held in place with four screws.)

4. Use a soft brush attachment to vacuum dust from the blades of the power supply's fan.

 TIP   If the fan blades rotate as you try to vacuum them, insert a screwdriver or long, thin vacuum attachment between the grill (if it's still on) to hold the fan blades in place while you vacuum.

5. Open the computer case.

→ To learn how to open the case, **see** "Opening the Computer Case," **p. 125**.

6. Use a soft brush attachment to vacuum the front of the power supply, as shown in Figure 1.7.

FIGURE 1.7

Vacuum the dust from the front of the power supply inside the case.

 CAUTION While you're on a roll, you might be tempted to open the power supply case to clean inside. Don't do it! Power supplies can retain huge voltages for long periods, so by messing around inside the power supply case, you risk a massive (and possible life-threatening) shock.

We'll continue our cleaning duties inside the case in the next section, so leave your case open for now if you're following along.

Cleaning the Interior

It's important both aesthetically and functionally to keep dust and other grime off the outside of your PC, but cleanliness is paramount on the inside of the machine because the most sensitive components are found there. Here's a general cleaning procedure to follow on the inside of the PC:

1. If you haven't done so already, turn off and unplug the PC and the monitor, remove any other cables attached to the PC, and open the case.

→ Again, to learn how to open the PC's case, **see** "Opening the Computer Case," **p. 125**.

2. It's always best to clean from the top to the bottom, so vacuum the front of the power supply, if you haven't already done so. (I'm assuming here that your case has a top-mounted power supply. If your power supply is bottom-mounted instead, clean it last.)

3. Use a soft brush attachment to vacuum the cables, the DVD/CD drive and hard drive connections, and the empty drive bays.

4. In the middle of the PC you should see a largish fan, which is the fan used to cool the processor. Use a soft brush attachment to vacuum the fan's blades.

5. If you have a small brush attachment, use it to clean the blades of the case fans, as shown in Figure 1.8.

FIGURE 1.8

Vacuum the dust from the case fan blades.

6. Use the softest brush attachment you have to carefully vacuum the expansion cards, as shown in Figure 1.9.

FIGURE 1.9

Use a soft brush attachment to vacuum dust from the expansion cards and their slots.

 CAUTION   Avoid using a really powerful vacuum to clean sensitive internal parts because the strong suction on such a vacuum could loosen or damage components. Either dial back the vacuum speed (if possible) or get a vacuum designed for electronics, which uses far less suction than most ordinary vacuums.

 TIP   If the grime on any component resists the vacuum, use a small brush—I use a photographer's lens-cleaning brush, but a new paint brush or makeup brush will also do the job—to loosen the dirt and then vacuum it up. Be sure to use slow, light strokes to avoid building up static electricity.

7. If you see dust accumulated in the slot used by an expansion card or memory module, remove the component, vacuum the slot, and then reinsert the component.

➜ To learn how to work with expansion cards, **see** "Installing an Expansion Card," **p. 135**.

➜ To learn how to work with memory modules, **see** "Pulling Out the Old Memory Modules," **p. 205**.

TIP   With the card or module out of its slot, this is a great time to clean the contacts. You can use a soft, lint-free cloth for this, or you can get contact cleaning solution specially designed for cleaning electronic contacts.

8. Vacuum the case floor.

9. If the case has one or more air filters, remove the filters, run them through warm water to remove the dust, use a lint-free cloth to dry the filters, and then reinsert them.

Checking Free Disk Space

Hard disks with capacities measured in the hundreds of gigabytes are standard even in low-end systems nowadays, and multiterabyte hard disks are now commonplace. This means that disk space is much less of a problem than it used to be. Still, you need to keep track of how much free space you have on your disk drives.

Follow these steps to check the free disk space on your PC's drives:

1. Open the Computer folder, which displays icons for the disk drives on your PC:

   • **Windows 8**—On the Start screen, type `computer` and then select Computer in the search results.

   • **Earlier versions of Windows**—Click Start and then click Computer.

2. In Windows 8, select the View tab; in earlier versions of Windows, pull down the View menu.

3. In the Layout list, select Tiles. Windows displays the disk drive icons as shown in Figure 1.10.

4. Examine the icons for your disk drives:

   • Each icon has a caption of the form X free of Y, where X is the number of gigabytes (GB) or megabytes (MB) of free space and Y is the total capacity of the drive.

   • Each icon displays a horizontal bar that uses a color strip to give you a visual indication of how full the drive is. If the colored portion of that bar is blue, it means the drive still has plenty of free space; if it's red, instead, it means the drive is running low on disk space.

NOTE   On your PC, the drive where the Windows files are installed is called the *system drive*. You can spot it in the Computer window by looking for the drive that has the Windows logo, as pointed out in Figure 1.10.

This logo tells you this is the Windows (system) drive

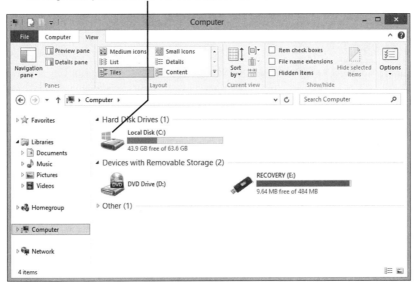

FIGURE 1.10

The Computer folder tells you the total size and free space on your system's disks.

Dealing with Hard Disk Errors

Our hard disks store our programs and, most important, our precious data, so they have a special place in the computing firmament. They ought to be pampered and coddled to ensure a long and trouble-free existence, but that's rarely the case, unfortunately. Just consider everything that a modern hard disk has to put up with:

- **General wear and tear**—If your computer is running right now, its hard disk is spinning away at probably 7,200 revolutions per minute. That's right, even though you're not doing anything, the hard disk is hard at work. Because of this constant activity, most hard disks simply wear out after a few years.

- **The old bump-and-grind**—Your hard disk includes *read/write heads* that are used to read data from and write data to the disk. These heads float on a cushion of air just above the spinning hard disk platters. A bump or jolt of sufficient intensity can send them crashing onto the surface of the disk, which could easily result in trashed data. If the heads happen to hit a particularly sensitive area, the entire hard disk could crash. Notebook computers are particularly prone to this problem.

> **NOTE** I should say that your hard disk is *probably* spinning away and *probably* has read/write heads. A type of hard drive called a *solid-state drive* (SSD, for short) is becoming increasingly popular, in part because it has no moving mechanical parts. This means that such drives are not prone to wear-and-tear and can survive even intense bumps with nary a hiccup.

- **Power surges**—The current supplied to your PC is, under normal conditions, relatively constant. It's possible, however, for massive power surges to assail your computer (for example, during a lightning storm). These surges can wreak havoc on a carefully arranged hard disk (although plugging your PC into a device called a *surge protector* can help prevent this).

So, what can you do about this? Before Windows 8 came along, you had basically two choices:

- Wait until Windows recognized a disk error (for example, when you tried to open a corrupted file). In this case, Windows would run a program called Check Disk that scanned your hard disk for problems and could repair them automatically.

- Run the Check Disk program yourself on a regular schedule (say, once a month or so) or when you suspected a hard disk error.

In both cases, Windows would not be able to run Check Disk right away on the Windows drive (usually drive C) because it had files in use. Instead, Windows would schedule Check Disk to run during the next boot. (Windows would be able to run Check Disk immediately on any other drive.)

The major downside to all this was that Check Disk would have to take the Windows drive out of commission temporarily to scan and repair it. That wasn't a big deal for a small hard disk, but with drive capacities getting into the hundreds and then thousands of gigabytes, these disk scans were taking forever. And the more full the drive was (technically, the more files it stored), the longer the check would take, sometimes several hours for extremely large disks with tons of files.

The solution to this dilemma is a Windows 8 feature called *self-healing*, where certain disk errors can be fixed on-the-fly without having to take the entire drive offline. This feature was introduced in Windows Vista, where it applied to only a few relatively rare errors, but in Windows 8, Microsoft has significantly increased the number of problems that can be self-healed. This means that many drive errors will get fixed behind the scenes without your even knowing an error occurred (and, more importantly, without having to take the Windows drive offline).

Understanding Hard Drive Health States

From a hard drive point of view, the main difference between Windows 8 and its predecessors is that Windows 8 now maintains a running assessment of the current health of the drive. Specifically, Windows 8 always sees your hard drive as currently in one of the five following states:

- **Healthy**—This state means that your hard drive is online and currently has no errors or corruption. When you open the Action Center's Maintenance section (press Windows Logo+W, type **action**, and then select Action Center), the Drive Status value shows "All drives are working properly," as you can see in Figure 1.11.

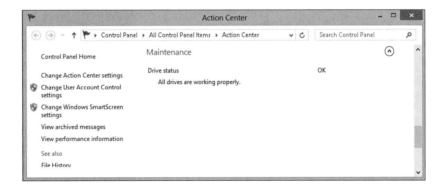

FIGURE 1.11

Action Center's Drive Status when your hard drives are healthy.

- **Self-healing**—This state means that Windows 8 has detected an error and is in the process of repairing it using self-healing. This transient state lasts a very short time, and you see no indication either on the desktop or in the Action Center.

- **Error verification**—This state means that Windows 8 has detected a possible hard drive error that it can't self-heal. I say "possible" because some problems that appear to be hard drive corruption are actually intermittent memory errors. Rather than just escalating the health status to the next level, Windows 8 runs a new feature called the *spot verification service*, which attempts to verify that the error is a drive-related one. This is also a transient state that lasts a very short time.

- **Scan required**—This state means that the spot verification service has confirmed the hard drive error and the system now needs to scan the hard drive. That scan is scheduled to run during the next automatic maintenance window. However, as you can see in Figure 1.12, the Action Center shows a `Scan drive for errors` message, and you can run the scan immediately by clicking the Run Scan button. The drive remains online, and you can work normally while the scan runs. During the scan, Windows 8 logs the error, determines the precise fix required, and escalates the health status to the next level.

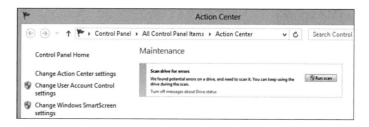

FIGURE 1.12

Action Center shows "Scan drive for errors" when Windows 8 detects a hard drive error.

- **Restart required**—This state occurs after the drive scan has logged the error and determined the repair that's required, which Windows 8 calls a *spot fix*. The notification area displays a `Restart to repair drive errors` message, and the same message appears in the Action Center, as shown in Figure 1.13. You can click Restart to begin the spot fix process. Because the full hard drive has already been scanned and the needed fix has already been determined, repairing the hard drive adds only a few seconds to the restart. Note that the restart is *required* to repair the system drive (which must go offline to affect the repairs), but is actually *optional* for all other drives. Windows 8 displays the restart message for all drives so that users don't have to take any direct action to repair the drive. However, for nonsystem drives, users can initiate the repair manually without a restart, as I describe in the next section.

FIGURE 1.13

Action Center shows "Restart to repair drive errors" when Windows 8 is ready to fix a hard drive problem.

Repairing a Drive Manually

On a multidrive system, when Windows 8 is ready to spot fix a drive and it alerts you that a restart is required, it is unfortunately vague as to which drive requires the repair. If you'd rather not restart at this time, you can check the drives yourself and, if the repair is required on a nonsystem drive, you can run the repair manually to avoid the restart.

If you're running an earlier version of Windows, if you're having trouble with your system (for example, a program is having trouble opening a file or is crashing), repairing the hard drive where the file or program is stored can sometimes help. Unlike in Windows 8, however, with earlier versions of Windows, you usually have to initiate the repair process yourself.

Follow these steps:

1. Open the Computer folder:

   - **Windows 8**—On the Start screen, type **computer** and then select Computer in the search results.

   - **Earlier versions of Windows**—Click Start and then click Computer.

2. Right-click the first hard drive (this is usually drive C, which is almost always the system drive; look for the Windows logo on the drive icon as pointed out earlier in Figure 1.10) and then click Properties. The drive's Properties dialog box appears.

3. Display the Tools tab.

4. Click the Check button. (In some versions of Windows, you click Check Now instead.)

5. In Windows 7 and earlier, make sure the Automatically Fix File System Errors check box is selected, select the Scan for and Attempt Recovery of Bad Sectors check box, then click Start.

6. Follow the instructions that appear onscreen. In Windows 8, one of two things will happen:

   - You see the message `You don't need to scan this drive`. This message means the drive is in the Healthy state, so no repair is necessary. You can click Cancel and then repeat steps 2–4 to check the next drive.

   - You see the message `Repair this drive`, as shown in Figure 1.14. If this is the system drive, you need to restart your computer to repair the drive. Otherwise, continue with step 5.

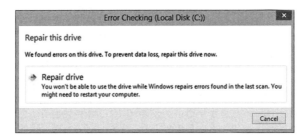

FIGURE 1.14

Check each hard drive until you see this message.

7. Click Repair Drive. Windows 8 repairs the nonsystem drive and returns its status to Healthy.

THE ABSOLUTE MINIMUM

This chapter got your PC maintenance education off to a good start by taking you through a few useful chores for keeping your hardware in top shape. Here are a few key points to take with you:

- Dust can cause untold havoc on sensitive PC parts, so your main PC cleaning goal should be to avoid dust bunnies in your PC.

- The main source of interior PC dirt is the fan that brings outside air into the PC for cooling. This fan also tends to bring in dust, hair, and other particles, so be sure to clean the fan both inside and out.

- Interior fans such as the one associated with the processor's cooler and the PC's exhaust fan are also prime dust areas.

- Take extra care when cleaning inside a PC to avoid loosening or damaging parts.

- The system drive is the hard drive where Windows is stored. To determine which drive is the system drive, open the Computer window and look for the drive that has the Windows logo.

- To check any drive's free space, open the Computer window and switch to the Tiles view.

- To repair a drive, open the Computer window, right-click the drive, click Properties, select the Tools tab, and then click Check (or Check Now).

IN THIS CHAPTER

- Decluttering your PC by getting rid of old files that it no longer needs
- Boosting your PC's performance by defragmenting your files
- Keeping your programs running smoothly by repairing and updating them
- Keeping Windows young at heart by installing the latest updates
- Giving the bum's rush to programs and devices that have worn out their welcome

2

MAINTAINING WINDOWS

Windows is your PC's operating system, which means that it controls, monitors, and oversees almost everything that happens with your PC's hardware and software. So a big part of PC maintenance involves maintaining Windows itself and using the tools that Windows provides to maintain your files, programs, and devices. This chapter is your guide to the most useful of these tools.

Deleting Unnecessary Files

In Chapter 1, "Maintaining Your PC," you learned how to check how much free space is left on your hard drive. What are you supposed to do if you find that your hard drive is getting low on free space? The first thing you should do is delete any unneeded files. How are you supposed to know which files are "unneeded"? Fortunately, you don't have to because Windows comes with a tool called Disk Cleanup that enables you to remove certain types of files quickly and easily, including the following:

- **Downloaded program files**—Small web page programs downloaded onto your hard drive.

- **Temporary Internet files**—Copies of web pages that Internet Explorer keeps on hand so the pages view faster the next time you visit them. Deleting these files slows down some of your web surfing slightly but also rescues lots of disk space.

- **Offline web pages**—Web page copies stored on your hard drive for offline viewing.

- **Recycle Bin**—The files that you've deleted recently. Windows stores them in the Recycle Bin just in case you delete a file accidentally. If you're sure you don't need to recover a file, you can clean out the Recycle Bin and recover the disk space.

- **Temporary files**—"Scratch pad" files that some programs use to doodle on while they're up and running. Most programs toss out these files, but a program or computer crash can prevent that from happening; delete these files at will.

- **Thumbnails**—Copies of picture files used by Windows to quickly display thumbnail versions of those files. If you delete them, Windows will re-create them as needed.

Here's how the process works:

1. Open the Computer folder, which displays icons for the disk drives on your PC:

    - **Windows 8**—On the Start screen, type **computer** and then select Computer in the search results.

    - **Earlier versions of Windows**—Click Start and then click Computer.

2. Right-click the drive you want to clean up and then click Properties. The drive's Properties dialog box appears.

3. Click Disk Cleanup. Disk Cleanup scans the drive to see which files can be deleted. Be patient. This process might take a few minutes.

4. Click Clean Up System Files. Disk Cleanup displays an expanded list of file types, as shown in Figure 2.1.

FIGURE 2.1

Disk Cleanup can automatically and safely remove certain types of files from a disk drive.

5. In the Files to Delete list, activate the check box beside each category of file you want to remove. If you're not sure what an item represents, select it and read the text in the Description box below. Note, too, that for most of these items, you can click View Files to see what you'll be deleting.

6. Click OK. Disk Cleanup asks whether you're sure that you want to delete the files.

7. Click Delete Files. Disk Cleanup deletes the selected files.

Defragmenting Your Hard Disk

Windows 8 comes with a utility called Defragment and Optimize Drives that's an essential tool for tuning your hard disk. (In earlier versions of Windows, this utility was called Disk Defragmenter.) The job of Defragment and Optimize Drives is to rid your hard disk of file fragmentation.

File fragmentation is one of those terms that sounds scarier than it actually is. It simply means that a file is stored on your hard disk in scattered bits, rather than all together. Having files stored this way is a performance drag because it means that when Windows tries to open such a file, it must make several stops to collect the various pieces. If a lot of files are fragmented, even the fastest hard disk can slow to a crawl.

The good news is that Windows configures Defragment and Optimize Drives to run automatically; the default schedule is once a week. This means you should never need to defragment your system manually. However, you might want to run a defragment before loading a particularly large software program.

Before using Defragment and Optimize Drives, you should delete any files from your hard disk that you don't need, as described in the "Deleting Unnecessary Files" section earlier in this chapter. Defragmenting junk files only slows down the whole process.

Follow these steps to use Defragment and Optimize Drives:

1. Start the program (see Figure 2.2):

   - **Windows 8**—On the Start screen, press Windows Logo+W to open the Settings search pane, type **defrag**, and then click Defragment and Optimize Your Drives in the search results.

   - **Earlier versions of Windows**—Select Start, All Programs, Accessories, System Tools, Disk Defragmenter.

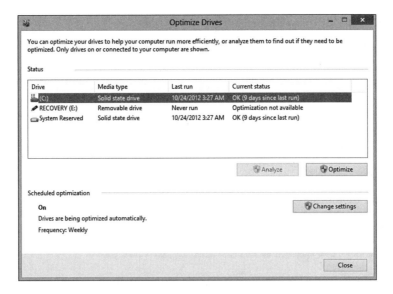

FIGURE 2.2

Use Defragment and Optimize Drives to eliminate file fragmentation and improve hard disk performance.

2. Click the drive you want to defragment.

3. Click Optimize (in earlier versions of Windows, the button is named Defragment Disk or Defragment Now). Windows defragments your hard drive.

4. When the defragment is complete, click Close.

 TIP In some cases, you can defragment a drive even further by running Defragment and Optimize Drives on the drive twice in a row. (That is, run the defragment, and when it's done, immediately run a second defragment.)

Repairing, Updating, and Uninstalling Programs

A big part of your routine PC maintenance chores will involve working with the programs installed on your computer, whether they're apps that you run using the new Windows 8 interface, or programs that run on the desktop. The next few sections show you how to repair, update, and uninstall programs.

Repairing a Software Installation

If you find that an application is crashing or behaving erratically, one common cause is that one or more of the application's internal files have become corrupted. You can often resolve such problems by uninstalling and then reinstalling the application. However, some desktop programs come with a repair feature that examines the program's files and replaces any that are corrupted or missing. Here's how it works:

1. Open the Programs and Features window, which operates as a kind of one-stop shop for your installed desktop programs (see Figure 2.3):

   - **Windows 8**—On the Start screen, press Windows Logo+W to open the Settings search pane, type **programs**, and then click Programs and Features in the search results.

   - **Earlier versions of Windows**—Select Start, Control Panel, Uninstall a Program.

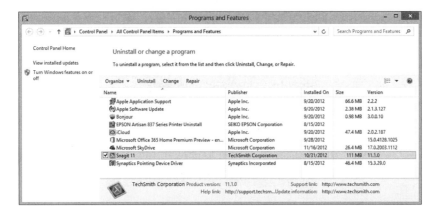

FIGURE 2.3

You use the Programs and Features window to modify, repair, and uninstall desktop programs.

2. Click the program you want to fix.

3. Click the Repair command in the taskbar (see Figure 2.3 for an example), if one exists for the program (not all programs offer this feature).

When you click Repair, one of two things happens:

- Windows launches the application's repair program immediately.

- Windows launches the application's install program, and you then select the repair option.

Updating Windows 8 Apps

After a software company releases an app, its programmers continue to work on it. They add new features, improve existing features, fix problems, and close security holes. After fully testing these improvements and fixes, they place the new version of the app in the Windows Store. This new version is obviously an improvement on the original, so it makes sense to install the updated version as soon as possible. But how do you know when app updates are available? On the Windows 8 Start screen, check out the Store tile. If you see a number in the lower-right corner of the tile (see Figure 2.4 for an example), that number tells you how many app updates are currently ready to be installed.

FIGURE 2.4

The number in the lower-right corner of the Store tile tells you how many apps are ready to be updated.

Follow these steps to update one or more apps:

1. In the Start screen, click Store. The Windows Store app appears.

2. Click Updates in the upper-right corner of the window. The Windows Store displays a list of the available updates, as shown in Figure 2.5.

FIGURE 2.5

In the Windows Store app, click Updates to see a list of the available app updates.

3. If you want to update only some of the apps, click Clear. (If you later decide that you prefer to update all the apps at once, click Select All.)

4. Click each update that you want to install.

5. Click Install. Windows 8 installs the app updates.

Uninstalling Windows 8 Apps

If you have an app that you no longer use, you can free up some disk space and reduce clutter on the Start screen by uninstalling that app. Here's how you do that:

1. Use the Start screen or the Apps screen to locate the Windows 8 app that you want to uninstall.

2. Right-click or swipe down on the app tile. Windows 8 displays the app bar.

3. Click Uninstall. Windows 8 asks you to confirm.

4. Click Uninstall. Windows 8 removes the app.

Uninstalling Desktop Programs

If your PC has a desktop program that has worn out its welcome, you need to uninstall it so that it's out of your life forever. Here are the steps to follow:

1. Open the Programs and Features window (refer to Figure 2.3):

   - **Windows 8**—On the Start screen, press Windows Logo+W to open the Settings search pane, type **programs**, and then click Programs and Features in the search results.

   - **Earlier versions of Windows**—Select Start, Control Panel, Uninstall a Program.

2. Click the program you want to remove.

3. Click the Uninstall command in the taskbar. In some cases, the corresponding command is Uninstall/Change.

4. Windows asks you to confirm you want to uninstall this program. Click Yes.

When you click Uninstall (or Uninstall/Change), Windows launches the application's setup program, and you follow the instructions to uninstall the program.

Checking for Windows Updates

Microsoft is constantly working to improve Windows with bug fixes, security patches, new program versions, and device driver updates. All these new and improved components are available online, so you should check for updates and patches often.

You might think you'd have to go online to get these updates, but that's not the case. Windows comes with an automatic updating feature that can download and install updates automatically.

Configuring Automatic Updates

If you prefer to know what's happening with your computer, you're able to control the automatic updating by following these steps:

1. Open the Control Panel window:

    - **Windows 8**—On the Start screen, press Windows Logo+X and then click Control Panel.

    - **Earlier versions of Windows**—Select Start, Control Panel.

2. Click System and Security.

3. Click Windows Update. This opens the Windows Update window, which shows you the current update status and enables you to view installed updates.

     NOTE To view the updates installed on your PC, click the View Update History link.

4. Click the Change Settings link to display the Change Settings window, shown in Figure 2.6.

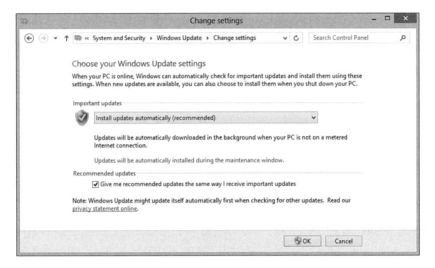

FIGURE 2.6

Use the Change Settings window to configure automatic updating in Windows.

5. In the **Important Updates** list, select one of the following options to determine how Windows 8 performs the updating:

- **Install Updates Automatically**—This option tells Windows to download and install updates automatically. Windows checks for new updates during the automatic maintenance window.

 NOTE The automatic maintenance window is defined by default as follows:

- Maintenance is performed each day at 3:00 a.m.
- If you are using your computer, maintenance is postponed until you are no longer using it.
- If your computer is in sleep mode, maintenance is postponed until the computer is awake.
- If the maintenance server is running late, maintenance is postponed until the server is ready, as long as your computer is not being used and is awake.

- **Download Updates, but Let Me Choose Whether to Install Them**— If you select this option, Windows checks for new updates and then automatically downloads any updates available. Windows then displays a notification to let you know that the updates are ready to install. Click the notification to see the list of updates. If you see an update that you don't want to install, deactivate its check box.

- **Check for Updates but Let Me Choose Whether to Download and Install Them**—If you select this option, Windows checks for new updates and then, if any are available, displays a notification to let you know that the updates are ready to download. Click the notification to see the list of updates. If you see an update that you don't want to download, deactivate its check box. Click Start Download to initiate the download. When the download is complete, Windows displays another notification to let you know that the updates are ready to install. Click the notification and then click Install to install the updates.

- **Never Check for Updates**—Activate this option to prevent Windows from checking for new updates.

6. If you want the setting from step 5 to apply only to important updates and not recommended updates, be sure to deactivate the check box in the Recommended Updates section.

7. Click OK to put the new settings into effect.

Checking for and Installing Updates Manually

If you chose the Never Check for Updates option in the preceding section, it's up to you to manually check for updates, which you should do regularly to keep your PC safe and sound. Even if you're using one of the automatic checking options, you might still want to do a manual check if you're waiting for an important security patch or some other crucial update that you'd prefer to install now rather than waiting for the automatic maintenance window.

Whatever the reason, follow these steps to check for and install updates:

1. Open the Control Panel window:

   - **Windows 8**—Press Windows Logo+X and then click Control Panel.

   - **Earlier versions of Windows**—Select Start, Control Panel.

2. Click System and Security.

3. Click Windows Update. The Windows Update window appears.

4. Click Check for Updates. Windows Update connects to the update server and checks for updates. If Windows Update determines that one or more updates are available, it lets you know under the status. As you can see in Figure 2.7, you see one link for the important updates and a second link for the optional updates, each of which tells you how many updates are available.

FIGURE 2.7

After you check for updates, Windows Update lets you know how many import and optional updates are available.

5. If you have important updates, click the X Important Updates Are Available link. The Select Updates to Install window appears.

6. If there are any important updates you don't want to install, deactivate their check boxes.

> **CAUTION**   Generally speaking, important updates are identified as important for a reason: they are designed to enhance your computer's security, stability, or performance. Therefore, I recommend that you always install all the available important updates.

7. Click Optional. Windows Updates displays a list of the optional updates available for your system.

8. If there are any optional updates you don't want to install, deactivate their check boxes.

9. Click Install. Windows 8 installs the selected updates.

Installing a New Device

Before you install a device, it's best to find out in advance whether the device is compatible with your version of Windows. The easiest way to do this is to look for the Designed for Windows X logo on the box (where X is the Windows version, such as 8, 7, or Vista). For older devices, check the manufacturer's website to see whether the company tells you that the program can be run under your version of Windows or if an upgrade is available. Alternatively, Microsoft has a web page that enables you to search on the name of a device or manufacturer to find out compatibility information (this works for Windows 8, Windows RT, and Windows 7):

> http://www.microsoft.com/en-us/windows/compatibility/en-US/ CompatCenter/Home

If you see your device (and, in some cases, the correct device version) in the hardware list, you can install it secure in the knowledge that it will work properly with Windows.

Installing Plug and Play Devices

Computing old-timers will remember (none too fondly) the days when installing devices required flipping DIP switches; fiddling with jumpers; or fussing with various IRQ, I/O port, and DMA combinations. If, on the other hand, all the abbreviations in the preceding sentence are incomprehensible to you, think yourself lucky that you live in a time when all the devices manufactured in recent years support Plug and Play, which means you simply attach the device, and Windows automatically recognizes it and installs the necessary software.

How do you know this is happening? If you're on the desktop, you see the Device Setup icon appear on the taskbar, and the icon shows a green background moving in from the left. That background is actually a progress bar that's showing you the state of the device installation. Click the icon to see the install details, as shown in Figure 2.8.

FIGURE 2.8

When you attach a new device, click the taskbar's Device Setup icon to watch the progress of the install.

When the install is done, the Device Setup dialog box and taskbar icon disappear, and your device is ready to go.

Using Action Center to Complete a Device Install

Plug and Play device installations almost always go off without a hitch. *Almost always.* In some cases, Windows might encounter a problem, or it might not have access to the necessary files to complete the install. If you're using Windows 8, open the PC Settings app's Devices tab, and the status of the new device will say something like the following (see Figure 2.9):

"Setup incomplete. Go to Action Center to install software."

FIGURE 2.9

Every now and then Windows 8 fumbles an install.

To rectify the situation, open Action Center (in Windows 8, press Windows Logo+W, type **action**, and then click Action Center; in Windows 7, click Action Center [the flag icon] and then click Open Action Center; for Windows Vista or XP, see "Updating a Device Driver," in Chapter 5, "Troubleshooting Devices"). In the Messages section, you see an `Install software for your devices` message, as shown in Figure 2.10. Click Install to complete the installation. In most cases, Windows scours the Web for the needed software, downloads it, and then proceeds with the installation.

FIGURE 2.10

You can use Action Center to complete the device installation.

Uninstalling a Device

When you remove a Plug and Play device, the hardware system informs Windows that the device is no longer present. Windows, in turn, updates its device list, and the hardware no longer appears in Device Manager.

If you're removing an older device, however, you need to tell Device Manager that the device no longer exists. To do that, follow these steps:

1. Run Device Manager:

    - **Windows 8**—Press Windows Logo+X and then click Device Manager.

    - **Windows 7 and Vista**—Select Start, type **device**, and then click Device Manager in the search results.

    - **Windows XP**—Select Start, right-click My Computer, click Properties, click the Hardware tab, and then click Device Manager.

2. Click the device.

3. Select Action, Uninstall. (Alternatively, click Uninstall in the toolbar or double-click the device, display the Driver tab, and then click Uninstall.)

4. When Windows warns you that you're about to remove the device, click OK.

THE ABSOLUTE MINIMUM

This chapter continued your look at PC maintenance by showing you how to use some Windows tools to maintain your PC's software and hardware. Here are the highlights:

- As you use your PC, Windows constantly generates files that it requires only temporarily. You don't need them either, so you can reclaim a significant amount of hard drive real estate by periodically running Disk Cleanup to delete those files.

- Windows is a bit sloppy about storing files on your hard drive, so they end up scattered about the drive. This file fragmentation slows down your system, so Windows automatically defragments your hard drive once a week, although you should feel free to "optimize" (as they say) your drive more often.

- If a Desktop program is behaving oddly or crashing, you can often solve the problem by repairing the installation.

IN THIS CHAPTER

- Assuming the worst will someday happen to your PC and preparing your PC (and yourself) for that day
- Backing up your precious (and irreplaceable) files
- Taking "snapshots" of your system's current state just in case you need to revert to that state in the future
- Creating a handy recovery drive or system repair disc that lets you get your PC back on its feet even if your hard drive goes down for the count
- Making an exact copy of your system and its files so that you can recover everything down the road, if necessary

3

PREPARING FOR TROUBLE

You're in what I like to call *ounce-of-prevention mode* when you're taking active steps to guard against and prepare for PC problems. A big part of ounce-of-prevention mode is the unwavering belief that someday something *will* go wrong with your computer. That might sound unduly pessimistic, but hey, this is a *PC* we're talking about here, and it's never a question of *if* the thing will go belly up one day, but rather *when* that day will come.

With that gloomy mindset, the only sensible thing to do is to prepare for that dire day so that you're ready to get your system back on its feet, and that's just what you learn in this chapter.

Backing Up Your Files

In theory, theory and practice are the same thing; in practice, they're not. That old saw applies perfectly to data backups. In theory, backing up data is an important part of everyday computing life. After all, we know that our data is valuable to the point of being irreplaceable, and there's no shortage of causes that can result in a hard disk crashing: power surges, rogue applications, virus programs, or just simple wear and tear. In practice, however, backing up our data always seems to be one of those chores we'll get to "tomorrow." After all, that old hard disk seems to be humming along just fine, thank you.

When it comes to backups, theory and practice don't usually converge until that day you start your system and you get an ugly `Invalid system configuration` or `Hard disk failure` message. Believe me: Losing a hard disk that's crammed with unarchived (and now lost) data brings the importance of backing up into focus real quick. To avoid this sorry fate, you have to find a way to take some of the pain out of the practice of backing up. The next few sections take you through some easy backup techniques in various versions of Windows.

Backing Up File Versions with Windows 8's File History

Windows 8 has the capability to store previous versions of files and folders, where a "previous" version is defined as a copy of an object that has subsequently changed. For example, suppose that you make changes to a particular document each day for three days in a row. This means that you'll end up with three previous versions of the document: the original, the one with yesterday's changes, and the one with today's changes.

Taken together, these previous versions represent the document's *file history*, and you can access and work with previous versions by activating the File History feature. When you turn on File History and specify an external drive to store the data, Windows 8 begins monitoring your libraries, your desktop, your contacts, and your Internet Explorer favorites. Once an hour, Windows 8 checks to see whether any of this data has changed since the last check. If it has, Windows 8 saves copies of the changed files to the external drive.

When you have some data saved, you can then use it to restore a previous version of a file, as described in Chapter 6, "Recovering from Problems."

→ To learn how to restore file versions, **see** "Restoring Backed-Up Data," **p. 82**.

To start, connect an external drive to your PC. The drive should have enough capacity to hold your user account files, so an external hard drive is probably best. Now you need to set up the external drive for use with File History.

The easiest way to do this is to look for the notification that appears a few moments after you connect the drive. Click the notification and then click Configure This Drive for Backup.

If you miss the notification, follow these steps instead:

1. In the Windows 8 Start screen, press Windows Logo+W to open the Settings search pane, type **history**, and then click File History. The File History window appears.

2. Examine the Copy Files To section of the window. If you see your external hard drive listed, as shown in Figure 3.1, you can skip the rest of these steps.

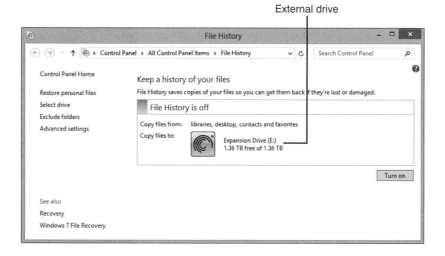

FIGURE 3.1

Windows 8 should recognize your external drive and add it to the File History window.

3. Click Select Drive. The Change Drive window appears.

4. Select the drive you want to use and then click OK. Windows 8 displays the external drive in the File History window.

At long last, you're ready to start using File History. In the File History window, click Turn On. If Windows 8 asks whether you want to recommend the drive to your homegroup, click Yes or No, as you see fit. File History immediately goes to work saving the initial copies of your files to the external drive or network share.

Backing Up Files in Windows 7

In Windows 7, you launch Windows Backup by selecting Start, typing **backup**, and then clicking Backup and Restore in the search results. Figure 3.2 shows the initial version of the window.

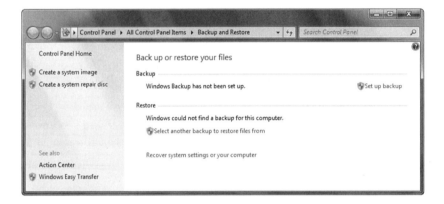

FIGURE 3.2

When you first launch Windows Backup, you see this version of the Backup and Restore window.

Follow these steps to configure and activate Windows 7's automatic file backup feature:

1. Click Set Up Backup to start the Set Up Backup Wizard.

2. The wizard first wants to know the backup destination. You have two choices. (Click Next when you're ready to continue.)

    - **Local hard disk or optical drive**—The Save Backup On list shows the available drives on your system, and you use this list to select the drive you want to use.

    - **Network share**—This is the way to go if you want to use a shared network folder to store the backup. Click Save On a Network; then either type the network address of the share or click Browse to use the Browse for Folder dialog box to select the shared network folder. Type a username and password for accessing the share, and then click OK. Make sure the network share is selected in the Save Backup On list.

3. In the What Do You Want to Back Up dialog box, you have two choices. (Click Next after you've made your choice.)

- **Let Windows Choose**—Select this option to leave it up to Windows 7 to select what gets backed up. This includes everything in your user profile, including your documents, pictures, videos, and email.

- **Let Me Choose**—This is the way to go if you want more control over what gets backed up. When you click Next, you see the dialog box shown in Figure 3.3. The folders in your user profile are all selected by default. If you want to include any other folder, open the Computer branch, drill down to the folder, and then activate its check box. Click Next when you're done.

FIGURE 3.3

Activate the check box beside each folder on your system that you want to include in the backup.

4. In the Review Your Backup Settings dialog box, click Change Schedule to open the How Often Do You Want to Back Up dialog box.

5. Make sure the Run Backup on a Schedule check box is activated, and then set up your preferred backup schedule. (Click OK when you're done.)

   - **How Often**—Select Daily, Weekly, or Monthly.

   - **What Day**—If you chose Weekly, select the day of the week you want the backups to occur; if you chose Monthly, select the day of the month you want the backups to occur.

   - **What Time**—Select the time of day you want the backup to run. (Choose a time when you won't be using your computer.)

6. Click Save Settings and Run Backup to save your configuration and launch the backup. Windows 7 returns you to Backup and Restore and shows the progress of the backup.

When the backup is done, the Backup and Restore window now offers all kinds of useful information here, including the backup size, the free space on the backup drive, the previous and next backup dates, and the schedule. The window also sprouts three new options:

- **Back Up Now**—Click this option to rerun the entire backup.

- **Change Settings**—Click this option to change your backup configuration by running through the Configure Backup Wizard's dialog boxes again.

- **Turn Off Schedule**—Click this link to disable the automatic backup feature. (Click the Turn On Schedule link to reinstate automatic backups.)

Backing Up Files in Windows Vista

In Windows Vista, when you first launch the Backup program (select Start, All Programs, Accessories, System Tools, Backup Status and Configuration), it displays the window shown in Figure 3.4.

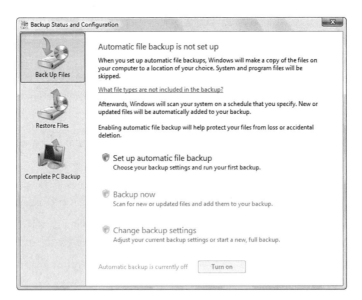

FIGURE 3.4

In Vista, when you first launch Windows Backup, the program prompts you to configure and start the Automatic File Backup feature.

 **NOTE** The Backup utility is available only in the Premium, Business, Enterprise, and Ultimate versions of Windows Vista.

Follow these steps to configure and activate Vista's Automatic File Backup feature:

1. Click Set Up Automatic File Backup and then enter your user account control credentials to load the Back Up Files Wizard.

2. The wizard first wants to know the backup destination. You have two choices (click Next when you're ready to continue):

    • **On a Hard Disk, CD, or DVD**—Select this option if you want to use a disk drive on your computer. If you have multiple drives, use the list to select the one you want to use.

    • **On a Network**—Select this option if you want to use a shared network folder. Either type the network address of the share or click Browse to use the Browse for Folder dialog box to select the shared network folder.

3. If your system has multiple hard drives, the wizard asks you to select which of them you want to include in the backup. Deactivate the check box beside any drive you don't want to include in the backup (you can't exclude the system drive, however), and then click Next.

4. The next dialog box provides you with a long list of file types to back up, including documents, pictures, videos, and email, as shown in Figure 3.5. Leave the check boxes activated for those document types you want to include in the backup and then click Next.

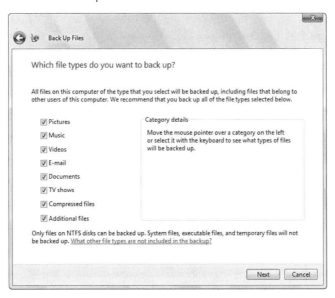

FIGURE 3.5

Use this wizard dialog box to specify the file types you want to include in the backup.

5. The next dialog box asks you to set up a backup schedule:

   • **How Often**—Select Daily, Weekly, or Monthly.

   • **What Day**—If you chose Weekly, select the day of the week you want the backups to occur; if you chose Monthly, select the day of the month you want the backups to occur.

   • **What Time**—Select the time of day you want the backup to run. (Choose a time when you won't be using your computer.)

6. Click Save Settings and Start Backup to save your configuration and launch the backup. Windows Backup lets you know that it will perform a full backup of your system now.

7. Click Yes.

8. Follow any instructions that appear onscreen, particularly if Windows Backup asks you to insert or format a disc. After the backup starts, click the File Backup Is Running icon in the notification area to watch the progress.

9. When the backup is done, click Close.

The next time you run Windows Backup, the initial window shows you the backup status, when your system was last backed up, and when the next backup will occur. The window also shows several new options:

• **Back Up Now**—Click this option to rerun the entire backup.

• **Change Backup Settings**—Click this option to change your backup configuration by running through the Back Up Files Wizard's dialog boxes again.

• **Automatic Backup Is Currently On**—Click the Turn Off button to disable the automatic backup feature.

Backing Up Files in Windows XP

In Windows XP, a *backup job* is a file that specifies a few particulars about your backup. These particulars include the files you want backed up, the location where the files will be backed up, and any backup options you specify along the way. These backup options include the *backup type*, which can make backing up easier and more convenient. That is, after you've decided on all the files that should be part of the backup job, don't waste time by backing up every single one of those files each time you do a backup. Instead, it's possible to use backup types to tell Windows XP to back up only those files that have changed. Windows XP supports no fewer than five backup types:

- **Normal**—Backs up each and every file, each and every time. (Note that by "each and every file," I mean "each and every file in the backup job.") All files are marked to indicate they've been backed up.

- **Incremental**—Backs up only those files that have changed since the most recent Normal or Incremental backup. This is the fastest type because it includes only the minimum number of files. Again, the files are marked to indicate they've been backed up.

- **Differential**—Backs up only those files that have changed since the most recent non-Differential backup. That is, the files are not marked to indicate they've been backed up. So, if you run this type of backup again, the same files get backed up (plus any others that have changed in the meantime).

- **Daily**—Backs up only those files that were modified on the day you run the backup.

- **Copy**—Makes copies of the selected files. This type of backup does not mark the files as having been backed up. This means you can use it for quick backups without interfering with your backup strategy (discussed next).

So a typical strategy might go something like this:

- Run a Daily backup each day.

- Run an Incremental backup once a week. Delete the previous week's Daily and Incremental backups.

- Run a Normal backup once a month. When done, delete the previous month's Incremental and Normal backups.

 NOTE   If you're using Windows XP Home Edition, note that you need to install Backup from the Windows XP Home Edition CD. In the VALUEADD\MSFT\NTBACKUP folder, launch the Ntbackup.msi file.

To get started, select Start, All Programs, Accessories, System Tools, Backup. After a second or two, the Backup or Restore Wizard pulls itself out of a hat. This wizard's step-by-step approach makes it easy to create and launch a backup job. Here's what happens:

1. In the initial Backup or Restore Wizard dialog box, click Next.

2. Activate the Back Up Files and Settings option and then click Next.

3. The next wizard dialog box gives you four choices (click Next when you're done):

- **My Documents and Settings**—Choose this option to back up your My Documents folder, your Favorites folders, your desktop, and your cookies.

- **Everyone's Documents and Settings**—Choose this option if you have multiple users on the computer and you want to back up their documents and settings as well as your own.

- **All Information on This Computer**—Choose this option to be able to completely recover your system in the event of a catastrophe.

- **Let Me Choose What to Back Up**—Choose this option to pick out exactly which files to back up.

 NOTE Windows XP has a collection of files that store what's known as the *system state*. This is the Windows XP configuration, so these are absolutely crucial files, and you'll be able to recover your system much faster if you back them up. To include the system state files in your backup job, open the My Computer branch and activate the System State check box.

4. If you elected to choose what to back up, you'll see the Items to Back Up dialog box shown in Figure 3.6. The idea here is that you use the items in the Items to Back Up list to choose which drives, folders, or files you want to include in the backup. You do this by activating the check box beside each item you want to back up. (Now you see why I suggested you include all your documents in subfolders within My Documents. To back up all your data files, all you have to do is activate the My Documents check box. One click and you're done. What could be easier?) Click Next when you're ready to proceed.

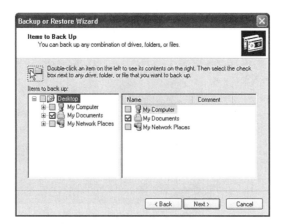

FIGURE 3.6

If you decided to select the backup job files yourself, you'll get this dialog box coming at you.

5. Now the wizard wants to know the backup destination. Use the Select the Backup Type list to choose the type of backup medium (such as a file or a tape device) you want to use. Use the Choose a Place to Save Your Backup list to specify the location of the backup. (You can click Browse to choose the location from a dialog box.) You can also enter a name in the Type a Name for This Backup text box. Click Next to continue.

6. In the summary of the backup job settings, click Advanced. You'll then run through a series of dialog boxes. Here's a quick summary (click Next after each one):

- **Type of Backup**—Use the Select the Type of Backup list to choose a backup type (Normal, Incremental, and so on).

- **How to Back Up**—If you have ultra important data and you don't want anything to go wrong, activate the Verify Data After Backup check box. This ensures that your data was backed up without mishap, but it basically doubles the total backup time.

- **Backup Options**—You can either append this backup to an existing backup job (this is your best choice in most situations) or have this backup replace an existing backup job.

- **When to Back Up**—Choose Now to start the backup immediately. Alternatively, select Later and click Set Schedule to run the backup at a future time.

7. Click Finish. Backup gathers the files and then starts backing them up. If the backup medium gets full, you'll be prompted to insert another one. When the backup job is complete, you'll see a report. (If the report tells you that errors occurred during the backup, check to see which files were involved and then back them up again.)

8. Click Close.

Setting System Restore Points

One of the biggest causes of system instability is the tendency of some newly installed programs simply to not get along with Windows. The problem could be a program that doesn't mesh with the Windows system or a settings change that causes havoc on other programs or on Windows. Similarly, hardware installations often cause problems by adding faulty device drivers to the system or by corrupting some Windows files.

To help guard against software or hardware installations that bring down the system, Windows offers the System Restore feature. Its job is straightforward, yet clever: to take periodic snapshots—called *restore points* or *protection points*—of your system, each of which includes the currently installed program files, system settings, and other crucial system data. The idea is that if a program or device installation causes problems on your PC, you use System Restore to revert your system to the most recent restore point before the installation (I show you how to do this in Chapter 6).

To learn how to recover your PC using a restore point, **see** "Recovering Using System Restore," **p. 95**

System Restore automatically creates restore points under certain conditions. For example, it creates an automatic restore point (called a *system checkpoint*) once a week, and it creates a restore point before installing certain programs and devices.

You also are able to create a restore point manually using the System Restore feature, which is a good idea if you're installing a large program or an older device that might not work properly with Windows. Here are the steps to follow:

1. Start System Restore:

    • **Windows 8**—Press Windows Logo+W to open the Settings search pane, type **restore point**, and then click Create a Restore Point in the search results. This displays the System Protection tab of the System Properties dialog box (see Figure 3.7).

    • **Windows 7 and Vista**—Click Start, right-click Computer (or My Computer), click Properties, and then click System Protection.

    • **Windows XP**—Select Start, All Programs, Accessories, System Tools, System Restore.

FIGURE 3.7

In Windows 8, 7, and Vista, use the System Protection tab to set a restore point.

2. Click Create to display the Create a Restore Point dialog box.

3. Type a description for the new restore point and then click Create. System Protection creates the restore point and displays a dialog box to let you know.

4. Click Close to return to the System Properties dialog box.

5. Click OK.

Creating a Windows 8 Recovery Drive

We all hope our computers operate trouble-free over their lifetimes, but we know from bitter experience that this is rarely the case. Computers are incredibly complex systems, so it is almost inevitable that a PC will develop glitches. If your hard drive is still accessible, you can boot to Windows 8 and access the recovery tools, as I describe in Chapter 6.

→ To learn about the Windows 8 recovery tools, **see** "Accessing the Windows 8 Recovery Environment," **p. 89**

If you can't boot your PC, however, you must boot using some other drive. If you have your Windows 8 installation media, you can boot using that drive. If you don't have the installation media, you can still recover if you've created a USB recovery drive. This is a USB flash drive that contains the Windows 8 recovery environment, which enables you to refresh or reset your PC, use System Restore, recover a system image, and more.

Before you can boot to a recovery drive, such as a USB flash drive, you need to create the drive. Follow these steps:

1. Insert the USB flash drive you want to use. Note that the drive must have a capacity of at least 256MB. Also, Windows 8 will erase all data on the drive, so make sure it doesn't contain any files you want to keep.

     NOTE You might see a notification a few moments after you insert the flash drive. If so, you can ignore it.

2. In the Start screen, press Windows Logo+W, type **recovery**, and then click Create a Recovery Drive. User Account Control appears.

3. Click Yes or enter administrator credentials to continue. The Recovery Drive Wizard appears.

4. Click Next. The Recovery Drive Wizard prompts you to choose the USB flash drive, as shown in Figure 3.8.

FIGURE 3.8

Select the flash drive that you inserted in step 1.

5. Click the drive, if it isn't selected already, and then click Next. The Recovery Drive Wizard warns you that all the data on the drive will be deleted.

6. Click Create. The wizard formats the drive and copies the recovery tools and data.

7. Click Finish.

Remove the drive, label it, and then put it someplace where you'll be able to find it later, just in case.

 TIP   To make sure your recovery drive works properly, you should test it by booting your PC to the drive. Insert the recovery drive and then restart your PC. How you boot to the drive depends on your system. Some PCs display a menu of boot devices, and you select the USB drive from that menu. In other cases, you see a message telling you to press a key.

Creating a System Image Backup

The worst-case scenario for PC problems is a system crash that renders your hard disk or system files unusable. Your only recourse in such a case is to start from scratch with either a reformatted hard disk or a new hard disk. This usually means that you have to reinstall Windows 8 and then reinstall and reconfigure all your applications. In other words, you're looking at the better part of a day or, more likely, a few days, to recover your system. However, Windows 8 has a feature that takes most of the pain out of recovering your system. It's called a *system image backup,* and it's part of the system recovery options that I discuss in Chapter 6.

The system image backup is actually a complete backup of your Windows installation. Creating a system image takes a long time (at least several hours, depending on how much stuff you have), but doing so is worthwhile for the peace of mind. Here are the steps to follow to create the system image:

1. Depending on your version of Windows, use one of the following to get started:

    • **Windows 8**—Press Windows Logo+W, type `file recovery`, and then click Windows 7 File Recovery. The Windows 7 File Recovery window appears.

    • **Windows 7**—Select Start, type `backup`, click Backup and Restore in the search results.

- **Windows Vista**—Select Start, type **backup**, click Backup and Restore Center in the search results.

 NOTE Windows XP doesn't offer a system image backup feature. Or, technically, it does offer a similar feature called Automated System Recovery, but that feature requires a floppy disk drive, and I'm assuming your PC doesn't have one of those. However, if you use XP to perform a full backup of your system, including the system state, as I described earlier, you'll have enough backed up to perform a full recovery of your system.

2. Click Create a System Image. (In Windows Vista, click Back Up Files.) The Create a System Image Wizard appears.

3. The wizard asks you to specify a backup destination. You have three choices, as shown in Figure 3.9. (Click Next when you're ready to continue.)

- **On a Hard Disk**—Select this option if you want to use a disk drive on your computer. If you have multiple drives, use the list to select the one you want to use.

- **On One or More DVDs**—Select this option if you want to use DVDs to hold the backup. Depending on how much data your PC holds, you might need to use dozens of discs for this (at least!), so I don't recommend this option.

- **On a Network Location**—Select this option if you want to use a shared network folder. Either type the address of the shared folder (if you know it) or click Select and then click Browse to use the Browse for Folder dialog box to choose the shared network folder. Make sure it's a share for which you have permission to add data. Type a username and password for accessing the share and then click OK.

FIGURE 3.9

You can create the system image on a hard drive, on DVDs, or on a network shared folder.

4. The system image backup automatically includes your internal hard disk in the system image, and you can't change that. However, if you also have external hard drives, you can add them to the backup by activating their check boxes. Click Next. Windows Backup asks you to confirm your backup settings.

5. Click Start Backup. Windows Backup creates the system image. When the backup is complete, Windows 8 asks whether you want to create a system repair disc.

6. You don't need a system repair disc if you already created a recovery drive, so click No. If you don't have a recovery drive and don't have a USB flash drive to create one, click Yes and follow steps 2–5 in the next section.

7. Click Close.

8. Click OK.

If you used a hard drive and you have multiple external drives lying around, be sure to label the one that contains the system image so you'll be able to find it later.

 CAUTION Many people make the mistake of creating the system image once and then ignoring it, forgetting that their systems aren't set in stone. Over the coming days and weeks, you'll be installing apps, tweaking settings, and, of course, creating lots of new documents and other data. This means that you should periodically create a fresh system image. Should disaster strike, you'll be able to recover most of your system.

Creating a System Repair Disc

In Windows Vista, you could attempt to get a badly behaving machine up and running again by booting to the Vista install disc and then accessing the system recovery options. That was a nice feature, but only if you could find your install disc (or if you ever had one in the first place)! Windows 7 fixed that problem by giving you the option of creating your own system repair disc and, despite the more convenient feature of the USB recovery drive, Windows 8 still offers that option (although slightly deprecated as a "Windows 7 recovery tool"). Here's how you go about doing this using Windows 8 or 7:

1. Insert a blank recordable CD or DVD into your burner. If an AutoPlay notification shows up, close it.

2. Depending on your version of Windows, use one of the following to get started:

   - **Windows 8**—Press Windows Logo+W, type **file recovery**, and then click Windows 7 File Recovery. The Windows 7 File Recovery window appears.

   - **Windows 7**—Select Start, type **backup**, click Backup and Restore in the search results.

3. Click Create a System Repair Disc. The Create a System Repair Disc dialog box appears, as shown in Figure 3.10.

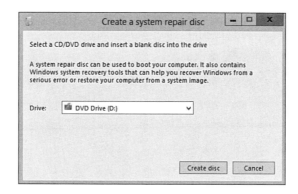

FIGURE 3.10

Both Windows 8 and Windows 7 offer the system repair disc option.

4. If you have multiple CD/DVD burners, use the Drive list to select the one you want to use

5. Click Create Disc. Windows creates the disk (it takes a minute or two) and then displays a particularly unhelpful dialog box.

6. Click Close and then click OK.

Eject the disc, label it, and then put it someplace where you'll be able to find it later.

THE ABSOLUTE MINIMUM

In this chapter you learned several techniques for protecting your PC by getting into "ounce-of-prevention" mode. Here are some important points to remember:

- The biggest key to PC preventative maintenance is that a healthy dose of paranoia is a good thing. That is, assume—no, *expect*—that your PC will one day crash, so take steps now to prepare.

- Backing up isn't hard to do, so just do it.

- Feel free to create restore points before performing any major (or even semi-major) tasks, particularly installing new hardware and software.

- By performing regular backups, keeping your system image backup current, and creating a recovery drive or system repair disc, you'll be able to recover your system no matter what happens to your PC.

UNDERSTANDING BASIC TROUBLESHOOTING

If you find yourself in a bit of a pickle because your PC is acting wonky (or not acting at all), you've come to the right place. This chapter provides you with a number of strategies and techniques for not only diagnosing the problem, but also fixing whatever's gone haywire with your PC. If these basic troubleshooting steps don't solve the problem, not to worry: the next three chapters take you deeper into troubleshooting territory.

Determining the Source of a Problem

One of the ongoing mysteries that all Windows users experience at one time or another is what might be called the "now you see it, now you don't" problem. This is a glitch that plagues you for a while and then mysteriously vanishes without any intervention on your part. (This situation also tends to occur when you ask a nearby user or someone from the IT department to look at the problem. Like the automotive problem that goes away when you take the car to a mechanic, computer problems often resolve themselves as soon as a knowledgeable user sits down at the keyboard.) When this happens, most people just shake their heads and resume working, grateful to no longer have to deal with the problem.

Unfortunately, most computer ills aren't resolved so easily. For these more intractable problems, your first order of business is to hunt down the source of the glitch. This is, at best, a black art, but it can be done if you take a systematic approach. Over the years, I've found that the best approach is to ask a series of questions designed to gather the required information or to narrow down what might be the culprit. The next few sections take you through these questions.

Did You Get an Error Message?

Unfortunately, most computer error messages are obscure and do little to help you resolve a problem directly. However, error codes and error text can help you down the road, either by giving you something to search for in an online database or by providing information to a tech support person. Therefore, you should always write down the full text of any error message that appears.

 TIP If the error message is lengthy and you can still use other programs on your computer, don't bother writing down the full message. Instead, while the message is displayed, press Windows Logo+Print Screen to place an image of the current screen as a file in your Windows 8 Pictures library. If you're using an earlier version of Windows, press Print Screen to place an image of the screen in memory and then paste it into Paint or some other graphics program.

Did You Recently Change Any Windows Settings?

If the problem started after you changed your Windows configuration, try reversing the change. Even something as seemingly innocent as activating a screensaver can cause problems, so don't rule out anything. If you've made a number of recent changes and you're not sure about everything you did, or if it would take too long to reverse all the changes individually, use System Restore, as described in Chapter 6, "Recovering from Problems," to revert your system to the most recent checkpoint before you made the changes.

→ To learn how to use System Restore to revert to an earlier state, **see** "Recovering Using System Restore," **p. 95**

Did You Recently Change Any Application Settings?

If you've recently changed an application setting, try reversing the change to see whether doing so solves the problem. If that doesn't help, here are three other things to try:

- Check the developer's website to see whether an upgrade or patch is available.

- As described in Chapter 2, "Maintaining Windows,", run the application's Repair option (if it has one), which is often useful for fixing corrupted or missing files.

→ For the details on repairing a program, **see** "Repairing a Software Installation," **p. 29**

- Reinstall the program.

 NOTE If a program freezes, you cannot shut it down using conventional methods. If you try, you might see a dialog box warning you that the program is not responding. If so, click End Now to force the program to close. If that doesn't work, right-click the taskbar and then click Task Manager. You should see your stuck application listed. Click the program and then click End Task.

Did You Recently Install a New Program?

If you suspect a new program is causing system instability, restart Windows and try operating the system for a while without using the new program. If the problem doesn't reoccur, the new program is likely the culprit. Try using the program without any other programs running.

You should also examine the program's readme file (if it has one) to look for known problems and possible workarounds. It's also a good idea to check for a version of the program that's compatible with your version of Windows. Again, you can also try the program's Repair option (if it has one), or you can reinstall the program.

Similarly, if you recently upgraded an existing program, try uninstalling the upgrade.

Did You Recently Install a New Device or Update a Driver?

If you recently installed a new device or updated an existing device driver, the new device or driver might be causing the problem. Check Device Manager to see whether there's a problem with the device, as described in Chapter 5, "Troubleshooting Device Problems."

→ For more information on using Device Manager for troubleshooting purposes, **see** "Troubleshooting with Device Manager," **p. 72**

General Troubleshooting Tips

Figuring out the cause of a problem is often the hardest part of troubleshooting, but by itself it doesn't do you much good. When you know the source, you need to parlay that information into a fix for the problem. I discussed a few solutions in the preceding section, but here are a few other general fixes you need to keep in mind:

- **Close all programs**—You can often fix flaky behavior by shutting down all your open programs and starting again. This is a particularly useful fix for problems caused by low memory or low system resources.

- **Log off Windows**—Logging off clears the memory and thus gives you a slightly cleaner slate than merely closing all your programs.

- **Reboot the computer**—If you have problems with some system files and devices, logging off won't help because these objects remain loaded. By rebooting the system, you reload the entire system, which is often enough to solve many computer problems.

- **Turn off the computer and restart**—You can often solve a hardware problem by first shutting off your machine. Wait for 30 seconds to give all devices time to spin down, and then restart.

- **Check connections, power switches, and so on**—Some of the most common (and some of the most embarrassing) causes of hardware problems are the simple physical things. Therefore, make sure that a device is turned on, check that cable connections are secure, and ensure that insertable devices are properly connected.

Troubleshooting Startup

Computers are often frustrating beasts, but few things in computerdom are as maddening as a computer that won't compute or an operating system that won't operate. After all, if your PC won't even start Windows, then Windows can't start any programs, which means *you* can't get any work done.

What you've got on your hands is a rather expensive boat anchor, not to mention a hair-pullingly, teeth-gnashingly frustrating problem that you have to fix *now*. To help save some wear and tear on your hair and teeth, this chapter outlines a few common startup difficulties and their solutions.

Startup problems generally are either trivially easy to fix or are take-it-to-the-repair-shop difficult to solve. Fortunately, startup conundrums often fall into the former camp, and in many cases one of the following solutions will get your PC back on its electronic feet:

- Some boot problems mercifully fall into the Temporary Glitch category of startup woes. That is, it could be that your PC has just gone momentarily and temporarily haywire. To find out, shut down the computer and leave it turned off for at least 30 seconds to give everything time to spin down and catch its breath. Turn your PC back on and cross whatever parts of your body you think might help.

- Every now and then a defective device will interfere with the boot process. To ensure that this isn't the case, disconnect every device that's disconnectable and then try booting your newly naked PC. If you get a successful launch, one of the devices was almost certainly the culprit. Attach the devices one by one and try rebooting each time until you find out which one is causing the boot failure. You could then reboot without the device, upgrade the device driver, and try again. If that still doesn't work, the device is probably defective and so should be repaired or replaced.

- If you get no power when you flick your PC's On switch, you've likely got a defective power supply on your hands, or one or more of the power supply connections have come loose. Check the connections or, if they're fine, replace the power supply.

→ To learn how to install a new power supply in your PC, **see** Chapter 10, "Replacing the Power Supply"

More Troubleshooting Tools

Windows comes with diagnostic tools that not only help finding the source of many common disk, memory, and network problems, but can also detect impending failures and alert you to take corrective or mitigating action (such as backing up your files). The next few sections describe these tools.

Running the Windows Troubleshooters

Windows Vista introduced the idea of the *troubleshooter*, a Help system component that offered a series of solutions that led you deeper into a problem in an attempt to fix it. In Windows 7, the troubleshooters were beefed up and given their own home within the Control Panel interface, and that home remains in place in Windows 8. To see the Windows troubleshooters, use one of the following techniques:

- **Windows 8**—Press Windows Logo+W, type `trouble`, and then choose Troubleshooting in the search results.

- **Windows 7**—Click Start, type `trouble`, and then click Troubleshooting in the search results.

- **Windows Vista**—Select Start, Help and Support and then click Troubleshooting.

The Troubleshooting window (see Figure 4.1) is divided into several categories (Programs, Hardware and Sound, and so on), each of which offers a few links to general troubleshooting tasks. (If you see a message asking whether you want the most up-to-date troubleshooting content, be sure to click Yes.)

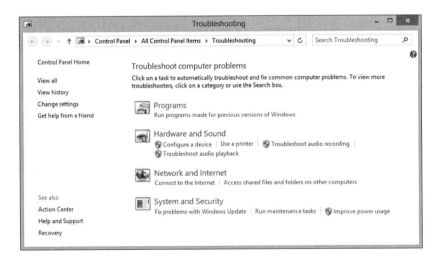

FIGURE 4.1

The Troubleshooting window offers links to various troubleshooting categories and tasks.

When you click a category, Windows queries the Windows Online Troubleshooting service for the latest troubleshooting packs and then displays the complete list for that category. For example, Figure 4.2 shows the troubleshooters that were available for the Programs category as I wrote this chapter.

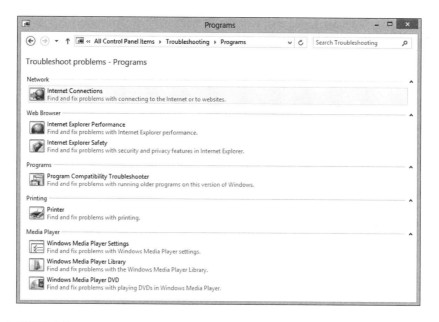

FIGURE 4.2

Click a category to see its available troubleshooters.

 TIP   If you want to see all the available troubleshooters, click the View All link in the Troubleshooting window.

Running the Memory Diagnostics Tool

Few computer problems are as maddening as those related to physical memory defects because they tend to be intermittent and they tend to cause problems in secondary systems, forcing you to waste time on wild goose chases all over your system.

Therefore, it is welcome news indeed that Windows 8, 7, and Vista ship with a Memory Diagnostic tool that works with Microsoft Online Crash Analysis to determine whether defective physical memory is the cause of program crashes. If so, Memory Diagnostic lets you know about the problem and schedules a memory test for the next time you start your computer. If it detects actual problems, the system also marks the affected memory area as unusable to avoid future crashes.

Windows also comes with a Memory Leak Diagnosis tool that's part of the Diagnostic Policy Service. If a program is leaking memory (using up increasing amounts of memory over time), this tool will diagnose the problem and take steps to fix it.

To run the Memory Diagnostic tool yourself, follow these steps:

1. Launch the Memory Diagnostic tool (shown in Figure 4.3):

   - **Windows 8**—Press Windows Logo+W, type **memory**, and then click Diagnose Your Computer's Memory Problems in the search results.

   - **Windows 7**—Click Start, type **memory**, and then click Windows Memory Diagnostic.

   - **Windows Vista**—Click Start, type **memory**, and then click Memory Diagnostics Tool.

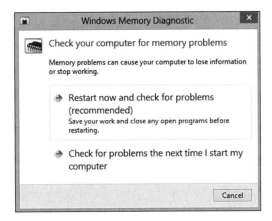

FIGURE 4.3

Use the Memory Diagnostic tool to check for memory problems.

2. Click one of the following options:

   - **Restart Now and Check for Problems**—Click this option to force an immediate restart and schedule a memory test during startup. Be sure to save your work before clicking this option.

   - **Check for Problems the Next Time I Start My Computer**—Click this option to schedule a memory test to run the next time you boot.

After the test runs (it takes 10 or 15 minutes, depending on how much RAM is in your system), Windows restarts and you see (for a short time) the Windows Memory Diagnostic icon in the taskbar's notification area. This icon displays the results of the memory test.

Checking for Solutions to Problems

Microsoft constantly collects information about Windows from users. When a problem occurs, Windows usually asks whether you want to send information about the problem to Microsoft and, if you do, it stores these tidbits in a massive database. Engineers then tackle the "issues" (as they euphemistically call them) and hopefully come up with solutions.

One of the most promising features in Windows 8, 7, and Vista is called Problem Reporting. It's designed to make solutions available to anyone who goes looking for them. Windows keeps a list of problems your computer is having, so you can tell it to go online and see whether a solution is available. If a solution is waiting, Windows will download it, install it, and fix your system.

Here are the steps to follow to check for solutions to problems:

1. Launch the Memory Diagnostic tool (refer to Figure 4.3):

   - **Windows 8**—Press Windows Logo+W, type **problem**, and then click View Solutions to Problems in the search results.

   - **Windows 7**—Click Start, type **problem**, and then click View Solutions to Problems.

   - **Windows Vista**—Click Start, type **problem**, and then click Problem Reports and Solutions.

2. In Windows 8 and 7, open the Maintenance section and then click Check for Solutions. In Windows Vista, click Check for New Solutions. Windows begins checking for solutions.

3. If you see a dialog box asking whether you want to send more information about your problems, you can click View Problem Details to see information about the problems, as shown in Figure 4.4. When you're ready to move on, click Send Information.

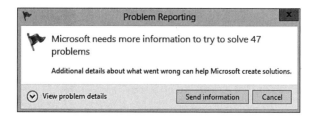

FIGURE 4.4

If Windows tells you it needs more information, click View Problem Details to see the problems.

4. If a solution exists for your computer, you see it listed in the Maintenance section of the window. Click the solution to install it.

THE ABSOLUTE MINIMUM

In this chapter you learned a few troubleshooting fundamentals that you can use to begin tackling just about any PC problem. Here are some highlights:

- If a problem occurs but then just as quickly goes away, don't give it a second thought. Many PC problems are temporary glitches, and there's no sense scratching your head over them.

- For less tractable woes, you need to track down the source of the problem. Error messages can help with this, but in the absence of any such message, you should look to your recent actions on the PC, particularly changing a setting or installing a new program or device.

- The number one solver of a huge number of PC problems is a simple system reboot. If closing your running programs doesn't solve the glitch, rebooting just might do it.

- The Windows troubleshooters are excellent problem-solving tools, so don't forget about them.

- You'd be surprised how often Microsoft already has a solution to a problem, so be sure to check for solutions before trying more involved troubleshooting steps.

IN THIS CHAPTER

- Solving device dilemmas with Device Manager
- Getting your head around device drivers
- Learning the fine art of locating device drivers on the Web
- Troubleshooting hardware problems by updating device drivers
- Troubleshooting *new* hardware problems by rolling back a device driver update

5

TROUBLESHOOTING DEVICE PROBLEMS

If you buy Windows-friendly devices, you should have a mostly trouble-free computing experience. Of course, *mostly* doesn't mean *completely* because hardware is not foolproof—far from it. Things still can, and will, go wrong, and when they do, you'll need to perform some kind of troubleshooting. (Assuming, of course, that the device doesn't have a physical fault that requires a trip to the repair shop.) Fortunately, Windows also has some handy tools to help you both identify and rectify hardware ills.

Troubleshooting with Device Manager

Device Manager (press Windows Logo+X and then click Device Manager) not only provides you with a comprehensive summary of your system's hardware data, but also doubles as a decent troubleshooting tool. To see what I mean, first start Device Manager:

- **Windows 8**—Press Windows Logo+X and then click Device Manager.

- **Windows 7 and Vista**—Select Start, type **device**, and then click Device Manager in the search results.

- **Windows XP**—Select Start, right-click My Computer, click Properties, click the Hardware tab, and then click Device Manager.

Check out the Device Manager window shown in Figure 5.1. See how the Other Devices branch has an Unknown Device item that has an exclamation mark superimposed on its icon? This icon tells you that there's a problem with the device.

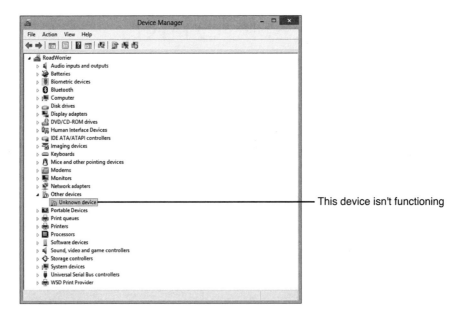

FIGURE 5.1

The Device Manager uses icons to warn you there's a problem with a device.

If you double-click the problem device to open its properties, as shown in Figure 5.2, the Device Status area tells you a bit more about what's wrong. As you can see in Figure 5.2, the problem here is that the device drivers aren't installed.

Device Manager usually offers a suggested remedy (such as the Update Driver button shown in Figure 5.2).

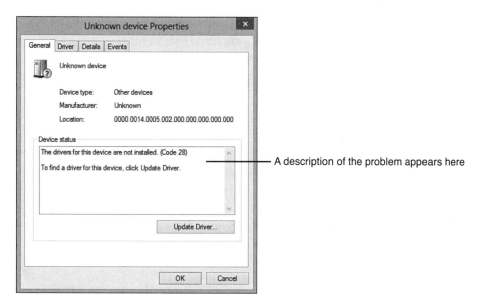

A description of the problem appears here

FIGURE 5.2

The Device Status area tells you if the device isn't working properly.

Device Manager uses three different icons to give you an indication of the device's current status:

- A black exclamation mark (!) on a yellow field tells you that there's a problem with the device.

- A red *X* tells you that the device is disabled or missing.

- A blue *i* on a white field tells you that the device's Use Automatic Settings check box (on the Resources tab) is deactivated and that at least one of the device's resources was selected manually. Note that the device might be working just fine, so this icon doesn't indicate a problem. If the device isn't working properly, however, the manual setting might be the cause.

If your system flags a device, but you don't notice any problems, you can usually get away with just ignoring the flag. I've seen lots of systems that run perfectly well with flagged devices, so this falls under the "If it ain't broke..." school of troubleshooting. The danger here is that tweaking your system to try to get rid of the flag can cause other—usually more serious—problems.

Troubleshooting Device Driver Problems

Device drivers are small chunks of software that Windows uses to contact and control (that is, "drive") your PC's hardware. As the middlemen brokering the dialogue between Windows and our devices, these complex bits of code perform a crucial task. After all, unleashing the full potential of your system is just not possible unless the hardware and the operating system coexist harmoniously and optimally.

Other than problems with the hardware itself, device drivers are the cause of most device woes. This is true even if your device doesn't have one of the problem icons mentioned in the preceding section. That is, if you open the device's properties sheet, Windows might tell you that the device is "working properly," but all that means is that Windows can establish a simple communications channel with the device. So if your device isn't working right, but Windows says otherwise, suspect a driver problem.

Basic Device Driver Troubleshooting

Here are a few basic techniques for correcting device driver problems:

- **Reinstall the driver**—A driver might be malfunctioning because one or more of its files have become corrupted. You can usually solve this problem by reinstalling the driver. Just in case a disk fault caused the corruption, you should check the hard drive where the driver is installed (usually drive C) for errors before reinstalling.

→ To learn more about hard disk error checking, **see** "Dealing with Hard Disk Errors," **p. 17**

- **Upgrade to a signed driver**—*Unsigned* drivers—that is, device drivers that don't come with a security signature from Microsoft that verifies the drivers are safe to install—are accidents waiting for a place to happen in Windows, so you should upgrade to a signed driver, if possible. How can you tell whether an installed driver is unsigned? In Device Manager, double-click the device to open its Properties dialog box and then display the Driver tab. Signed driver files display a name (such as "Microsoft Windows") beside the Digital Signer label (see Figure 5.3), whereas unsigned drivers display "Not digitally signed" instead.

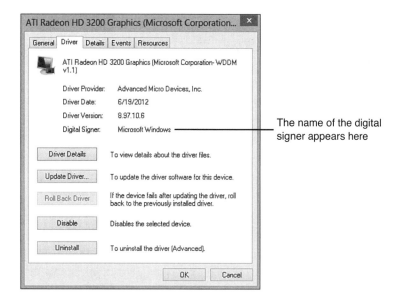

The name of the digital signer appears here

FIGURE 5.3

In the Driver tab, the Digital Signer label tells you whether the device driver is signed.

- **Disable an unsigned driver**—If an unsigned driver is causing system instability and you can't upgrade the driver, try disabling it. In Device Manager, double-click the device to open its Properties dialog box, click the Driver tab, and then click Disable.

- **Try the manufacturer's driver supplied with the device**—If the device came with its own driver (say, on a CD or DVD), either try updating the driver to the manufacturer's (see "Updating a Device Driver," later in this chapter) or try running the device's setup program from the disc.

- **Download the latest driver from the manufacturer**—Device manufacturers often update drivers to fix bugs, add new features, and tweak performance. Go to the manufacturer's website to see whether an updated driver is available. See "Tips for Downloading Device Drivers," next, for more info.

- **Roll back a driver.** If the device stops working properly after you update the driver, try rolling it back to the old driver as described a bit later in the "Rolling Back a Device Driver" section.

Tips for Downloading Device Drivers

Finding device drivers on the Web is an art in itself. I can't tell you how much of my life I've wasted rooting around manufacturer websites trying to locate a device driver. Most hardware vendor sites seem to be optimized for sales rather than service, so although you can purchase, say, a new printer with just a mouse click or two, downloading a new driver for that printer can take a frustratingly long time. To help you avoid such frustration, here are some tips from our hard-won experience:

- If the manufacturer offers different sites for different locations (such as different countries), always use the company's "home" site. Most mirror sites aren't true mirrors, and (Murphy's law still being in effect) it's usually the driver you're looking for that a mirror site is missing.

- The temptation when you first enter a site is to use the search feature to find what you want. This works only sporadically for drivers, and the site search engines almost always return marketing or sales material first.

- Instead of the search engine, look for an area of the site dedicated to driver downloads. The good sites will have links to areas called Downloads or Drivers, but it's far more common to have to go through a Support or Customer Service area first.

- Don't try to take any shortcuts to where you *think* the driver might be hiding. Trudge through each step the site provides. For example, it's common to have to select an overall driver category, then a device category, then a line category, and then the specific model you have. This is tedious, but it almost always gets you where you want to go.

- If the site is particularly ornery, the preceding method might not lead you to your device. In that case, try the search engine. Note that device drivers seem to be particularly poorly indexed, so you might have to try lots of search text variations. One thing that usually works is searching for the exact filename. How can you possibly know that? A method that often works for me is to use Google (www.google.com), Google Groups (groups.google.com), or some other web search engine to search for the driver. Chances are, someone else has looked for your file and will have the filename (or, if you're really lucky, a direct link to the driver on the manufacturer's site).

- When you get to the device's download page, be careful which file you choose. Make sure it's designed for your version of Windows, and make sure you're not downloading a utility program or some other nondriver file.

- When you finally get to download the file, be sure to save it to your computer rather than opening it. If you reformat your system or move the device to another computer, you'll be glad you have a local copy of the driver so that you don't have to wrestle with the whole download rigmarole all over again.

Updating a Device Driver

As I mentioned earlier, one of basic troubleshooting techniques for hardware troubles is to update the device's driver to either the version that comes on a disc that shipped with the device, or a version that you downloaded from the manufacturer's website. Either way, follow these steps to update a device driver:

1. If you have a disc with the updated driver, insert it. If you downloaded the driver from the Internet, decompress the driver file, if necessary (which generally means double-clicking the file).

2. Open Device Manager as described earlier in this chapter.

3. Click the device you want to work with.

4. Select Action, Update Driver Software. (You can also click the Update Driver Software button in the toolbar or double-click the device, display the Driver tab, and click Update Driver.) The Update Driver Software Wizard appears.

5. You have two choices:

   - **Search Automatically for Updated Driver Software**—Click this option to have Windows check Windows Updates for the driver.

   - **Browse My Computer for Driver Software**—Click this option if you have a local device driver, whether on a disc or in a downloaded file. In the dialog box that appears, click Browse and then select the location of the device driver.

 NOTE If your driver download comes packaged in a setup file, it's almost always best just to launch the setup file and let it perform the update for you.

Rolling Back a Device Driver

It's an unfortunate fact of computing life that sometimes the attempts we make at fixing a problem only lead to worse or different problems. Sigh. So if you updated a device driver as described in the previous section but that has only made things worse in some way, not to worry. Windows has tools that let you easily *roll back* the driver update, which means it reverts to using the previous device driver.

You have two ways to fix things:

- If updating the driver was the last action you performed on the system, restore the system to the most recent restore point.

→ To learn how to restore your system, **see** "Recovering Using System Restore," **p. 95**

- If you've updated other things on the system in the meantime, a restore point might cause you to lose updates you want to keep. In that case, you need to roll back just the device driver that's causing problems.

Follow these steps to roll back a device driver:

1. Run Device Manager as described earlier in this chapter.

2. Double-click the device to open its Properties dialog box.

3. Display the Driver tab.

4. Click Roll Back Driver and then click OK.

THE ABSOLUTE MINIMUM

This chapter continued your troubleshooting tour by looking at a few tools and techniques that you can use to get wonky devices back on their digital feet. Here are the highlights:

- Device Manager is the Windows troubleshooting tool of choice.

- In Device Manager's list of devices, look for a black exclamation mark (!) on a yellow field, which tells you that there's a problem with the device. Alternatively, a red X tells you that the device is disabled or missing.

- A device driver is a cute, little bundle of software that enables Windows and a device to communicate with each other.

- An unsigned device driver is one that doesn't come with a security certificate from Microsoft that verifies the driver is safe to install. Ideally, you should upgrade any unsigned drivers to signed versions.

- Device driver troubleshooting step #1: Reinstall the driver that came with the device.

- Device driver troubleshooting step #2: Update the driver to the one on the disc that came with the device.

- Device driver troubleshooting step #3: Download the latest version of the driver from the manufacturer's website and then update the driver to this new version.

- If the driver update causes more problems, roll it back either by using System Restore or by using the Roll Back Driver command in Device Manager.

IN THIS CHAPTER

- Restoring a lost or damaged file that you prudently backed up
- Taking advantage of Windows 8's Recovery Environment
- Starting up your PC in Safe mode
- Reverting your PC to an earlier—and working—state using System Restore
- Solving problems by refreshing your Windows 8 system files
- Getting your PC back on its feet by restoring a system image

6

RECOVERING FROM PROBLEMS

Ideally, solving a problem requires a specific tweak to the system: a setting change, a driver upgrade, a program uninstall. But sometimes you need to take more of a "big picture" approach to revert your system to some previous state in the hope that you'll leap past the problem and get your system working again. Fortunately, Windows comes with a boatload of tools that can help in such scenarios, and I use this chapter to tell you about these tools.

Restoring Backed-Up Data

As you saw in Chapter 3, "Preparing for Trouble," all the effort you put into getting your PC prepared for some future calamity is really about only one thing: keeping your precious and irreplaceable data from becoming digital dust in the wind. So the most fundamental form of recovery is restoring a lost or damaged file or folder from a backup which, when complete, is one of the sweetest feelings in all of computerdom. (I talk about the much bigger operation of restoring your PC from a system image backup later in this chapter; see the section "Restoring a Windows 8 System Image.") The next few sections take you through the backup restore tools in various versions of Windows.

Restoring a Previous Version of a File in Windows 8

When you activate File History on your PC, as described earlier in Chapter 3, Windows 8 periodically—by default, once an hour—looks for files that have changed since the last check. If it finds a changed file, it takes a "snapshot" of that file and saves that version of the file to the external drive that you specified when you set up File History. This gives Windows 8 the capability to reverse the changes you've made to a file by reverting to an earlier state of the file. An earlier state of a file is called a *previous version*.

Why would you want to revert to a previous version of a file? One reason is that you might improperly edit the file by deleting or changing important data. In some cases, you may be able to restore that data by going back to a previous version of the file. Another reason is that the file might become corrupted if the program or Windows 8 crashes. You can get back a working version of the file by restoring a previous version.

 NOTE Windows 8 also keeps track of previous versions of folders, which is useful if an entire folder becomes corrupted because of a system crash.

Follow these steps to restore a previous version of a file in Windows 8:

1. In the Start screen, press Windows Logo+W, type **history**, and then click File History to open the File History window.

2. Click Restore Personal Files. The File History window appears.

3. Double-click the library that contains the file you want to restore.

4. Open the folder that contains the file.

5. Click Previous Version (see Figure 6.1) or press Ctrl+Left arrow until you open the version of the folder you want to use. If you'd prefer a more recent version, click Next Version or press Ctrl+Right arrow.

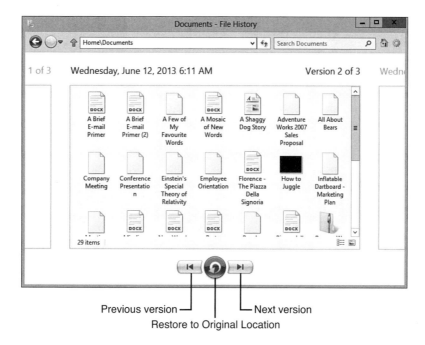

Previous version ——   —— Next version
Restore to Original Location

FIGURE 6.1

Use the File History window to choose which previous version you want to restore.

6. Click the file you want to restore.

7. Click Restore to Original Location (pointed out in Figure 6.1). If the original folder has a file with the same name, File History asks what you want to do.

8. Select an option:

- **Replace the File in the Destination Folder**—Click this option to overwrite the existing file with the previous version.

- **Skip This File**—Click this option to skip the restore and do nothing.

- **Compare Info for Both Files**—Click this option to display the File Conflict dialog box (see Figure 6.2), which shows the original and the previous version side by side, along with the last modification date and time and the file size. Activate the check box beside the version you want to keep and then click Continue. To keep both versions, activate both check boxes. File History restores the previous version with (2) appended to its filename.

FIGURE 6.2

If the original folder has a file with the same name and you're not sure which one to keep, use the File Conflict dialog box to decide.

Restoring a Backed-Up File in Windows 7

If you've been farsighted (or paranoid) enough to make backups of your Windows 7 data, nice going! Your reward is that you can follow these steps to restore the data you seek:

1. Select Start, type **backup**, and then click Backup and Restore in the search results.

2. Select Restore My Files. The Restore Wizard appears and displays the Browse or Search Your Backup for Files and Folders to Restore dialog box.

3. If you backed up using a removable medium such as a CD, DVD, or memory card, insert the medium that contains the backups.

TIP Windows Backup keeps track of your previous backups, and although you'll most often want to restore a file from the most recent backup, you can restore files from any stored backup. In the Browse or Search Your Backup for Files and Folders to Restore dialog box, click the Choose a Different Date link and then use the Restore Files dialog box to choose backup you want to work with.

4. Select Browse for Files. If you want to restore an entire folder, select Browse for Folders instead. The Browse the Backup for Files dialog box appears.

5. Open the folder that contains the file you want to restore and then select the file you want to restore. To restore multiple files from the same folder, press and hold Ctrl and click each file.

6. Select Add Files. The Restore Files Wizard adds the file you selected to the list, as shown in Figure 6.3.

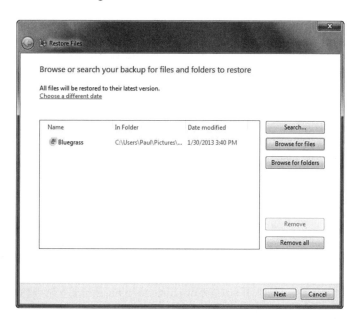

FIGURE 6.3

Use this dialog box to select the files or folders you want to restore.

7. Repeat steps 4 to 6 to select other files to restore.

8. Select Next. The Where Do You Want to Restore Your Files? dialog box appears.

9. Select the In the Original Location option and then select Restore. If a file with the same name exists in the original location, you see the Copy File dialog box; otherwise, skip to step 12.

10. If you want Windows Backup to handle all conflicts the same way, select the Do This for All Conflicts check box.

11. Choose how you want Windows 7 to handle the conflict:

- Click Copy and Replace if you want to overwrite the existing file.

- Click Don't Copy if you want to keep the original.

- Click Copy, But Keep Both Files if you want to see both files.

12. Click Finish. Windows 7 restores the data.

Restoring a Backed-Up File in Windows Vista

If you have a backup of your Windows Vista data, good news: You can restore a file or folder by following these steps:

1. Select Start, All Programs, Accessories, System Tools, Backup Status and Configuration. The Backup Status and Configuration window appears.

2. Select the Restore Files tab and then select Restore Files. Vista launches the Restore Files Wizard.

3. If you backed up using a removable medium such as a CD, DVD, or memory card, insert the medium that contains the backups.

4. Select the Files from the Latest Backup option. If you prefer to restore from an earlier backup, select the Files from an Older Backup option instead.

5. Click Next.

6. Select Browse Files. If you want to restore an entire folder, select Browse Folders instead. The Browse the Backup for Files dialog box appears.

7. Open the folder that contains the file you want to restore and then select the file you want to restore. To restore multiple files from the same folder, press and hold Ctrl and click each file.

8. Select Restore. The Restore Files Wizard adds the file you selected to the list, as shown in Figure 6.4.

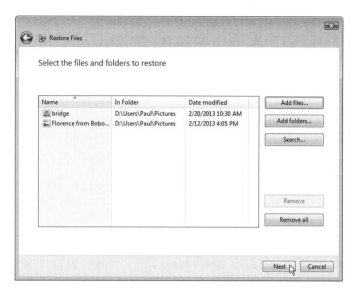

FIGURE 6.4

Use this dialog box to select the files or folders you want to restore.

9. Repeat steps 6 to 8 to select other files to restore.

10. Select Next. The Where Do You Want to Save the Restored Files? dialog box appears.

11. Select the In the Original Location option and then select Start Restore. If a file with the same name exists in the original location, you see the Copy File dialog box; otherwise, skip to step 14.

12. If you want Windows Backup to handle all conflicts the same way, select the Do This for All Conflicts check box.

13. Choose how you want Windows Vista to handle the conflict:

- Click Copy and Replace if you want to overwrite the existing file.

- Click Don't Copy if you want to keep the original.

- Click Copy, But Keep Both Files if you want to see both files.

14. Click Finish. Windows Vista restores the data.

Restoring a Backed-Up File in Windows XP

Here are the steps to follow if you want to restore a file from a backup using Windows XP:

1. Select Start, All Programs, Accessories, System Tools, Backup. The Backup or Restore Wizard appears.

2. Select Next. The Backup or Restore dialog box appears.

3. Select the Restore Files and Settings options and then select Next. The What to Restore dialog box appears.

4. Expand the File branch and then expand the branch of the backup file from which you want to restore the files.

5. Expand the folders until you locate the one that contains the file you want to restore, and then select that folder.

6. Select the check box beside the file you want to restore, as shown in Figure 6.5.

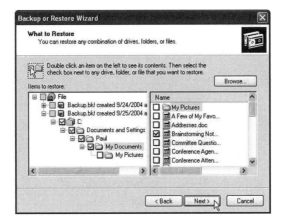

FIGURE 6.5

Use this dialog box to select the files or folders you want to restore.

7. Repeat steps 4 to 6 to select other files to restore, and then select Next. The Completing the Backup or Restore Wizard dialog box appears.

8. Insert the medium that contains the backup file.

9. Select Finish. Windows XP restores the data.

Accessing the Windows 8 Recovery Environment

Windows 8 offers a Recovery Environment (RE) that gives you a simple, easily navigated set of screens that offer a number of troubleshooting tools and utilities. Windows 8 offers many other ways to get to the RE and its advanced startup options, including the following:

- Use the PC Settings app within Windows 8.

- Boot to a recovery drive.

- Boot to your Windows 8 installation media.

The next few sections discuss each method in more detail.

Accessing the RE via PC Settings

If you're having trouble with your PC, but you can still start Windows 8, you can use the PC Settings app to access the RE. Follow these steps to boot to the RE using the PC Settings app within Windows 8:

1. Press Windows Logo+W to open the Settings search pane.

2. Type **advanced** and then click Advanced Startup Options in the search results. Windows 8 opens the PC Settings app and displays the General tab.

3. In the Advanced Startup section, click Restart Now. The Choose an Option screen appears, as shown in Figure 6.6.

4. Click Troubleshoot.

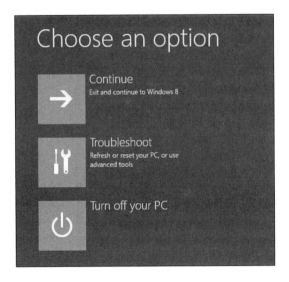

FIGURE 6.6

When you boot to the Choose an Option screen, click Troubleshoot to see the Recovery Environment tools.

Accessing the RE via a Recovery Drive

If you're having a problem with your system and are unable to start Windows 8 and can't even access your hard drive, you can still access a version of the RE if you created a recovery drive, as I described in Chapter 3.

→ For the details on building your own recovery drive, **see** "Creating a Windows 8 Recovery Drive," **p. 53**

Follow these steps to boot to the RE using the recovery drive:

1. Insert the recovery drive.

2. Restart your PC and boot to the USB flash drive:

   - If you have a newer PC, Windows 8 should recognize the flash drive automatically and display the Use a Device screen. Click your flash drive in the list that appears.

- If you have an older PC, you need to access your PC's settings and configure them to boot to the flash drive. Look for a message right after you turn on the PC that says something like `Press Del to access BIOS/Start settings`. Press the key and then use the settings for the boot options to configure your PC to boot to the USB flash drive.

3. Click a keyboard layout. The Choose an Option screen appears.

4. Click Troubleshoot.

Accessing the RE via Windows 8 Install Media

If you didn't create a recovery drive, but you have your Windows 8 installation media, follow these steps to boot to the RE using the install media:

1. Insert your Windows 8 install media.

2. Restart your PC and boot to the install drive.

3. When the Windows Setup dialog box appears, click Next.

4. Click Repair Your Computer. The Choose an Option screen appears.

5. Click Troubleshoot.

 TIP If your system doesn't boot from the Windows 8 install media (or the recovery drive), you need to adjust the system's settings to allow it to boot. Restart the computer and look for a startup message that prompts you to press a key or key combination to modify the PC's settings (which might be called Setup or something similar). Find the boot options and either enable a media drive–based boot or make sure that the option to boot from the media drive comes before the option to boot from the hard disk. If you use a USB keyboard, you may also need to enable an option that lets the system recognize keystrokes after the POST but before Windows starts.

Navigating the Recovery Environment

In the preceding few sections, each procedure dropped you off at the Troubleshoot screen, shown in Figure 6.7.

FIGURE 6.7

The Troubleshoot screen offers a few troubleshooting tools.

From here, you can refresh or reset your PC (I discuss these options later in this chapter; see sections, "Refreshing Your Windows 8 PC" and "Resetting Your Windows 8 PC"). You can also click Advanced Options to display the Advanced Options screen, shown in Figure 6.8.

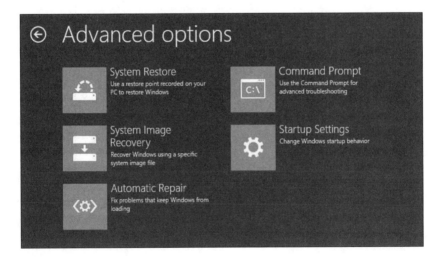

FIGURE 6.8

The new Advanced Options screen offers even more troubleshooting tools.

From here, you can run System Restore (see "Recovering Using System Restore," later in this chapter), recover a system image (see "Restoring a Windows 8 System Image"), and more.

In most cases, you can also click Startup Settings and then click Restart to access even more startup settings. (Note that you don't see the Windows Startup Settings option if you boot to a recovery drive or the Windows 8 install media.) Windows 8 restarts your PC and displays the Startup Settings screen, shown in Figure 6.9.

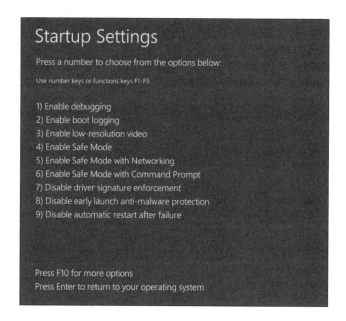

FIGURE 6.9

The Startup Settings screen offers several startup options.

Press Enter to load Windows 8 in the usual fashion. You can use the other options to control the rest of the startup procedure. Here are the most useful of these options:

- **Enable Low-Resolution Video**—This option loads Windows 8 with the video display set to 640×480 and 256 colors. This capability is useful if your video output is garbled when you start Windows 8. For example, if your display settings are configured at a resolution that your video card can't handle, boot in the low-resolution mode and then switch to a setting supported by your video card.

- **Safe Mode**—The three Safe mode options enable you to run a barebones version of Windows 8 for troubleshooting. See "Booting Up in Safe Mode."

- **Disable Driver Signature Enforcement**—This item prevents Windows 8 from checking whether device drivers have digital signatures. Choose this option to ensure that Windows 8 loads an unsigned driver, if failing to load that driver is causing system problems.

- **Disable Early Launch Anti-Malware Protection**—This option prevents Windows 8 from scanning device drivers for malware during startup. If Windows 8 doesn't start, it's possible that the anti-malware scan is messing with a driver.

Booting Up in Safe Mode

If you're having trouble with Windows—for example, if a corrupt or incorrect video driver is mangling your display, or if Windows doesn't start—you can use the Safe Mode option to run a stripped-down version of Windows that includes only the minimal set of device drivers that Windows requires to load. Using this mode, you could, for example, reinstall or roll back the offending device driver and then load Windows normally.

 TIP To get to the Safe Mode option in Windows 7 or earlier, restart your computer, wait until the POST is complete, and then press F8 to display the Windows Boot Manager menu, and then press F8 again to open the Advanced Boot Options screen. If your computer is set up to "fast boot," it might not be obvious when the POST ends. In that case, just turn on your computer and press F8 repeatedly until you see the Windows Boot Manager menu. Note, however, that if your system picks up two separate F8 presses, you might end up directly in the Advanced Boot Options menu. From there, select Safe Mode.

When you start in Safe mode, Windows uses the all-powerful Administrator account, which is the account to use when troubleshooting problems. However, caution is required when doing so.

When Windows finally loads, as shown in Figure 6.10, the desktop reminds you that you're in Safe mode by displaying `Safe Mode` in each corner. (Also, Windows Help and Support appears with Safe mode–related information and links.)

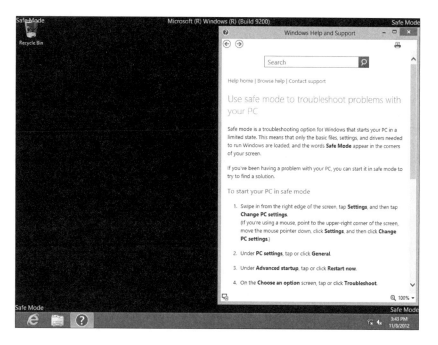

FIGURE 6.10

Windows 8 in Safe mode.

 TIP Safe mode is a lifesaver if your PC becomes infected with a virus, spyware, or some other form of so-called *malware*, which in most cases can't run in Safe mode. When you get to the Safe mode screen, run an antimalware utility to disinfect your system. If you don't have such a utility and can't get to the store to buy one, select Safe Mode with Networking at startup, which gives you basic Internet access so you can download an antimalware utility.

Recovering Using System Restore

If you make a change to your system—such as adding new hardware, updating a device driver, installing a program, or modifying some settings—and then find that the system doesn't start or acts weirdly, it's a good bet that the change is the culprit. In that case, you can tell Windows to revert to an earlier configuration that worked (that is, a configuration that doesn't include your most recent change). The theory is that by using the previous working configuration, you can make your problem go away because the system is bypassing the change that caused the problem.

You revert Windows to an earlier configuration by using System Restore. I showed you how to use System Restore to set restore points in Chapter 3.

→ For information on setting restore points, **see** "Setting System Restore Points," **p. 51**

To revert your system to a restore point, follow these steps:

1. Launch System Restore:

   • **If you can boot Windows 8**—In the Start screen, press Windows Logo+W, type **recovery**, click Recovery, and then click Open System Restore.

   • **If you can't boot Windows 8**—Boot to the Recovery Environment, as described earlier (see section, "Navigating the Recovery Environment"), click Advanced Options, and then click System Restore. Click your user account, type your account password, and then click Continue.

> **TIP** Use one of the following techniques to start System Restore in earlier versions of Windows:
>
> • **Windows 7 and Vista**—Select Start, type **restore**, and then select System Restore in the search results.
>
> • **Windows XP**—Select Start, All Programs, Accessories, System Tools, System Restore.

2. In the initial System Restore dialog box, click Next. System Restore displays a list of restore points.

3. If you don't see the restore point you want to use, click to activate the Show More Restore Points check box, which tells Windows to display all the available restore points.

> **NOTE** By default, Windows displays only the restore points from the previous five days. When you activate the Show More Restore Points check box, you tell Windows to also show the restore points that are more than five days old.

4. Click the restore point you want to use.

5. Click Next. If other hard disks are available in the restore point, Windows displays a list of the disks. Activate the check box beside each disk you want to include in the restore and then click Next.

6. Click Finish. Windows asks you to confirm that you want your system restored.

7. Click Yes. System Restore begins reverting to the restore point. When it's done, it restarts your computer and displays a message telling you the results of the restore.

8. Click Close.

Refreshing Your Windows 8 PC

If the System Restore feature didn't solve your problem, the next recovery step to try is Refresh Your PC. This new tool reinstalls a fresh copy of Windows 8 while keeping your data, settings, and Windows 8 apps intact. When you refresh your PC, the computer boots to the Recovery Environment, gathers up your data, copies it to another part of the hard drive, reinstalls Windows 8, and then restores your data.

Here's what gets saved when you refresh your PC:

- The files in your user account

- Your personalization settings, wireless network connections, mobile broadband connections, and drive letter assignments

- Any Windows 8 apps you've installed

 CAUTION Because the refresh first makes a copy of your data and settings, you must have enough free space on your hard drive to hold this data. If you don't have the space, you can't refresh your PC.

Here's what does *not* get saved during the refresh:

- All other PC settings (which are reverted to their defaults).

- Any desktop programs you installed. However, Windows 8 does generate a list of these programs for you.

Here are the steps to follow to refresh your PC:

1. Launch Refresh Your PC:

    - **If you can boot Windows 8**—In the Start screen, press Windows Logo+W, type **refresh**, and then click Refresh Your PC.

- **If you can't boot Windows 8**—Boot to the Recovery Environment's Troubleshoot screen, as described earlier (see section, "Accessing the Windows 8 Recovery Environment"), and click Refresh Your PC. Windows 8 reboots the PC and asks you to choose your user account. Click your user account, type your account password, and then click Continue.

2. Click Next. Refresh Your PC prompts you to insert your installation media or a recovery drive.

3. Insert the media. Refresh Your PC validates the media and prompts you to start the process.

4. Click Refresh. Refresh Your PC reboots the computer and runs the refresh.

Resetting Your Windows 8 PC

Refreshing your PC should solve most problems. If it doesn't for some reason, or if you don't have enough room on your hard drive to perform the refresh, your next option is to completely reset your PC. (However, you should first consider restoring a system image, if you have one, as described in the next section.) This procedure completely erases your data, reformats your hard drive, and then reinstalls Windows 8, so it's a fairly drastic step.

 NOTE Resetting your PC is perfect if you're going to be giving your PC to someone else or selling it. This way, you don't have to worry about the new owner seeing any of your data or programs.

Follow these steps to reset your PC:

1. Launch Reset Your PC:

   - **If you can boot Windows 8**—In the Start screen, press Windows Logo+W, type **reset**, and then click Remove Everything and Reinstall Windows.

   - **If you can't boot Windows 8**—Boot to the Recovery Environment's Troubleshoot screen, as described earlier (see section, "Accessing the Windows 8 Recovery Environment"), and click Reset Your PC.

2. Click Next. Windows 8 reboots the PC and prompts you to insert your installation media or a recovery drive.

3. Insert the media. Reset Your PC asks how you want to remove your personal files.

4. Make your choice:

- **Thoroughly**—Choose this route if you're resetting your PC to give or sell to someone else. This option erases your personal data by overwriting it with random data at the sector level, but the process can take a few hours to complete.

- **Quickly**—Choose this option if you're keeping your computer and want to get it back on its feet as soon as possible.

 CAUTION The thorough data removal option is indeed thorough, but it is *not* 100% secure. Reset Your PC erases your data with a single pass of random data, but that's not enough to prevent someone with extremely sophisticated (and expensive) equipment from recovering some of your data. The thorough option is fine for the vast majority of us, but consider more robust erasure methods if your PC contains extremely sensitive or secret data. I suggest a free program called Eraser, which you can download from http://eraser.heidi.ie/.

5. Click Reset. Reset Your PC begins the recovery. Along the way, you need to enter your Windows 8 product key, accept the license terms, name your PC, sign in with your Microsoft account, and perform a few other setup chores.

Restoring a Windows 8 System Image

If you can't reset your PC because you don't have your Windows 8 install media or a recovery drive, you can still get your system back on its feet if you created a backup system image, as I described in Chapter 3.

→ For the details on creating system image backups, **see** "Creating a System Image Backup" **p. 55**

Follow these steps to restore a system image:

1. If you saved the system image to an external hard drive, connect that hard drive. If you used DVDs, insert the last DVD in the set.

2. Boot to the Recovery Environment, as described earlier (see section, "Accessing the Windows 8 Recovery Environment").

TIP Use one of the following techniques to initiate a system image restore in earlier versions of Windows:

- **Windows 7**—Restart your computer, press F8 to display the Windows Advanced Options Menu, select the Repair Your Computer option, click Next, type your Windows 7 username and password, click OK, and then select System Image Recovery.

- **Windows Vista**—Insert your Windows Vista CD and reboot your computer. If you're prompted to press a key to boot from the CD, go ahead and press whatever key you like. Click Next, click System Recovery Options, click Next, click Next yet again, and then click CompletePC Restore.

3. Click Advanced Options. The Advanced Options screen appears.

4. Click System Image Recovery. Windows 8 asks you to choose a target operating system.

5. Click Windows 8. System Image Recovery prompts you to select a system image backup and offers two options:

   - **Use the Latest Available System Image**—Activate this option to restore Windows 8 using the most recently created system image. This is almost always the best way to go because it means you'll restore the maximum percentage of your data and programs. If you choose this option, click Next and skip to step 8.

   - **Select a System Image**—Activate this option to select from a list of restore points. This is the way to go if you saved a system image to your network, or if the most recent system image includes some change to your system that you believe is the source of your system problems. Click Next and continue with step 6.

6. Click the location of the system image and then click Next.

7. Click the system image you want to use for the restore and then click Next. If you want to use a system image saved to a network share, click Advanced and then click Search for a System Image on the Network.

8. If you replaced your hard drive, activate the Format and Repartition Disks check box.

9. Click Next. System Image Recovery displays a summary of the restore process.

10. Click Finish. System Image Recovery asks you to confirm.

11. Click Yes. System Image Recovery begins restoring your computer and then reboots to Windows 8 when the restore is complete.

THE ABSOLUTE MINIMUM

PC problems might be inevitable, but losing your data most certainly is not. With a bit of pre-problem prep and the tools available with Windows, you can recover from most calamities with your files (and your sanity) intact:

- If you're running Windows 8, use the File History feature to restore a previous version of a lost, damaged, or otherwise inaccessible file or folder.

- For earlier versions of Windows, load the backup utility and use it to restore your data from a backup file.

- Windows 8 fans can gain access to tons of useful troubleshooting tools via the Recovery Environment, which you can access via PC Settings, a recovery drive, or your Windows 8 install media.

- Safe mode comes in handy when your PC won't boot to Windows, your display is garbled beyond recognition, or your system has contracted a virus or other form of malware.

- You can work around most recent problems by using System Restore to revert your PC to a state prior to the start of the problem.

- If you have Windows 8, refreshing your system files can solve many problems without messing with your data.

TROUBLESHOOTING YOUR NETWORK

Networking can be a complex, arcane topic that taxes the patience of all but the most dedicated wireheads (an affectionate pet name often applied to network hackers and gurus). There are so many hardware and software components to deal with that networks often seem like accidents looking for a place to happen. If your network has become a "notwork," this chapter offers a few solutions that might help.

Repairing a Network Connection

Windows comes with a Network Diagnostics tool that digs deep into all layers of the network connection to try to identify and resolve problems. Windows gives you several ways to launch the Network Diagnostic tool, but the following are probably the easiest:

- If you're using Windows 8, press Windows Logo+W to open the Search pane, type **network problem**, and then select Identify and Repair Network Problems in the search results.

- From the desktop, right-click the notification area's Network icon and then click Troubleshoot Problems.

When you launch the diagnostics, various troubleshooters work behind the scenes to create a list of possible solutions to the problem. If only one solution can be performed automatically, Windows attempts the solution. If there are multiple solutions (or a single solution that requires user input), you see a Windows Network Diagnostics dialog box similar to the one shown in Figure 7.1. Click the solution or follow the instructions that appear.

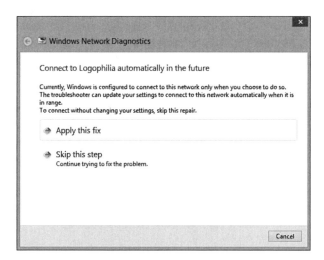

FIGURE 7.1

An example of a Windows Network Diagnostics dialog box.

Checking the Connection Status

The first thing you should check when you suspect a network problem is the Windows Network icon, which appears in the desktop's notification area. It has four states:

- **Wired connection with Internet access**—This state (see Figure 7.2) means that you have access to both the network and to the Internet via a wired network connection.

FIGURE 7.2

The Network icon for a wired connection with Internet access.

- **Wireless connection with Internet access**—This state (see Figure 7.3) means that you have access to both the network and to the Internet via a wireless network connection.

 NOTE In Windows 8, if you see the wireless bars, but they're grayed out with an asterisk in the upper-left corner, it means that you're not connected to a wireless network, but nearby networks are available.

FIGURE 7.3

The Network icon for a wireless connection with Internet access.

- **Connected, but with an error**—This state (see Figure 7.4) means that you have access to the network, but either your computer cannot access the Internet, or you have limited access to the network.

FIGURE 7.4

The Network icon for a connection that has either no Internet access or limited network access.

- **Not connected**—This state (see Figure 7.5) means that you are completely cut off from the network.

FIGURE 7.5

The Network icon for a broken network connection.

Checking Connectivity with the PING Command

As you might know, a submarine can detect a nearby object by using sonar to send out a sound wave and then seeing whether the wave is reflected. This is called *pinging* an object.

Windows has a PING command that performs a similar function. PING sends out a special type of message to a remote location. This message requests that the remote location send back a response. PING then tells you whether the response was received. In this way, you can check your network configuration to see whether your computer can connect with a remote host.

To use PING, first open a command-line session:

- **Windows 8**—Press Windows Logo+X and then select Command Prompt.

- **Earlier versions of Windows**—Select Start, All Programs, Accessories, Command Prompt.

At the command prompt, type **ping**, a space, and then the name of an Internet location. Here's an example that pings google.com:

```
C:\Users\Paul>ping google.com

Pinging google.com [64.233.187.99] with 32 bytes of data:

Reply from 64.233.187.99: bytes=32 time=43ms TTL=240
Reply from 64.233.187.99: bytes=32 time=42ms TTL=239
Reply from 64.233.187.99: bytes=32 time=43ms TTL=239
Reply from 64.233.187.99: bytes=32 time=42ms TTL=240

Ping statistics for 64.233.187.99:
    Packets: Sent = 4, Received = 4, Lost = 0 (0% loss),A
Approximate round trip times in milli-seconds:
    Minimum = 42ms, Maximum = 43ms, Average = 42ms
```

Here, you see that each message received a reply. If you can't connect to the remote host, PING returns a Request timed out error for each message.

If you can't connect to a remote host, here are some notes on using PING to troubleshoot problems:

- First, check to see whether you can use PING successfully on the this address:

  ping 127.0.0.1.

  The only reason this PING would fail is if your computer doesn't have the software required to connect to a network. However, all Windows machines have the software installed by default, and the option to uninstall it is disabled, so pinging this address will almost certainly work. The only reason to include it in your troubleshooting is that if it doesn't work, it means you have a serious problem with your machine. Either revert to a working configuration using System Restore, as described in Chapter 6, "Recovering from Problems"; refresh Windows 8 (or reinstall Windows, if you're using an earlier version); or take your machine to a computer repair professional.

- Now ping the name of another computer on your network. If PING fails, check your cable or wireless connections.

- If you get this far, try using PING on the Internet site you're trying to contact. If you're unsuccessful, check the cable connections and make sure the router is turned on. You may need to power cycle the router and your broadband modem.

General Solutions to Network Problems

Figuring out that a problem exists is one thing, but it's often quite another to come up with a fix for the problem. I discuss a few solutions in later sections, but here are a few other general fixes you need to keep in mind:

- **Enable network discovery**—If you can't access your network, by far the most common cause is that you have the Windows network discovery feature turned off. Make sure network discovery is turned on, as described later in this chapter (see the section "Turning On Network Discovery").

- **Close all programs**—You can often fix flaky behavior by shutting down all your open programs and starting again. This is a particularly useful fix for problems caused by low memory or low system resources.

- **Log off Windows**—Logging off clears the memory and gives you a slightly cleaner slate than merely closing all your programs.

- **Reboot the computer**—If there are problems with some system files and devices, logging off won't help because these objects remain loaded. By rebooting the system, you reload the entire system, which is often enough to solve many computer problems.

- **Turn off the computer and restart**—You can often solve a hardware problem by first shutting off your machine. Wait for 30 seconds to give all devices time to spin down and then restart. This is called *power cycling* the computer.

- **Power cycle the router**—If you're getting a network error or you can't access the Internet, the router may be at fault. Power off the router and then power it on again. Wait until the status lights stabilize and then try accessing the network.

- **Power cycle the modem**—If you can't get Internet access, you could have a problem with your broadband modem. Power off the modem and then power it on again. Wait until the status lights stabilize and then try accessing the Internet.

- **Check connections, power switches, and so on**—Some of the most common (and some of the most embarrassing) causes of hardware problems are the simple physical things. So, you want to make sure that a device (for example, your router) is turned on, check that cable connections (particularly between the NIC and router) are secure, and ensure that insertable devices (such as a USB or PC Card NIC) are properly inserted.

- **Check for solutions to your problem**—Open the Action Center, as described in Chapter 4, "Understanding Basic Troubleshooting," and, in the list of problems, check to see if your problem is listed and whether a solution exists.

→ To learn how to open the Action Center in your version of Windows, **see** "Checking for Solutions to Problems," **p. 69**.

- **Revert to a working configuration**—If you could access the network properly in the past, you may be able to solve the problem by reverting your system to that working state, as described in Chapter 6.

→ To learn how to use System Restore, **see** "Recovering Using System Restore," **p. 95**.

- **Upgrade the router's firmware**—Some network problems are caused by router bugs. If the manufacturer has corrected these bugs, the fixes will appear in the latest version of the router firmware, so you should upgrade to the new version, as described later in this chapter (see the section "Updating the Router Firmware").

- **Reset the router**—Network problems may result if you misconfigure your router or if the router's internal settings become corrupted somehow. Almost all routers come with a reset feature that enables you to return the router to its factory settings. Ideally, the device comes with a Reset button that you can push; otherwise, you need access to the router's setup pages.

Turning On Network Discovery

Networking your computers is all about access. You may want to access another computer to view one of its files or use its printer, and you may want other computers to access your machine to play your digital media. In Windows 8 and 7, however, this access is not always automatic. Windows 8 and 7 come with a feature called network discovery that, when turned on, means you can see (discover) the other computers on your network and the other computers can see (discover) yours. In networking, it's generally true that it you can see something, you can access it. (I say that this is generally true because there may be security issues that prevent or restrict access to a computer.)

Whether you have discovery turned on for a network depends on the type of network you're connected to:

- In a private network such as the one in your home or office, you want to see other computers and have them see you, so network discovery should be turned on.

- In a public network, such as a wireless hot spot, network discovery should be turned off because you probably don't want other users in the coffee shop (or wherever) to see your computer.

These aren't hard-and-fast rules, however, and sometimes you might need to flaunt these rules. For example, you might have one computer on your home or office network that you don't want others to see because, for instance, it contains sensitive information. In this case, it makes sense to turn off network discovery for that computer. Similarly, you and a friend might want to see each other's computers in a public setting so that you can perform a quick file exchange. In such a scenario, you can turn on network discovery, if only temporarily.

Here are the steps to follow to change the current network discovery setting:

1. In Windows 8, select the Desktop tile.

2. Right-click the taskbar's Network icon and then click Open Network and Sharing Center. Windows displays the Network and Sharing Center.

3. Click the Change Advanced Sharing Settings link. The Advanced Sharing Settings window appears.

4. Open the Private section (in Windows 8; see Figure 7.6) or the Home or Work section (in Windows 7).

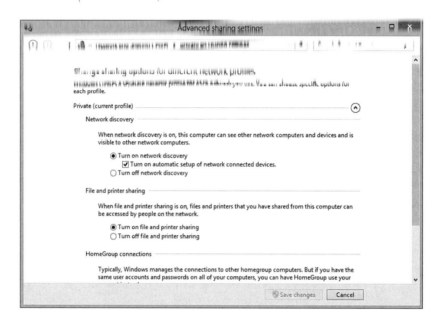

FIGURE 7.6

In the Advanced Sharing Settings window, open the Private section (or Home or Work if you're using Windows 7).

5. Select Turn On Network Discovery (which works only while you're connected to a network).

6. Open the Guest or Public section.

7. Select Turn Off Network Discovery.

8. Click Save Changes to put the new settings into effect.

If you have network discovery turned off and you open the Network folder (in any Windows Explorer window, click Network in the navigation pane), Windows displays an information bar message warning you that network discovery is turned off (see Figure 7.7), which is why you don't see any icons in the window. If you want to turn on network discovery, click the information bar and then click Turn On Network Discovery and File Sharing.

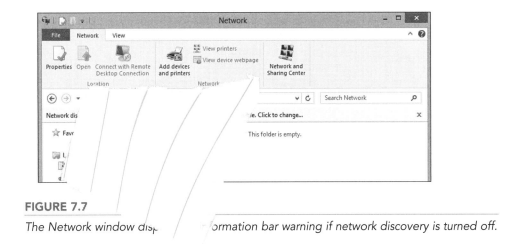

FIGURE 7.7

The Network window disp̣   ̣ormation bar warning if network discovery is turned off.

Updating the Router Firmware

The *router firmware* is the internal program that your network router uses to perform its routing chores and to display the setup pages and process any configuration changes you make. Router manufacturers frequently update their firmware to fix bugs, to improve performance, and to add new features. For all these reasons, it's a good idea to update the router's firmware to get the latest version. In case you're wondering, updating the firmware doesn't cause you to lose any of your settings.

TIP   The router's setup pages usually show you the current firmware version. However, you can usually get the router's firmware version through Windows. In Windows 8, open File Explorer and then click Network in the navigation pane; for earlier versions of Windows, select Start, Network. Right-click the router's icon and then click Properties. In the dialog box that appears, click the Network Device tab. The current firmware version usually appears as the Model Number value in the Device Details group.

The specifics of updating router firmware vary from device to device, so it's best to check either the manual that came with your router or the manufacturer's website. However, here's the general procedure for finding, downloading, and installing the latest firmware version:

1. Use Internet Explorer to navigate to the router manufacturer's website.

2. Navigate to the Support pages.

3. Navigate to the Download pages.

4. Use the interface to navigate to the download page for your router.

TIP   Most product support pages require the name and model number of the router. You can usually find this information on the underside of the router.

5. You should now see a list of firmware downloads. Examine the version numbers and compare them to your router's current firmware version.

6. If the latest version is later than the current version on your router, click the download link and save the firmware upgrade file on your computer.

 TIP   A good place to save the firmware upgrade file is the `Downloads` folder, which is a subfolder of your main Windows user account folder.

 CAUTION   Most router manufacturers require that you upgrade the firmware using a wired link to the router. Using a wireless link can damage the router.

7. Open and log in to the router's setup pages.

8. Navigate to the firmware upgrade page. Figure 7.8 shows a typical firmware upgrade page.

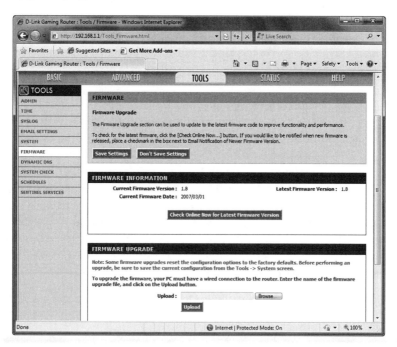

FIGURE 7.8

A typical firmware upgrade page for a router.

9. Locate the upload section, click Browse, and then select the firmware file that you downloaded.

10. Click Upload. The router uploads the file and then performs the upgrade.

Troubleshooting Cables

If one of the problems discussed so far isn't the cause of your networking quandary, the next logical suspect is the cabling that connects the workstations (of course, if your network is wireless, feel free to skip this section). This section discusses cabling, gives you a few pointers for preventing cable problems, and discusses some common cable kinks that can crop up.

Although most large-scale cabling operations are performed by third-party cable installers, home setups are usually do-it-yourself jobs. You can prevent some cable problems and simplify your troubleshooting down the road by taking a few precautions and "ounce of prevention" measures in advance:

- First and foremost, always buy the highest-quality cable you can find (for example, Category 5e or Category 6 or higher for twisted-pair cable). With network cabling, you get what you pay for.

- Good-quality cable is labeled. You should also add your own labels for things such as the source and destination of the cable.

- To avoid electromagnetic interference, don't run cable near electronic devices, power lines, air conditioners, fluorescent lights, motors, and other electromagnetic sources.

- Try to avoid phone lines because the ringer signal can disrupt network data carried over twisted-pair cable.

- To avoid the cable being stepped on accidentally, don't run it under carpet.

- To avoid people tripping over a cable (and possibly damaging the cable connector, the NIC port, or the person doing the tripping!), avoid high-traffic areas when laying the cable.

- If you plan to run cable outdoors, use conduit or another casing material to prevent moisture damage.

- Don't use excessive force to pull or push a cable into place. Rough handling can cause pinching or even breakage.

If you suspect cabling might be the cause of your network problems, here's a list of a few things to check:

- **Watch for electromagnetic interference**—If you see garbage on a workstation screen or experience random packet loss or temporarily missing nodes, the problem might be electromagnetic interference. Check your cables to make sure that they are at least 6 to 12 inches from any source of electromagnetic interference.

- **Check your connections**—Loose connections are a common source of cabling woes. Be sure to check every cable connection associated with the workstation that's experiencing network difficulty, including connections to the network adapter, router, switch, and so on.

- **Check the lay of the line**—Loops of cable could be generating an electrical field that interferes with network communication. Try not to leave your excess cable lying around in coils or loops.

- **Inspect the cable for pinching or breaks**—A badly pinched cable can cause a short in the wire, which could lead to intermittent connection problems. Make sure that no part of the cable is pinched, especially if the back of the computer is situated near a wall. A complete lack of connection with the network might mean that the cable's copper core has been severed completely and needs to be replaced.

Troubleshooting Wireless Network Problems

Wireless networking adds a whole new set of potential snags to your troubleshooting chores because of problems such as interference, compatibility, and device ranges. Here's a list of a few troubleshooting items that you should check to solve any wireless connectivity problems you're having:

- **Repair the connection**—The Windows network repair tool seems to work particularly well for solving wireless woes, so you should always start with that (see the section "Repairing a Network Connection," earlier in this chapter).

- **Reboot and power cycle devices**—Reset your hardware by performing the following tasks, in order: Log off Windows, restart your computer, power cycle your computer, power cycle the wireless router, and then power cycle the broadband modem.

- **Check connections**—Make sure your wireless adapter is installed properly and that the antenna is attached securely.

- **Move the antenna**—If the wireless adapter's antenna is on a cable, move the antenna to a higher position.

- **Check your notebook wireless adapter switch**—Many notebook computers come with a switch or program that turns the internal wireless adapter on and off. Make sure you haven't inadvertently turned off the adapter.

- **Look for interference**—Devices such as baby monitors and cordless phones that use the 2.4GHz radio frequency (RF) band can play havoc with wireless signals. Try either moving or turning off such devices if they're near your wireless adapter or wireless router.

> **CAUTION** You should also keep your wireless devices and router well away from a microwave oven; microwaves can jam wireless signals.

- **Change the channel**—You can configure your wireless access to broadcast signals on a specific channel. Sometimes one channel gives a stronger signal than another, so try changing the channel. You do this by logging on to the wireless router's configuration pages and looking for a setting that determines the broadcast channel.

- **Check your range**—If you're getting no signal or a weak signal, your wireless device could be too far away from the wireless router. You usually can't get much farther than about 115 feet away from a wireless router before the signal begins to degrade (230 feet if you're using 802.11n devices). Either move closer to the wireless router or turn on the wireless router's range booster feature, if it has one. You could also install a wireless range extender.

- **Check 802.11b/g/n/ac compatibility**—For your wireless device to work properly with your wireless router, both must use a compatible version of the wireless 802.11 standard. For example, if your wireless adapter supports only 802.11n, but your wireless router supports only 802.11g, the two are not able to connect.

- **Reset the router**—As a last resort, reset the router to its default factory settings. (Refer to the device documentation to learn how to do this.) Note that if you do this, you need to set up your network from scratch.

THE ABSOLUTE MINIMUM

This chapter extended your troubleshooting toolkit into the network realm. Here's a summary of the main points:

- If you're having trouble transferring data, accessing the Internet, or seeing other network computers, first check the connection status by examining the notification area's Network icon.

- To use `PING` for basic connectivity checks, open a Command Prompt session, type **ping**, a space, the name of the remote location you want to check, and then press Enter.

- If you can't see other computers on your network, make sure network discovery is turned on.

- Most network problems solve themselves when you reboot the PC, the router, or the broadband modem.

- If none of the basic solutions solves a wireless connection problem, try adjusting the antenna or moving the PC either away from a source of interference (such as a microwave oven) or closer to the router.

IN THIS CHAPTER

- Learning what tools you need (and don't need) for your PC repair jobs
- Setting up your PC-repair workshop for comfort and convenience
- Getting hip to a few common-sense (and not evenly remotely paranoid) safety precautions
- Getting inside the PC case
- Learning about computer cables and their myriad connections
- Getting an expansion card safely installed inside a PC

8

BASIC PC REPAIR SKILLS

Repairing a desktop PC is an art that anybody can master. If you can wield a knife and fork without poking yourself in the eye, you have the requisite dexterity to perform any PC upgrade or repair task. If you can dress yourself in the morning, you have the needed organizational abilities to coordinate any PC repair project.

What Tools Do You Need?

These days, you can almost get away with repairing a PC without requiring *any* tools at all! This is mostly thanks to the "toolless" designs of many modern computer cases, which enable you to install expansion cards, hard drives, and other internal drive bay components, such as optical drives and memory card readers, using clips (or variations on the clip theme) instead of screws.

I said *almost* because you still need a Phillips-head screwdriver to install a few components. In other words, you can perform probably 99% of all PC upgrade and repair chores using just an average Phillips screwdriver (see Figure 8.1)!

FIGURE 8.1

The simplest PC-builder's toolkit: a single Phillips screwdriver!

Of course, if you're anything like me, the tools are almost as much fun as the components themselves, so a single screwdriver doth not a toolkit make. If you're just starting out, one option is to buy a preassembled computer toolkit. For example, Figure 8.2 shows a toolkit that includes almost everything a budding PC repairer could want: a couple of Phillips- and flat-head screwdrivers, tweezers, pliers, extra screws, and more.

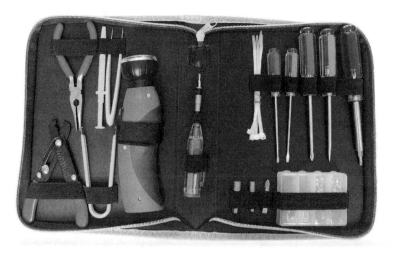

FIGURE 8.2

A preassembled computer toolkit.

The problem with almost all preassembled toolkits is that they're never perfect. For example, the kit shown in Figure 8.2 originally included a cheap soldering iron that's simply not going to be useful for most people. If they'd asked me, I'd have told them to replace the soldering iron with a decent flashlight, which is what I've done in Figure 8.2. So if you want to assemble your own toolkit (which is much more fun, anyway), here are my recommendations, more or less in descending order of importance:

- **Phillips-head screwdrivers**—This is the only essential computer tool. Note that not all Phillips screws are the same size, so I suggest getting several sizes of Phillips heads. At a minimum, get a #2 and a #1, and throw in a #0 if your budget permits it. (The smaller the number, the smaller the head; see Figure 8.3.)

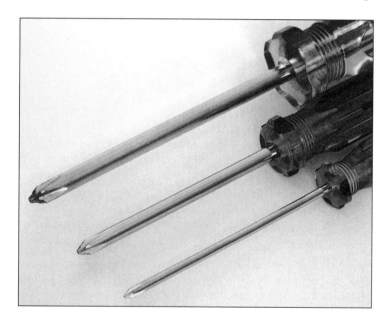

FIGURE 8.3

Several Phillips-head screwdrivers.

- **Flashlight**—Although your work area should be well lit (see "Setting Up Your Work Area," later in this chapter), computer cases can have dark areas where it's tough to see what you're doing. A good flashlight can help illuminate these areas.

- **Tweezers**—You'll be surprised how often you have to manipulate tiny parts such as screws that have fallen into one nook or another. Trying to maneuver these parts with your fingers is an exercise in frustration. The solution is a good pair of tweezers. I like to keep around both a regular pair of tweezers and a screw grabber, which is often easier to maneuver into tight spots (see Figure 8.4). Instead of tweezers, you can use needle-nose pliers, particularly a pair with a long nose.

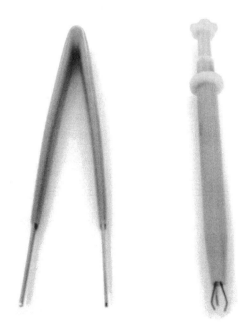

FIGURE 8.4

Regular tweezers and a screw grabber often come in handy when manipulating small objects.

- **Nut driver**—A 1/4-inch (or 7mm) nut driver is useful for screws that need to be inserted into or removed from tight spaces.

- **Cable ties**—To improve the air flow in your case, you need to combine cables and move them out of the way. Nylon cable ties make this easy.

- **Canned air**—A can of compressed air is great for thoroughly cleaning the dust off any component you've scavenged from an old PC.

- **Spare parts box**—A small plastic box provides a handy way to store extra screws, washers, jumpers, and other teensy parts that will get lost in five minutes unless you have a place to store them.

- **Flat-head screwdrivers**—These are also called *slotted screwdrivers* because the screws they work with include a slot across the top. You don't see these screws very often when working with PCs, but they sometimes come in handy with Phillips screws that also include a slot.

- **TORX screwdrivers**—You use these screwdrivers to manipulate tiny screws with star-shaped slots (see Figure 8.5). You'll never need a TORX screwdriver when installing PC components, but they're often used in the components themselves. So, for example, if one day you decide you want to see what the inside of a hard drive looks like, chances are you'll need a TORX screwdriver to remove the cover.

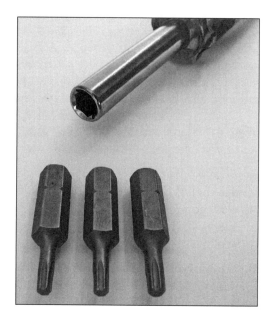

FIGURE 8.5

Some TORX bits.

 CAUTION   The inside of a PC case is no place for a power screwdriver (corded or cordless). The risk of overtightening a screw is just too great with these otherwise-useful tools, so you can easily break your motherboard or some other component. Also, power screwdrivers are bulky beasts that can easily slip off the screw and damage the board circuits.

Setting Up Your Work Area

Repairing a PC doesn't require a high-tech workshop, but it's not a task you should perform on the living room carpet, either. A proper PC-repair area is one that makes the job easier, so here are a few considerations to help you set up the perfect construction zone:

- **You need lights, lights, and more lights**—When it comes to cobbling together a PC, you simply can't have too much light. Some of the tasks you face take place in dim corners of the case or require you to make fairly precise connections. All this is much easier if you have a lot of light. A bright overhead light is great, but I also suggest a table lamp with some kind of adjustable neck so you can concentrate the light where you need it.

 TIP A good flashlight helps you illuminate even the murkiest corners of a case, but when it comes time to work in those corners, you almost always need two hands, so you have to put down the flashlight and try to angle it just so, which rarely works. Technology rides to the rescue here, too, by offering hat lights (sometimes called cap lights) that clip to the brim of a hat for hands-free illumination.

- **You need power**—Your area must have at least one power outlet nearby to plug in any lamps you use.

- **Get up off the floor**—A hardwood floor or other noncarpeted surface makes a nice even surface, but it's not a comfortable place for most people over a certain age. It's also more of a problem if dogs, cats, children, and other pets (kidding!) come along. It's better to build your new machine on a table or some other surface.

- **Give yourself plenty of elbow room**—Speaking of a table, be sure you use one that has a reasonable amount of room. It should be big enough to hold your case lying flat and still give you plenty of room around the case to hold your tools and parts.

- **Set up a work area of your own**—The ideal work surface is one you can claim as your own for the duration of your repair. That way, you can leave things as they are until you get a chance to resume the job. If you use a kitchen table, coffee table, or dining room table, chances are you're going to have to clear out to let others use it at some point, and you run the risk of losing things or just forgetting where you left off.

Playing It Safe

We live in a world where concerns for our personal safety have become borderline absurd: An iron-on transfer for a T-shirt comes with a piece of paper that warns, "Do not iron while wearing shirt," and a letter opener has a label that says, "Caution: Safety goggles recommended." I'm hip to this over-the-top concern, so when I tell you that you need to observe a few safety precautions when working inside a PC, remember that I'm coming at this from necessity, not paranoia.

Keeping Yourself Safe

So just how dangerous is it to work inside a PC? The answer depends on the PC's current state:

- **The PC has never been turned on, or it has been off for a long time**—This is the safest state because you have to worry about only one thing: cutting or scratching yourself on something sharp. Many PC components are quite sharp. The solder points under most motherboards and expansion cards are nasty little daggers; devices such as power supplies and hard drives often have sharp, metal edges; and the cooling fins on some CPU coolers are razor thin. Handle all PC components carefully to avoid getting a nasty cut or abrasion.

- **The PC has only recently been turned off**—In this state, you still have to worry about sharp objects, but you also have two other things to watch out for:

    Heat—Components such as the processor, power supply, and hard drive work hard while the computer is on and so build up a tremendous amount of heat. Give everything a few minutes to cool down before diving into the case to prevent getting burned.

    Electricity—Most electronic components use capacitors to store electricity, and that voltage often drains out of the capacitors slowly after you turn off the PC and yank out the power cord. Because you're waiting a few minutes to let the PC's components cool down anyway, that's also enough time for most capacitors to drain. The exception is the power supply and its massive capacitors, which can retain life-threatening amounts of voltage for quite a while after you shut off the power. This is a concern only if you're going to open the power supply casing and, because you shouldn't ever do that, it's not a problem.

 CAUTION   Let me reiterate that when you shut down your computer and are going to open it to work inside, *always* disconnect the power cable. Doing so ensures that the computer has no incoming electricity, so the chances of electrocution are virtually nil.

- **The PC is powered up**—This is the PC at its most dangerous because the components remain sharp (duh), parts such as the processor and power supply can heat up to burn-inducing levels within a few minutes, and electricity is everywhere. Not only that, but a running PC has a fourth danger: spinning fans on the case, CPU cooler, and often the video card too. The danger here isn't so much that you might stick a finger in a fan (that would be unlikely to cause you much harm), but that you might get something caught in a fan, such as clothing, a bracelet, hair, and so on. Because of all this, the inside of a running PC is definitely a "hands-off" area. Feel free to open the case and look around, but touching things is just asking for trouble.

CAUTION   To be safe, open the case before you turn on the computer, and don't close the case until after you shut down the computer. Also, the open case wrecks the airflow inside the PC, so components can run hotter than usual; therefore, don't leave the computer running for an extended time with the case open.

Keeping Your Components Safe

Keeping yourself out of harm's way when working inside a PC is important, obviously, but it's not the only safety concern. Without proper precautions, you can also damage sensitive computer components, which means your PC either might run erratically or might not run at all. It also means you might have wasted good money. Fortunately, keeping your components safe takes only a few sensible precautions:

- **Discharge static electricity**—If you walk across a carpeted floor, or if your clothes rub together as you walk, your body builds up static electricity, perhaps as much as a few thousand volts! If you were to touch a sensitive component such as a processor or motherboard, the resulting electrical discharge could easily damage or destroy the part. To prevent this, after you open the PC case, you first should ground yourself by touching the chassis, the power supply unit, or some other metal object. Doing so discharges your static electricity and ensures that you won't damage any of the computer's sensitive electronic components. Ideally, you shouldn't walk around the room until you've finished working inside the PC. If you need to walk away from the computer for a bit—particularly if you're wearing socks on a carpeted surface—be sure to ground yourself again when you're ready to resume working.

TIP   If you find that you always forget to ground yourself, you can take the matter out of your hands, literally, by using an antistatic wrist strap. This is a device with a wrist strap on one end and a metal clip at the other. You attach the clip to a metal object to ground yourself full-time. However, if you move away from the computer, be sure to check that the clip hasn't fallen off before continuing to work with the PC.

- **Avoid liquids in your work area**—Liquids and computer components finitely don't mix, and spilling almost any amount of liquid on a part could mage the part or render it inoperable. Therefore, keep all liquids well away rom your work surface.

Don't touch electrical connectors—Many parts have electrical connectors that serve as conduits for data or power. The natural oils that reside on even the cleanest of hands can reduce the conductivity of these contacts, resulting in the part acting erratically. Therefore, never touch the connectors.

 TIP   If you do touch a contact, you can clean it either by using isopropyl alcohol (also called rubbing alcohol) and a cotton swab or with an unused pencil eraser.

- **Handle all components with care**—This means not only avoiding the contacts but also leaving components in their electrostatic discharge (ESD) bags (if they come with one) when not being used, carefully removing parts from their packaging to avoid breaking them, handling components with exposed electronics (such as resistors and capacitors) by the edges, setting down parts carefully, and allowing cold parts to heat up to room temperature before using them.

 CAUTION   After you take a component out of its ESD bag, if you need to put the component back down, don't lay it on the ESD bag because the outside of those bags can draw static electricity! Put the component back inside the bag.

Opening the Computer Case

All PC upgrade and repair jobs begin with an apparently simple task: opening the computer case, usually by removing a side panel. (If you're facing the case from the front, you almost always remove the left side panel.) Why is this an "apparently" simple task? Because the technology case manufacturers use to secure the side panel isn't universal. That wasn't the case a few years ago. In those days, the vast majority of side panels were attached using two or three screws, and removing the panel was a straightforward matter of removing the screws and sliding or lifting the panel away from the case. Figure 8.6 shows an example.

FIGURE 8.6

A case side panel attached with screws.

Those days are long gone. Yes, most cases still connect their side panels with screws, but this method is no longer even remotely universal. Nowadays case manufacturers have come up with an endless variety of ways to attach side panels. The goal in almost all cases is "tool-free access." That is, the older method required the use of a screwdriver, although many cases now use thumbscrews. In modern case designs, tools are verboten. Instead, you usually have to press a button or hold down a latch, sometimes while sliding the side panel at the same time!

My favorite case opening mechanism by far is the one that appears on some models of Cooler Master cases. As you can see in Figure 8.7, the back of the case contains a simple lever. Lift that lever up, and the side panel slides open as slowly and deliberately as if it were mechanized. Beautiful! To close the side panel, you simply snap it into place. Bliss!

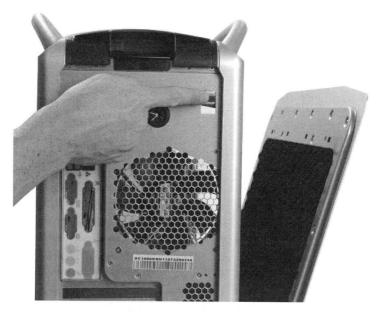

FIGURE 8.7

Some Cooler Master cases open with the lift of a simple latch.

Making Cable Connections

Great chunks of your PC repair time will be taken up connecting cables either to provide components with power or to provide a conduit along which the device can send and receive data. There are many cable types, and at first blush you might think this is just the computer industry's way of confusing novice upgraders. In fact, the opposite is the case: There are so many types because that's the only way to ensure that the connections you make are pretty close to foolproof. In other words, because each cable connector has a unique shape and configuration, it's nearly impossible for you to insert the cable in the wrong port or to insert the cable incorrectly in the right port.

Before going any further with all this, I should establish some terminology:

- **Connector**—This is a generic term for any piece of hardware that enables one thing to connect to another. So, the hardware at the end of a cable is a connector, as is the corresponding hardware on the other device to which you want the cable attached.

- **Male**—This is a connector that has protruding pins. Each pin corresponds to a wire in the cable. A male connector is also called a *header* or *plug*.

- **Female**—This is a connector that has holes, and it's also called a *jack* or *port*.

The key issue here is that on a proper connection, each pin on a male connector maps to a corresponding hole in a female connector. (There are some exceptions to this, such as female connectors with more holes than there are pins on a male connector.)

For example, older hard drives connect to the motherboard using a 40-pin ribbon cable. In Figure 8.8, you can see that the cable has a 40-hole female connector, the motherboard has a 40-pin male connector, and the holes and pins match up perfectly. However, if you place the same cable beside a floppy drive connector, which uses a 34-pin male connector as shown in Figure 8.9, it's obvious that the two don't match. In other words, it isn't possible to insert this style of hard drive cable in a floppy drive header, even though they look similar.

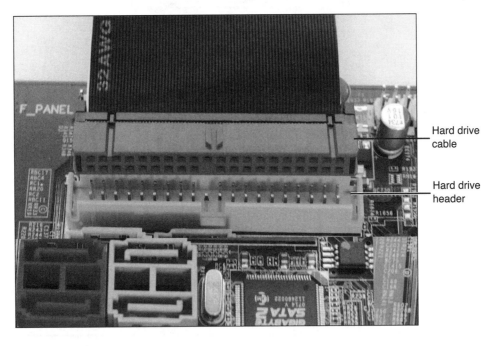

Hard drive cable

Hard drive header

FIGURE 8.8

The holes on an ATA hard drive ribbon cable connector match up perfectly with the pins on the motherboard's ATA cable connector.

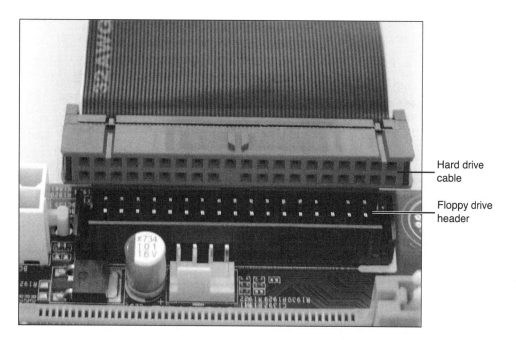

Hard drive
cable

Floppy drive
header

FIGURE 8.9

*The pin configuration on a motherboard's floppy drive header doesn't match the ATA hard
drive connector.*

So, your first clue when deciding where to insert a cable is to look for a connector
that has the corresponding number of pins (or holes). Next, you often have to
decide which way to insert the cable connector. As you can see in Figure 8.8, you
can either insert the cable as shown or turn the cable 180° and try it that way. The
pin configuration is the same both ways, so how do you know which is correct?

In this particular case, you need to look for the notch that appears in the back
of the plastic shroud that surrounds the pins. That notch corresponds with a
protrusion that appears on one side of the cable connector (you can see it in
Figure 8.9). The only way to insert the cable is to match up the protrusion and the
notch.

Another way system designers help you orient a cable connector correctly is by
using a nonsymmetrical pin layout. For example, a motherboard's USB header has
nine pins: five in one row and four in another. The case's USB jack has nine holes:
five in one row and four in another. As you can see in Figure 8.10, there's only
one way to match up the holes and pins, so there's only one way to connect the
header and jack.

USB connector

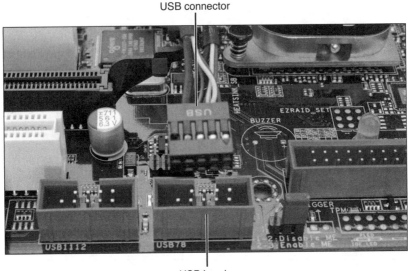

USB header

FIGURE 8.10

The arrangement of the pins on a USB header matches the arrangement of the holes on the USB jack, so there's only one way to make the connection.

A third way system designers ensure that you don't insert a connector incorrectly is to use a nonsymmetrical shape for the connector. For example, the 4-pin Molex power jack is designed to connect to a 4-pin Molex power header on a device. As you can see in Figure 8.11, two of the jack's four corners are rounded, and they match the rounded corners on the header. Again, there's only one way to make the connection.

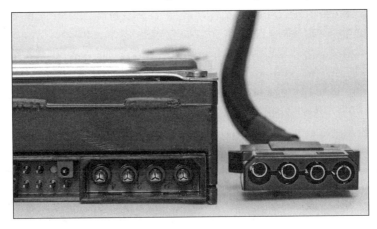

FIGURE 8.11

The rounded corners of the 4-pin Molex power jack match the rounded corners of the 4-pin Molex power header, so there's only one way to make the connection.

All this rigmarole of matching the numbers of pins, notches, and connector shapes is a complex business, so there has been a movement of late to reduce the complexity. System designers are accomplishing this by making connectors with a unique shape, period. With such connectors, you don't have to worry about pins or any other physical characteristics of the connector because there's only one kind of matching connector and only one way to insert the cable.

A good example is the newer hard drive data interface called SATA (Serial Advanced Technology Attachment). As you can see in Figure 8.12, the unique shape of the cable connector has a corresponding match on the hard drive. There's no danger here of inserting the cable in the wrong device or in the wrong way.

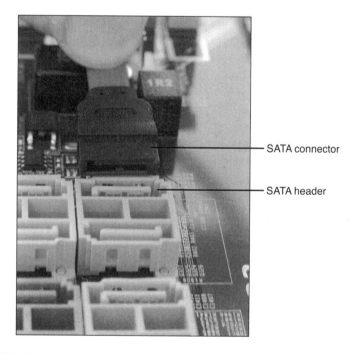

FIGURE 8.12

The unique shape of a SATA hard drive data cable connector matches the corresponding SATA hard drive data header for an unambiguous connection.

Working with Expansion Cards

Expansion cards are circuit boards that provide extra functionality such as networking, video, and sound. You install them by inserting them into slots inside your PC. So if want to upgrade your system, you can add a new card or replace an existing one. Similarly, if you're having trouble with one of these internal components, you can usually fix the problem by taking out the old expansion card and replacing it with a new one.

Note, however, that you can't install any type of card into any type of slot. The various card types use different slot configurations. That's good news for you as a system repairer because it means you can't insert a card into the wrong slot, and you can't insert a card into the correct slot with the wrong orientation.

Understanding Expansion Slot Types

Your PC's main internal component is the *motherboard*, which is the central connection point for all the devices inside your PC. In particular, all motherboards come with at least one *expansion slot*, and most come with four to six slots. These slots are an important part of the motherboard because they enable you to upgrade your system by inserting expansion cards. For example, if your motherboard comes with integrated video capabilities but you want to use your PC to play games or edit video, you need to insert a more powerful graphics card. Other common expansion cards add or upgrade your system's sound, enable you to watch and record TV signals, give you faster wired or wireless networking, or add more USB ports.

Not all expansions slots have the same configuration. There have been a number of slot standards over the years and, just to add more complication to our lives, each standard uses a different type of slot. So it's important to understand that if you want to add an expansion card to your system, that card must use a connector that fits one of your motherboard slots. That's the bad news. The good news is that these days you only have to worry about two slot types (see Figure 8.13):

- **PCI**—Variations on the PCI (Peripheral Component Interconnect) have been the standard expansion slot type for at least 15 years. Older motherboards (and even some new ones) offer regular PCI (often called *legacy* PCI) slots.

- **PCI Express**—Regular PCI is quite slow and is, in fact, too slow for intensive graphics work. To remedy this, PCI Express (also called PCIe) was created, and it's much faster than PCI. PCI Express has seen several versions over the years (2.0, 3.0, and now 4.0), and it comes in several configurations, such as x1, x4, and x16 (the higher the number, the more data the card can transfer).

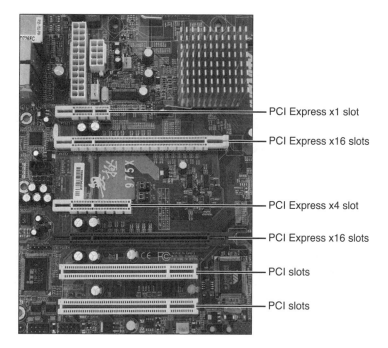

PCI Express x1 slot

PCI Express x16 slots

PCI Express x4 slot

PCI Express x16 slots

PCI slots

PCI slots

FIGURE 8.13

Most modern motherboards offer a selection of PCI Express expansion slots, and possibly a legacy PCI slot or two.

System designers ensure foolproof expansion card connections by using two configuration parameters:

- **Length**—The various slot types all use different lengths. For example, a PCI slot is larger than a PCI Express x4 slot, but smaller than a PCI Express x16 slot.

- **Slot ridges**—Each slot type has one or more ridges that correspond to notches in the expansion card's connector area. This ensures that you can't install a card with the incorrect orientation. For example, Figure 8.14 shows a PCI Express x16 card next to a PCI Express x16 slot. As you can see, the notches in the card match up perfectly with the ridges in the slot.

Card notch

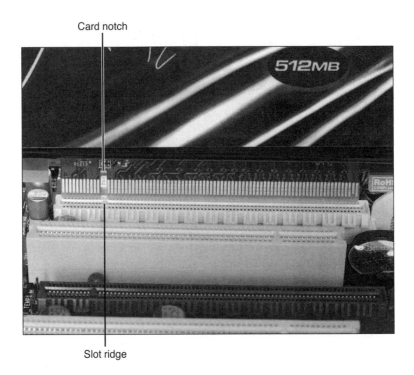

Slot ridge

FIGURE 8.14

The notches in an expansion card's connectors must match the ridges in the motherboard slot, as shown here with a PCI Express x16 card and slot.

Note that PCI Express provides certain exceptions to all this; that is, smaller PCI Express cards always fit into larger PCI Express slots. For example, a PCI Express x1 card fits into any other PCI Express slot (x4, x8, or x16). Figure 8.15 shows a PCI Express x1 card next to a PCI Express x16 slot. The card's notches match the slot's first two ridges, so you can successfully insert the card, even though it's the "wrong" length.

PCI Express x1 card   PCI Express x16 slot

FIGURE 8.15

You can always insert smaller PCI Express cards into larger PCI Express slots, such as the x1 card into the x16 slot shown here.

In days of yore (the 1990s), all case slot covers were attached using a screw. Now, as with case side panels, manufacturers have been experimenting with various tool-free slot covers—latches, levers, and so on—so there's no longer a universal way to either remove a slot cover or attach an expansion card to the slot. You need to consult your case manual to see how things work.

Installing an Expansion Card

With the preceding in mind, here are the generic steps to follow to install an expansion card:

1. Make sure the computer is turned off and the power cable is disconnected.

2. Remove the computer's side panel.

3. Touch something metal to ground yourself.

4. Locate the slot you want to use (see Figure 8.16).

5. Remove the slot cover. If the slot cover is held in place with a screw, use a Phillips screwdriver to remove the screw and then place the screw in a handy place. You will need this screw in step 8.

TIP   When the screw is out, the slot cover should come out easily; it might even fall out on its own, so it's a good idea to hold onto the slot cover with your free hand to ensure that it doesn't fall onto the motherboard and damage a component. If the slot cover doesn't budge, it's probably being held in place by the slot cover above it (or, less often, the slot cover below it). Loosen—but don't remove—the screw on the other slot cover. Doing so should give you enough slack to remove the cover for the empty slot. When that slot cover is out, you can tighten the screw on the other slot cover.

Slot covert   Empty slot

FIGURE 8.16

An empty PCI slot with an increasingly old-fashioned screw-on slot cover.

6. Place the expansion card so that its bracket is flush with the open slot cover and slowly slide the card toward the slot.

7. When the card's connectors are touching the slot and are perfectly aligned with the slot opening, place your thumbs on the edge of the card and press the card firmly into the slot (see Figure 8.17).

FIGURE 8.17

Press the card firmly into the slot.

 TIP   How do you know whether the card is completely inserted into the slot? The easiest way to tell is to look at the portion of the bracket that attaches to the case. If that portion isn't flush with the case, the card isn't fully inserted.

8. Attach the bracket to the case, as shown in Figure 8.18.

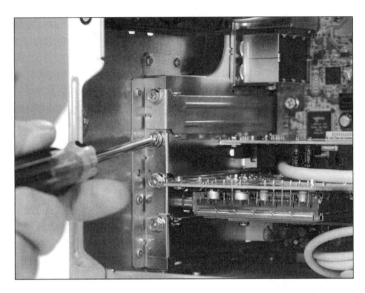

FIGURE 8.18

Screw (or whatever) the expansion card's bracket to the computer chassis.

THE ABSOLUTE MINIMUM

Let this chapter serve as your launch pad for your PC repair and upgrade projects. Here's a quick look at the basic skills you learned:

- For your PC repair toolkit, you need at least several Phillips-head screwdrivers, a flashlight, and some tweezers.

- When setting up your work area, you needs lots of the following: light, power, and elbow room.

- Never work inside a PC that's still running, and even after you turn off a PC, it's a good idea to wait a couple of minutes to give the components time to cool and drain their stored voltage.

- Before starting work inside a PC, always disconnect the power cord and discharge your static electricity.

- When making cable connections, remember that each pin on a male connector maps to a corresponding hole in a female connector.

- When installing an expansion card, remember that the card can be no wider than the slot you're using, and that the card notch (or notches) must line up with the slot's ridge (or ridges).

IN THIS CHAPTER

- Using the Web to research your purchases, including reading product reviews, comparing prices, and checking out retailer reputations

- Learning how to become a savvy PC parts shopper

- Getting the scoop on returning parts that don't work out

- Buying PC parts in the real world

9

BUYING PC PARTS

Fixing a PC is often a matter of software: tweaking a setting, uninstalling a program, updating a device driver, reverting your system to an earlier state, or refreshing the system files. Other PC repair jobs are hardware-related, such as checking cable connections, power cycling a device, or disconnecting a device from your computer. These solutions are "easy" in the sense that they don't require anything new, just a bit of time and know-how. However, there's a whole other class of PC problems for which the "fix" requires updating or replacing a part, such as the hard drive or a memory module. To make this happen, you need to purchase the replacement part, and this chapter gives you all the information you need to purchase parts like a pro.

Researching Parts Online

Sure, we use the Internet to communicate, connect, and have fun, but its main use for most of us is to do research. The reason is not only that the Web contains a vast amount of information (much of which is actually true!), but also that we can easily search and surf to the information we need. This is a boon to the PC repairer because it makes it absurdly easy to research components to find the right product at the right price. Whatever part you're looking to add to your PC, somebody has reviewed it and somebody else is selling it.

To help you get started, the next couple of sections list the best sites for checking hardware reviews and comparing component prices.

Checking Out Product Reviews

Whether you're looking for a new hard drive or more memory, it's a lead-pipe cinch that someone has reviewed it and posted that review online for all to read. I'm not talking here about little Johnny the budding computer geek proclaiming the latest digital doodad to be "Awesome!" on his blog (although, of course, there's no shortage of that kind of thing around). Rather, I'm talking about in-depth, nonpartisan reviews by hardware professionals who really put parts to the test and tell you the pros and cons of each piece of equipment.

Hardware-related sites are a dime a dozen (if that), but a few are really good. Here are my recommendations:

 TIP   When you read a review, be sure to note the date it was published. If it was quite a while ago, the review might be talking about an older version of the component.

- **AnandTech**—Although this site offers extras such as forums, blogs, product pricing, and hardware news, its heart—and its claim to fame—is the massive collection of incredibly in-depth reviews (see Figure 9.1). These reviews are often quite technical, but you should feel free to skim the mumbo-jumbo because there's still plenty of useful information for everyone.

  www.anandtech.com/

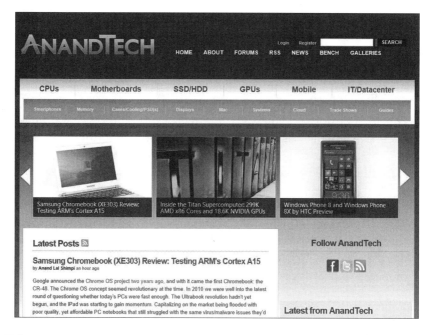

FIGURE 9.1

AnandTech is one of the best sites for hardware product reviews.

- **Ars Technica**—The name means "The Art of Technology," and that's an appropriate description of this deep, sprawling site aimed at computer enthusiasts. For system upgraders, the site includes buyer's guides, technology guides, how-to articles, and lots more.

  www.arstechnica.com/

- **CNET**—This massive site has a Reviews section that covers tons of products. Each review is simply laid out with headings such as Pros, Cons, Suitability, Value, and Suggestions. The layout of the site leaves something to be desired, so use the search engine to find what you want.

  www.cnet.com/

- **ExtremeTech**—This professional site (it's affiliated with *PC Magazine*) is loaded with in-depth product reviews and recommendations for the products suited to building your own PC.

  www.extremetech.com/

- **Maximum PC**—This is the Web home of the terrific print magazine *Maximum PC*. The website offers reviews of thousands of products in every conceivable category. The reviews aren't particularly exhaustive, but they give you a good overview of each product.

  www.maximumpc.com/

- **The Tech Report**—If you want your reviews to tilt more toward the obsessively detailed side of the spectrum, look no further than this site, which has some of the most in-depth reviews on the Web. It's not the best-looking website I've ever seen, but the content rules here.

  www.techreport.com/

- **Tom's Hardware**—If you want to know everything there is to know about a particular piece of technology, this jaw-droppingly impressive site is the place to go (see Figure 9.2). The reviews and technology articles are a geek's dream, and there's plenty of great information for everyone else too.

  www.tomshardware.com/

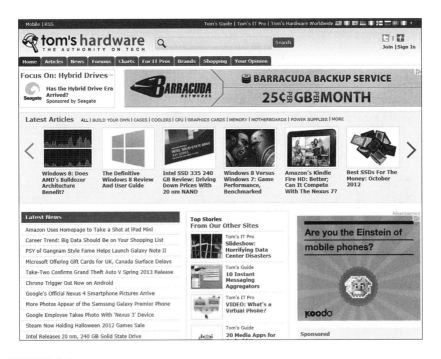

FIGURE 9.2

Tom's Hardware features awesomely in-depth product reviews.

TIP   Besides checking specific sites for reviews of a particular component, you can also try running a Google search that includes the product name and the word *review*. Be sure to search not only the Web but also Google Groups.

TIP   No time to read a long-winded review? No problem! Almost all reviews have a "summary" section at the end that recaps the highlights of the review, including the major pros and cons, the reviewer's kudos and caveats, and whether the reviewer recommends the product.

Performing Price Comparisons

After you've read the reviews and know exactly what you want, your next step as a savvy shopper is to find the best price. You could do that by jumping around to various online retailers, searching for your product, and making note of the price each time. However, plenty of sites out there will do all the hard work for you. I'm talking about the Web's price comparison sites (sometimes called *shopping portals*), where you select or specify the product you want and the site returns the product listings from a number of online retailers. You can then compare prices with just a few mouse clicks.

Here are some decent shopping portals to check out:

- **Become**—This site shows you not only the prices for each listing but also the product's rating at each store (one to five stars, based on user reviews).

  www.become.com/

- **CNET Shopper.com**—This is the Shopper.com section of the CNET site. Its nicest feature is that for each store returned in the listings, you get the store's rating (one to five stars) and whether the store currently has stock of the item—and if you enter your ZIP code, the taxes and shipping fees are displayed (see Figure 9.3).

  http://shopper.cnet.com/

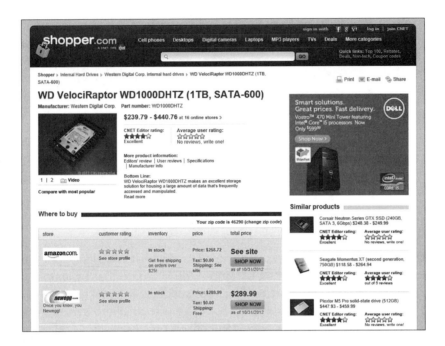

FIGURE 9.3

CNET's Shopper.com site not only compares prices, but also provides each store's rating, stock, taxes, and shipping costs to your ZIP code.

- **Google Product Search**—This site applies the awesome power of Google's search engine to online products. You search on the name of the product you want, and Google returns product listings from around the Web.

  www.google.com/shopping/

- **PriceGrabber.com**—This is one of the most popular shopping portals, and no wonder because, for each product, you get tons of information: price, stock, product details, user reviews and discussions, expert reviews, seller rating, and taxes and shipping for your ZIP code. What more could you want?

  www.pricegrabber.com/

- **Shopzilla**—This site doesn't have all the bells and whistles that you see with some of the other sites, but it often returns a broader array of listings and has all the basic information you need: price, taxes, shipping, product details, and product reviews.

  www.shopzilla.com/

- **Yahoo! Shopping**—Lots of people like this section of Yahoo! because it provides all the standard shopping portal data and gives you full product specifications, user ratings, and the ability to send listings to a mobile phone (perfect if you're doing your shopping offline).

  http://shopping.yahoo.com/

Researching Retailers Online

With hundreds of online retailers out there, how can you tell the e-commerce stars from the fly-by-night shysters? The best way is to ask your friends, family, and colleagues which retailers they've used and had good experiences with in the past. Because these are people you trust, you can rely on the information you get.

Besides that, you can also go by the ratings that online users have applied to retailers. These are usually stars (usually up to five stars, and the more stars the better). Many of the shopping portals in the preceding section also include user ratings for each store. For example, Google Product Search (www.google.com/shopping/) also doubles as a retailer ratings service. When you run a product search, the name of the reseller appears below the price and below that are a rating (one to five stars) and the number of user ratings that have produced the result. As you can see in Figure 9.4, you can also sort the results by seller rating, and the site has links to restrict the results based on seller rating (for example, to show only the results for sellers with four or more stars).

A site that's dedicated to rating resellers is the appropriately named ResellerRatings.com (see www.resellerratings.com/). This site uses a 1-to-10 scale, where the higher the rating, the better the store. You can use the site as a shopping portal, or you can look up an individual store to see its rating. (Usefully, you get two ratings for each store: a lifetime rating and a six-month rating; if the latter is much lower than the former, that's a sign something has gone seriously wrong at the store over the past few months and you might want to shop elsewhere.) The site also has interesting lists of the "Highest Rated Stores" (see Figure 9.5) and "Lowest Rated Stores."

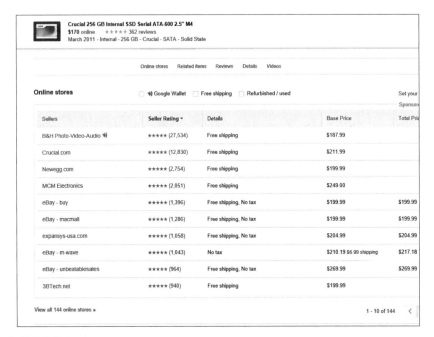

FIGURE 9.4

You can sort the Google Product Search results by reseller rating.

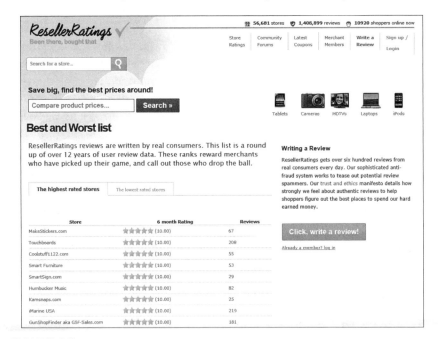

FIGURE 9.5

ResellerRatings.com is a massive database of online retailer ratings and reviews.

Buying Parts Online

Buying components online isn't the scary proposition it was a few years ago. You can choose from many reliable, reputable, and secure merchants now, so buying online is no longer a big deal. Even still, shopping online is different from buying at a retail store or via mail order. To ensure the best online transaction possible, bear in mind these few pointers:

- The three most important points to remember when buying online are compare, compare, compare. It's not at all unusual to find one store selling the same part for 10% or even 20% less than other stores, so use the shopping portals I mentioned earlier to get the best price.

- Keep an eye out for special deals. Many online retailers offer promotions on a particular day of the week or when they need to clear out inventory. Troll the sites of your favorite online retailers to watch out for these specials.

 TIP Some sites offer RSS feeds that alert you to upcoming promotions, which can be an easier way to stay on top of things. If a site doesn't have an RSS feed, look for a mailing list.

- Be wary of a price that seems too good to be true. Yes, some retailers occasionally offer a product as a loss leader—a price that's substantially lower than their competitors as a way of tempting you to buy something and thus establish a relationship with the store. (After you purchase at least one thing from a store, you're more likely to go back, particularly if the experience was a positive one.) However, it's also entirely possible for some of the shadier outfits to offer super-low prices on returned or refurbished parts without telling you what you're getting. Unless you know the store is reputable, assume really low prices are bogus and move on to the next store.

- Following on from the preceding point, note that a really cheap price might be the *net* price you pay after processing a mail-in rebate. Obviously, you'll pay a higher price up front, but some retailers don't tell you that, or they hide the fact in small print somewhere. Also, beware of extra "handling" charges and other fees that the retailer might try to tack on. Before committing to the sale, always give the invoice a thorough going-over so you know exactly what you're paying.

- Be sure you understand the difference between an original equipment manufacturer (OEM) version and a retail box version of a component. The OEM version of a product is the version that would normally go to a system builder. It's the same part but minus the extras that come with the retail box version, so it's often much cheaper. At best, this just means no-frills packaging, but it can also mean no manual, no device drivers, no extra parts such as hard drive data cables, and often a shorter warranty. If you just need the part itself, the OEM version can save you a few shekels, but be sure you know what you're getting.

 NOTE The term *OEM* is pretty universal, but some retailers use alternate terminology for specific products. For example, an OEM hard drive is sometimes called a *bare drive*.

- Buy just off the bleeding edge. It's a truism in PC component retailing that the latest-and-greatest parts cost the most. A top-of-the-line 3 terabyte (TB) internal hard drive can set you back hundreds of dollars, but a 1TB drive (which is still big enough for most people) can be had for under $100.

- Most good online vendors will give you a chance during checkout to enter your ZIP code or postal code so you can see exactly what your shipping charges will be. Because the cost of shipping can often be extravagant, whenever possible you should find out the cost in advance before completing the sale.

- Some retailers allow you to mail a check or money order and will ship the order when they receive the payment. You should avoid these payment options like the plague because, if something goes wrong (for example, the product never shows up), getting your money back could be a challenge. If you pay by credit card, however, you always have the option of charging back the cost to the vendor.

 CAUTION Watch out for online retailers who charge some kind of extra fee (usually a percentage of the product price) for accepting credit card payments. This is almost always a sign of a shady dealer who's either trying to squeeze an extra few percentage points out of you or is trying to discourage you from using a credit card.

- If the retailer offers a PayPal option, use it. Currently owned by eBay, PayPal is an online payment service that enables you to buy online without exposing your credit card data to the retailer. You sign up for a PayPal account at www.paypal.com and provide your credit card, debit card, or bank account information. (It's all super-secure and everything is verified before your account goes online.) When you buy something online with a PayPal-friendly retailer, that retailer tells PayPal the cost of the sale, and PayPal charges it to your credit card, debit card, or bank account and then passes along the money to the retailer. The retailer never sees your financial data, so you never have to worry about that data being stolen or accidentally exposed.

- When the checkout process is complete, leave the final window open on your Desktop so you have access to the order number, final total, tracking information, and other order details. After you get an email confirming the transaction and you've checked the email for accuracy, you can close the web window.

 NOTE   In the unlikely event that the retailer doesn't provide a confirmation email message, either print the screen or capture it to an image: in Windows 8, press Windows Logo+Print Screen (in earlier versions of Windows, just press Print Screen) and then paste the image into Paint.

Returning Parts Online

The arrival of a new PC part is often quite exciting. However, that initial excitement occasionally turns to disappointment when your new toy doesn't live up to expectations. It might be defective, incompatible, or just not what you want. Bummer. The good news is that the vast majority of the time you're not stuck with your part because almost all retailers offer returns for either refund or replacement. This process is usually fairly straightforward, but to ensure a smooth return, you need to know a few things; I detail them in this section.

 NOTE   With so many vendors offering returns privileges, you should avoid retailers that don't offer them. If resellers can't stand behind their products by offering returns, there's no reason you should ever stand in front of them!

First, when you get your package, resist the temptation to tear off the cellophane and dive into the box to eyeball your new bauble. A more deliberate pace should always be the norm when repairing a PC, but it also has ramifications in the returns department:

- You run the risk of scattering teensy-but-vital bits to the nether regions of your office. When you return an item, the retailer will check to see whether all the parts are present, and if anything's missing, it might disallow your refund.

- It's a general rule that hastily liberating the contents of a box means that those contents *never* go back in as neatly or at all! Your return stands far less chance of being rejected if you pack the contents back into the box exactly the way you found them originally.

- Don't throw anything away, even if you think you're *really, really* sure you're going to keep the component. First, the component might not work, which makes a return mandatory. Second, the component might not work the way you thought it would, and you can assuage your disappointment by sending the sucker back and getting something better. However, that's going to be a lot harder if you've already tossed the manual and other previously nonessential pieces.

- Open bags and containers as carefully as possible. If you just rip into things, you won't be able to put their components back in if the need for a return arises. This means either you have to leave them loose in the box (which could cause damage to other parts), or you need to improvise a new container (which is just a waste of your precious time).

- Don't remove any stickers, decals, or barcode labels. Try to keep the components as pristine as possible just in case they need to go back.

- Try the component as soon as possible. Most retailers offer returns for only a limited time—for refunds, it's sometimes as short as 14 days, but more typically it's 30 days—so give your product a whirl within that time frame.

- Check to ensure that you can send back your nondefective product. Many retailers have return exceptions for parts such as processors, batteries, and memory modules, as well as for special purchases such as open-box items.

- Check to see whether the retailer charges a restocking fee. This might be something like 15% of the cost, so find out in advance so that you're not surprised when an apparently too-small refund comes through on your next credit card statement.

 NOTE No reputable reseller will charge a restocking fee on an item you're returning for replacement. For refund returns, thumb your nose at any vendor that charges more than a 15% restocking fee. Unfortunately, fees in the 20% to 30% range aren't unheard of, so watch out for them and don't give any business to a company that would charge such an outrageous amount.

If, after all that, you do have something to return, you need to contact the retailer and ask for a return authorization number—usually called a return merchandise authorization (RMA) number. Most of the larger online retailers enable you to request an RMA number on their sites, usually by accessing your account. Otherwise, you need to contact the retailer's customer service department. After you have authorization, you're ready to make the return:

- Keep a box or three around for use with returns. Retailers often ship components in boxes filled with Styrofoam chips, so I keep a box of those around for safe shipping.

- If the retailer supplies you with a label, be sure to place the label on your box in a visible location. The label usually contains information—such as the retailer's address, the RMA number, and the original invoice number—that can help smooth the returns process.

- If you don't have a special label, write "RMA Number:" on the box, followed by the number the retailer supplied to you for the return. This helps steer the package to the retailer's returns department and helps the returns clerk process the package. If you want, you can also add the original invoice number to the box to help speed up processing.

- When sending back the component, use a traceable method such as registered mail or a courier. This enables you to keep track of the package. It's also a good idea to insure the contents, so you're not on the hook if the package gets lost or damaged.

- Keep an eye peeled on your credit card statement to look for the refund. (Having online access to your card statement is particularly handy here.) Most reputable retailers will process the return in just a few business days, and it shouldn't take more than another couple of business days for the credit to show up. If you don't see anything after a couple of weeks, see whether the retailer offers an option for checking the status of your return online. If not, contact the retailer's customer service department to see what the holdup is.

Buying Parts Offline

Should you buy your PC parts from a bricks-and-mortar store such as Best Buy, Circuit City, CompUSA, Costco, Fry's, Future Shop, Staples, or your local electronics store? Here's the simple answer to that question: It depends. Buying in person has its advantages, but doing so is not without its disadvantages. So the retail route you choose depends on what you need, when you need it, and a host of other factors.

Here are the main advantages of buying offline:

- **No shipping charges**—When you buy retail, the only "shipping charge" is the cost of gas for the trip to the store and back. This is particularly advantageous with large items such as computer cases and heavy items such as power supplies, which often generate exorbitant shipping charges when ordered online.

- **Faster**—If you need a part *now*, the only way to get it done (assuming you're not mid-repair at 3 a.m.) is to go to a store. Even the fastest online service can only offer overnight delivery (for big bucks, too).

- **Expertise**—In-store sales associates are often quite knowledgeable and can help you make a decision if you're having trouble finding the right part or choosing between two similar components. However, see also my comments below about aggressive salesmanship and the commission connection.

- **Easier returns**—If your component isn't right for whatever reason, you can drive it back to the store and get an instant refund or replacement, usually without any hassle. (Although someone will give the package a thorough going-over to ensure it's in returnable condition.) This is much easier than the online rigmarole of getting an RMA number, shipping the component (at your own expense), and waiting for the refund or replacement to show up.

- **Mail-in rebates**—Both online and offline retailers sometimes offer instant rebates that immediately reduce the price of a component. Real-world stores often go one better and also offer a mail-in rebate where you have to send a form and proof-of-purchase to a mailing address and a check comes your way a couple of weeks later.

NOTE Truth be told, mail-in rebates are a way for the retailer to make the product appear cheaper (because they usually show the after-rebate price prominently), and the retailer is counting on people not bothering to follow through on the rebate. Don't fall into their trap: Send in those rebates! Also, to make sure the rebate is honored, keep copies of the rebate forms and send the rebate via registered mail or some other traceable method.

Here are the main disadvantages of buying offline:

- **Smaller selection**—Due to the inevitable shelf space limitations, even the largest superstore can carry only a limited number of items in any one area. Even mid-size online retailers have access to many times more products.

- **More expensive**—Buying retail is almost always more expensive than buying online, although the big electronics superstores usually have fairly competitive prices. Not only that, but the retailer will have to charge you sales tax, and chances are an online retailer won't, depending on where you and the retailer are located. (Remember, however, that to compare retail apples with online apples, you also have to factor in the shipping costs that are part of most online orders.)

- **More time**—Besides the time it takes to get from your home to the store, more often than not you'll find yourself making a second or third stop at different stores to find the exact item you need.

- **Aggressive salesmanship**—Many electronics retailers put their sales staff on commission, which means the more they sell, the more money they make. That's a very simple recipe for aggressive and often annoying sales come-ons. Ask any overly insistent sales associate whether he's on commission and, if so, be sure to stick to your guns and purchase only what you need. Even better, take your business to a retailer that doesn't use commissioned sales staff.

- **Extended warranty**—Speaking of aggressive sales, many electronics stores pay their staff big commissions for signing people up for extended warranties. These extended warranties, which, for example, take the standard one-year warranty that a manufacturer might give and extend it to perhaps three years, are almost always a waste of money because if you're buying components from a reputable dealer, they'll almost certainly give you years of trouble-free service. So no matter how much pressure you feel from a salesperson, just say "No, thank you" to an extended warranty.

THE ABSOLUTE MINIMUM

When you're ready to purchase a part that you need for your PC repair, keep the following points in mind:

- Always begin your "purchase" by checking out the online reviews of the product you want to buy.

- Prices vary widely on the Web, so compare, compare, and then compare some more.

- If you come across your product at a good price from an online retailer you don't know, be sure to look for reviews of that retailer to make sure other people have had good experiences.

- For best results when buying online, be wary of too-good-to-be-true prices, buy just off the bleeding edge, know your shipping costs, and use PayPal, if you can.

- Open your package carefully just in case you have to return the product.

IN THIS CHAPTER

- Some surprisingly useful facts about power supplies
- A handy power supply buyer's guide
- Getting your old power supply out of your PC
- Shoehorning your new power supply into your PC

10

REPLACING THE POWER SUPPLY

Surprisingly, you can easily make a case that the power supply (sometimes called the PSU, short for *power supply unit*) is one of the three most important components in any system (the other two being the motherboard and the processor). Why? Because without the power supply, your PC—no matter how lovingly maintained—is nothing but an oversized paperweight. Almost every aspect of your PC requires a direct current (DC) source, and that source is the power supply. However, it isn't enough that the PSU doles out the watts to the motherboard and everything connected to it. The PSU must also supply that electrical power smoothly and efficiently, and a failure to do this (a symptom of many a cheap PSU) is often the cause of system glitches and crashes that are otherwise inexplicable. Low-end power supplies are also prone to simply dying, which at best shuts down your PC, but at worst can damage other components.

Getting to Know the Power Supply

From the standpoint of a budding PC fixer-upper, power supplies are relatively simple affairs that don't require tons of research or know-how. However, you need to know a few things to make the right choice when deciding on which power supply to get for your system:

- **Form factor**—Power supplies also come in different form factors that specify the dimensions of the power supply unit, as well as the types of motherboard power connections the unit supports. By far the most common is the ATX (Advanced Technology eXtended) form factor (see Figure 10.1), which fits most cases. The EPS form factor is the same size as the ATX but uses different connectors, as described in the next item.

FIGURE 10.1

A typical ATX form factor power supply.

- **Power connectors**—These are the main power connectors that supply power to the motherboard and the 12V power connector that supplies power to the processor. The three different combinations you might come across are as follows:
  - **ATX 1.3**—This older version of the ATX form factor uses a 20-pin main connector and a 4-pin 12V connector.
  - **ATX 2.2**—This more recent version of the ATX form factor uses a 24-pin main connector and a 4-pin 12V connector (see Figure 10.2).
  - **EPS (Entry-Level Power Supply Specification)**—This form factor uses a 24-pin main connector and an 8-pin 12V connector (called EPS12V; see Figure 10.3).

24-pin main connector   4-pin 12V connector

FIGURE 10.2

The ATX 2.2 form factor uses a 24-pin main connector and a 4-pin 12V connector.

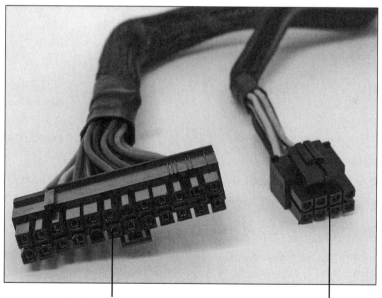

24-pin main connector   8-pin 12V connector

FIGURE 10.3

The EPS form factor uses a 24-pin main connector and an 8-pin 12V connector.

- **Other connectors**—A good power supply comes with a variety of wires so you can provide power to different types of components. Most power supplies come with wires for CD and DVD drives, older hard drives, and floppy drives. Most units should also have wires for SATA hard drives and for direct connections to high-end graphics cards.

- **Watts**—Perhaps the most important consideration with any power supply is the maximum number of watts the unit can handle. All your system's components—from the motherboard to the processor to the expansion cards to the drives—require a certain number of watts of power to function. Add up those watts and you get the total wattage of your PC; your power supply's maximum wattage must exceed that value. Of course, I don't expect you to actually add up the watts required by all your components! Instead, here are some general guidelines based on system type:

System	Recommended Wattage
Budget PC	300W
Basic Business PC	400W
Home Theater PC	400W
High-Performance PC	500W
Gaming PC	600W

Buying a Power Supply

By far the best advice I can give you about buying a power supply is this: buy a brand name. You might pay a few more dollars, but you are assured of getting a power supply that uses quality parts; is at least relatively quiet; and provides solid, smooth power to all your components. Here's a list of power supply manufacturers I recommend:

Antec (www.antec.com)

Coolermaster (www.coolermaster.com)

Corsair (www.corsair.com)

Enermax (www.enermax.com)

FSP (www.fsp-group.com)

PC Power & Cooling (www.pcpower.com)

Thermaltake (www.thermaltake.com)

Seasonic (www.seasonic.com)

Silverstone (www.silverstonetek.com)

Ultra (www.ultraproducts.com)

Zalman (www.zalman.com)

Here are a few points to bear in mind when purchasing a power supply:

- **Match the form factor to your motherboard**—When you're buying a power supply, make sure it comes with either 8-pin or 4-pin connector wires, as required by your motherboard.

 TIP Are you out of luck if your power supply has 4-pin wires but your motherboard has an 8-pin connector? Not at all. You can purchase a power cable adapter that converts the power supply's 4-pin ATX12V connector to an 8-pin EPS12V connector. (In addition, some adapters work the other way around, converting an 8-pin EPS12V connector to a 4-pin ATX12V connector.)

- **Look for detachable connectors**—For maximum flexibility when matching up your power supply with any motherboard, look for a unit that comes with detachable connectors. The most common such connector is a 24-pin main power connector with 4 of the pins detachable, which enables you to use the unit with a motherboard that has a 20-pin main connector. (This is often called a 20+4 connector and is shown in Figure 10.2.) Similarly, you can also get 8-pin EPS12V connectors where 4 of the pins are detachable, which enables you to use the unit with a motherboard that has a 4-pin 12V power connector. (This is often called a 4+4 connector.)

- **Look for a modular design**—A modular power supply is one that lets you use only the cables you need. The main and 12V cables are hard-wired, but all the other cables are optional and you just plug in the ones you need (see the power supply on the left in Figure 10.4). This reduces cable clutter and improves airflow through the case.

FIGURE 10.4

A modular power supply (left) lets you use only the power cables you need, whereas a regular power supply (right) comes with all its cables hard-wired.

- **Make sure the power supply has the connectors you need**—Check the connectors that come with the unit to ensure that it has everything you need for your devices, particularly SATA drives and graphics expansion cards that require a power connection.

- **Get a unit with high electrical efficiency**—*Electrical efficiency* measures the percentage of the AC that comes into the power supply and is converted into DC power. For example, a power supply that's only 50% efficient would convert 100W of AC into 50W of DC. Ideally, your power supply should be at least 80% efficient.

Removing the Old Power Supply

If your PC won't turn on, the most likely reason is that the power supply is no longer supplying power! This is surprisingly common, and it can occur for a number of different reasons, but overheating of the power supply is the most likely culprit. This is usually due to a lack of circulation inside the PC, particularly if any of the PC's internal fans are broken, the PC itself is located in a cramped area that prevents air from circulating, or the power supply's own fan no longer works.

If your PC's power supply is dead, or if you suspect that a wonky power supply is causing the PC to act even weirder than normal, it's time to yank out the old PSU and replace it with a new one. (This advice also applies if you plan on upgrading your PC—for example, by replacing the video card and adding new hard drives to the system—and you suspect your existing power supply doesn't have enough watts to handle the new load.)

Here are the steps to follow to remove a power supply:

1. Make sure the computer is turned off and the power cable is disconnected.

2. If the power supply has its own power switch, turn off the unit.

3. Remove the computer's side panel.

4. Touch something metal to ground yourself.

5. Locate the power supply unit. Some computers hide the PSU behind a plastic cover, so you might need to remove the cover to expose the unit.

6. Disconnect all the internal power cables. The unit is likely connected to at least some of the following components:

   Motherboard main connector

   Motherboard 12V connector

   Hard drive

   Optical drive

   Other internal drive bay components (such as a memory card reader)

   One or more case fans

   PCI Express video card

 TIP   To ensure you've disconnected all the power supply cables, trace each cable from the PSU to its connector.

 CAUTION   Make a note of each power connection and the type of connection it uses. That way, when you install your new power supply, you won't miss anything and you'll know exactly which power cable goes to which component.

7. Using a Phillips screwdriver, remove the four external screws that hold the power supply to the case, as shown in Figure 10.5. Be sure you place the screws in a handy place for easier retrieval later.

CAUTION Many power supplies are held in place *only* by the four screws in back. Therefore, it's a good idea to loosen only the four screws at first. Then use your free hand to support the underside of the power supply while you remove the screws.

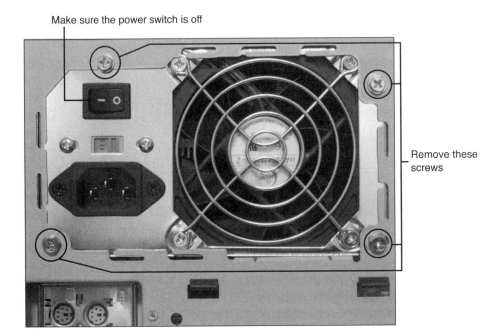

FIGURE 10.5

Most power supplies are attached to the case by four Phillips head screws.

8. Hold the power supply in one hand and the power cable in the other; then slowly remove the unit and cable from the case, taking care not to bang against any other component.

Installing a New Power Supply

With your old power supply removed from the PC, follow these steps to install the new one:

1. If you haven't done so already, remove the computer's side panel.

2. Touch something metal to ground yourself.

3. Orient the power supply unit so the back (the side with the power cable connector, on/off switch, and fan) is toward the back of the case.

4. Maneuver the power supply into the power supply bay on the bottom of the case.

5. Make sure the power supply is flush with the back of the case and that the screw holes line up with the holes in the case.

6. Attach the unit to the case with four screws, as shown in Figure 10.6.

7. Turn on the power supply's power switch, as shown in Figure 10.6.

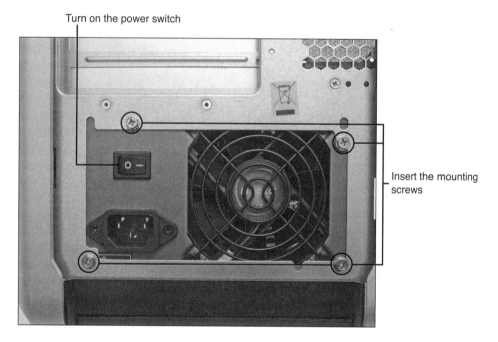

FIGURE 10.6

Use four screws to attach the power supply unit to the case, as shown here.

With the power supply onboard, you can now connect the power cables that supply juice to the motherboard. Your PC's motherboard has two power headers:

- A 24-pin main power header, into which you plug the power supply's 24-pin connector, as pointed out in Figure 10.7.

- A 4- or 8-pin 12V header to which you connect the power supply's corresponding 4- or 8-pin connector. Figure 10.7 shows an 8-pin connection.

TIP Most of the pins on a power cable connector are square, but a few are rounded on one side. These rounded pins have corresponding rounded holes on the header. To install a power cable connector with the correct orientation, match up the rounded pins with the rounded holes.

8-pin 12V connection

24-pin main connection

FIGURE 10.7

Connect the power supply's 24-pin and 8-pin connectors to the corresponding headers on the motherboard.

Finally, you need to get power to the rest of the devices:

1. Connect a power supply cable to each case fan.

2. If required, connect a power supply cable to the power connector on the video card.

3. Connect a power supply cable to the optical drive's power connector.

4. Connect a power supply cable to the hard drive's power connector.

THE ABSOLUTE MINIMUM

Here are a few notes to keep in mind during your power supply replacement projects:

- Make sure you get a power supply that can offer your PC enough watts to keep everything spinning.

- All power supplies come with two motherboard connections: a 24-pin main connector and either a 4- or 8-pin 12V connector.

- When buying your power supply, stick with brand names for best results.

- Ideally, get a power supply with a modular design so you use only the cables your PC needs.

- When removing and installing a power supply, look for all the power connections, including the motherboard main and 12V connections, the hard drive, the optical drive, the case fans, internal drive bay components, and possibly the video card.

IN THIS CHAPTER

- Looking under the hood at what drives a hard drive
- Getting a handle on how hard drives connect to your PC
- Learning the essentials for buying a hard drive
- Getting an old hard drive out of your PC
- Getting a new hard drive into your PC

UPGRADING THE HARD DRIVE

The hard drive is one of your PC's most vital components. Without it, Windows would have nowhere to store itself, and you would have nowhere to store your documents, photos, music, and other data. This chapter gives you a bit of background about how a hard drive works, gives you some pointers for buying a hard drive, and then gets down to the details as I show you how to install a new hard drive.

How a Hard Drive Works

Hard drives are an amazing combination of speed and precision, and their inner workings are fascinating. However, I'll save all that for another book because all we're interested in here are those hard drive principles that relate to fixing your PC. To that end, this section gives you a basic primer on how hard drives get the job done.

In simplest terms, a hard drive consists of three main parts:

- A rotating disk or platter (often more than one, but we can ignore that complication here) that's divided into concentric areas called *tracks*.

- A *read/write head* that floats just above the surface of the platter and performs the actual reading of data from and writing of data to the disk.

- An actuator arm on which the read/write head moves back and forth. The arm itself is controlled by a highly precise motor.

Figure 11.1 points out these hard drive parts.

FIGURE 11.1

The main parts of a typical hard drive.

Here's the basic procedure the hard drive follows when it needs to write data to the disk:

1. The processor locates a free storage location (called a *sector*) on the disk and passes this information (as well as the data to be written) to the hard drive.

2. The hard drive's actuator arm moves the read/write head over the track that contains the free sector. The time it takes the hard drive to do this is called the *seek time*.

3. The hard drive rotates the disk so that the free sector is directly under the read/write head. The time it takes for the hard drive to do this is called the *latency* (or sometimes the *rotational latency*).

4. The writing mechanism on the read/write head writes the data to the free sector. The time it takes the hard drive to do this is called the *write time*.

Reading data from the disk is similar:

1. The processor determines which sector on the disk contains the required data and passes this information to the hard drive.

2. The hard drive's actuator arm moves the read/write head over the track that contains the sector to be read.

3. The hard drive rotates the disk so the sector to be read is directly under the read/write head.

4. The reading mechanism on the read/write head reads the data from the sector. The time it takes the hard drive to do this is called the *read time*.

Understanding Hard Drive Specs

Hard drives are relatively simple devices, at least from the point of view of buying them. However, in your hard drive shopping excursions, you might still come across descriptions that look something like this:

> *Seagate Barracuda ST310005NA1AS SATA 6.0Gb/s*
>
> *3.5-inch Internal 1TB 7200 RPM*

As is so often the case, these descriptions are pure gobbledygook if you're not used to seeing them. The good news is that not only is it possible to translate this apparently foreign language without much fuss, but you'll also see that the translation itself offers tons of useful information that will help you make an informed choice. Here's a quick summary of what each item in the preceding description represents, and the sections that follow expand on most of them:

Seagate	This is the name of the hard drive manufacturer.
Barracuda	This is the manufacturer's hard drive product line.
ST310005NA1AS	This is the hard drive's model number.
SATA	This is the hard drive's interface.
6.0Gb/s (or Gbps)	This is the hard drive's throughput.
3.5-inch Internal	This is the hard drive's form factor.
1TB	This is the capacity of the hard drive.
7200 RPM	This is the speed or spin rate of the hard drive.

The Hard Drive Interface and Throughput

The hard drive *interface* refers to the method by which the drive connects to the motherboard, and the *throughput* (sometimes called the *data transfer rate* or the *bandwidth*) is a measure of how much data the drive can transfer per second. A number of interfaces are available, but the five you'll come upon most often when shopping for a hard drive are PATA, SATA, USB, IEEE 1394, and eSATA.

The PATA Interface

The Parallel Advanced Technology Attachment (PATA) interface is also known as the Integrated Device Electronics (IDE) interface and is the old hard drive standard that's now pretty much extinct, but you might still come across it if you're upgrading an older PC. Before going on, I should note that to differentiate this older drive standard from the newer SATA standard (discussed next), I'm using the term *PATA* here. However, most retailers (indeed, most people) instead use the term *ATA* for the older technology and *SATA* for the newer technology. This isn't strictly accurate (both PATA and SATA are part of the ATA standard), but there you go.

The two main PATA standards you'll see are

- **PATA/100**—This is also called ATA-6, ATA/100, or Ultra-ATA/100. In all cases, the "100" part tells you the throughput, which in this case means 100 megabytes per second (MBps).

- **PATA/130**—This is also called ATA-7, ATA/133, or Ultra-ATA/133. Here, the "133" tells you that the throughput for this standard is 133MBps.

The back of a PATA hard drive has three sections, pointed out in Figure 11.2.

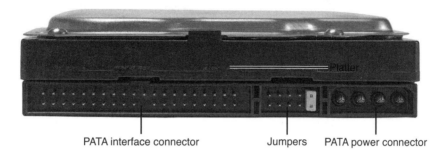

PATA interface connector   Jumpers   PATA power connector

FIGURE 11.2

The back of a PATA drive holds a couple of connectors and some jumpers.

The PATA interface connector accepts a 40-pin PATA interface cable, shown in Figure 11.3, and the other side of that cable connects to a corresponding 40-pin connector on the motherboard, as shown in Figure 11.4. The PATA power connector accepts a 4-pin power cable, shown in Figure 11.3, and that cable comes from the computer's power supply. The jumpers are mostly used to determine whether the drive is the *master* (the first or only drive on the PATA cable) or a *slave* (the second drive on a PATA cable).

 TIP See your hard drive documentation to learn which jumpers control the master/slave configurations. The docs may be available online if you no longer have them. If you don't have any documentation, many drives print a jumper diagram on the label. If you don't have that either, you can usually place a jumper on the far left pins for a master configuration and remove the jumper entirely for a slave configuration.

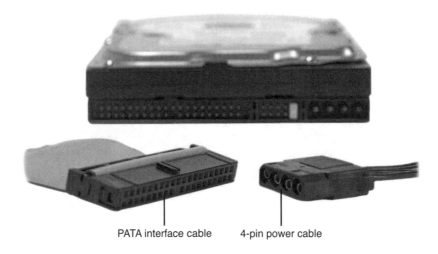

PATA interface cable   4-pin power cable

FIGURE 11.3

A PATA interface cable connects the drive to the motherboard, and the PATA power cable connects the drive to the power supply.

PATA connector

FIGURE 11.4

Most PCs come with at least one PATA interface connector.

The SATA Interface

The Serial Advanced Technology Attachment (SATA) interface is the current gold standard for PCs, and it's the only standard you should really consider for the internal hard drive (or drives) on your PC. Why? Two reasons: SATA drives cost about the same as the equivalent PATA drive, but the SATA drive will be significantly faster. How much faster? Anywhere from 1.5 times to 6 times faster! To see why, consider the three SATA standards you'll encounter:

- **SATA/150**—This is also called SATA 1. The "150" part tells you the throughput, which in this case means 150 megabytes per second (MBps). You might also see a SATA/150 drive's throughput listed as 1.5 gigabits per second (Gbps). Technically, that's the rate at which the hard drive transfers data, but some of that is overhead, so the actual rate is closer to 1.2Gbps, which is the same as 150MBps, because there are 8 bits in a byte.

- **SATA/300**—This is also called SATA 2. The "300" part tells you the throughput, which in this case means 300MBps. Again, you sometimes see a SATA/300 drive's throughput listed as 3.0Gbps. Taking signaling overhead into account, the actual rate is closer to 2.4Gbps, which is the same as 300MBps.

- **SATA/600**—This is also called SATA 3. The "600" part tells you the throughput, which in this case means 600MBps. You sometimes see a SATA/600 drive's throughput listed as 6.0Gbps, but the actual rate is closer to 4.8Gbps, which is the same as 600MBps.

The back of a SATA hard drive usually has two main sections, pointed out in Figure 11.5.

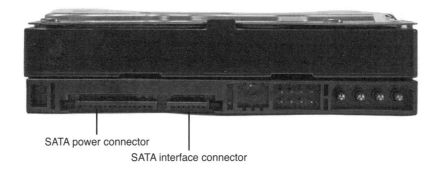

SATA power connector
SATA interface connector

FIGURE 11.5

The back of a SATA drive usually holds several connectors and some jumpers.

The SATA interface connector accepts a 7-pin SATA interface cable, shown in Figure 11.6, and the other side of that cable connects to a corresponding 7-pin connector on the motherboard, as shown in Figure 11.7. The SATA power connector accepts a 15-pin power cable, shown in Figure 11.6, and that cable comes from the computer's power supply.

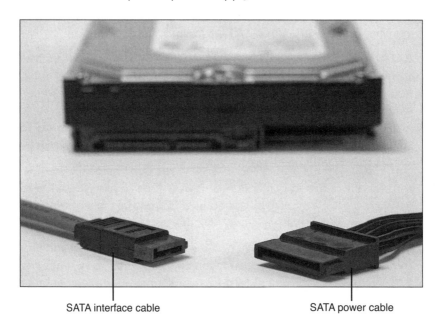

SATA interface cable   SATA power cable

FIGURE 11.6

A SATA interface cable connects the drive to the motherboard, and the SATA power cable connects the drive to the power supply.

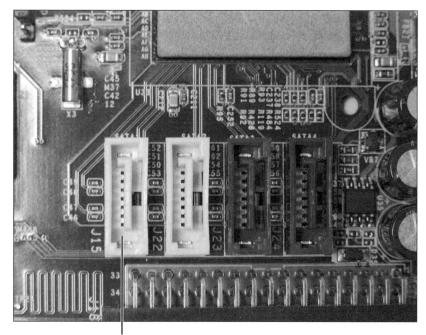

Internal SATA connectors

FIGURE 11.7

All PCs come with two or more SATA interface connectors.

External Drive Interfaces

The PATA and SATA hard drive interfaces are for internal drives. If your case has room for only a small number of internal drives (or if you want to add storage to a notebook PC), the only way to augment your local storage is to add one or more external drives. Note, too, that external drives also offer portability, which lets you attach the drive to another system, take important files with you, and so on. For external drives, you have three more choices:

- **USB 3.0**—These external drives attach to a USB 3.0 port. Make sure you get USB 3.0 (assuming your PC has at least one USB 3.0 port), which offers a transfer rate of 5Gbps, compared to 480Mbps for USB 2.0 and a mere 12Mbps for USB 1.1.

- **eSATA**—This is an external version of SATA (that's what the *e* stands for), and these drives attach to an eSATA connector. Other than the fact that it sits outside your PC, an eSATA drive is the same as an internal SATA/300 drive, which means you still get the 300MBps throughput.

- **IEEE 1394**—These external drives attach to an IEEE-1394 (also called FireWire) connector. You can get either IEEE 1394a (FireWire 400), which offers 400Mbps data throughput, or IEEE 1394b (FireWire 800), which offers 800Mbps data throughput.

For maximum flexibility, consider an external drive that offers two or more of these interfaces. For example, it's now fairly common to see external drives that offer both a USB 3.0 port and an eSATA port.

The Hard Drive Form Factor

The hard drive *form factor* refers to the dimensions of the drive—and more specifically to the approximate width of the drive. By far the most common hard drive form factor is 3.5 inches (the actual width is closer to 4 inches). Almost every case you buy will have hard drive bays that support 3.5-inch drives. The other common hard drive form factor is 2.5 inches (the actual width is closer to 2.75 inches), which is most often present in notebook drives. Figure 11.8 shows a 3.5-inch and a 2.5-inch hard drive for comparison.

3.5-inch hard drive   2.5-inch hard drive

FIGURE 11.8

The two most common hard drive form factors are 3.5 inches and 2.5 inches.

 NOTE Keep your eyes peeled on the new *solid-state* hard drives (SSDs) that are becoming quite popular. These 2.5-inch drives are made from solid-state semiconductors, which means they have no moving parts. As a result, SSDs are faster than HDDs, last longer, use less power, weigh less, and are completely silent. The downside is price. This is still bleeding-edge technology, so expect to pay around $200 for a 240GB SSD. Prices are dropping fast, however, so I'm sure it won't be long before SSDs become a viable alternative to regular drives.

The Hard Drive Speed

The hard drive *speed* is a measure of how fast the drive's internal platters spin, measured in revolutions per minute (RPM). In general, the higher the RPM value, the better the drive's performance. Most PATA and SATA hard drives spin at 7200RPM, although some older drives spin at 5400RPM. You should avoid these older drives because the performance hit is substantial, and they're not that much cheaper than the equivalent 7200RPM drive. If money is no object, you can find SATA drives that spin at 10000RPM, which offers a substantial performance boost.

Buying a Hard Drive

Purchasing a hard drive for your PC doesn't have to be a complex exercise. In fact, you can make a smart hard drive choice by paying attention to just three numbers:

- **Cost/GB**—This is the cost per gigabyte, which you calculate by dividing the price of the hard drive by its storage capacity. Here are some examples for internal hard drives:

Price	Capacity	Cost/GB
$44.99	250GB	$0.18
$59.99	500GB	$0.12
$69.99	750GB	$0.09
$79.99	1TB	$0.08
$199.99	2TB	$0.10

As you can see, the low end and the high end cost more per gigabyte, and the sweet spot is the 1TB drive. Note that, from a cost/GB perspective, there's not a lot of difference between the 750GB, 1TB, and 2TB drives. So, if you have only minimal storage needs on your system, get the 750GB drive; if you need a bigger drive to store lots of media, get the 2TB drive.

- **Cache**—The hard drive *cache* refers to a memory area embedded in the hard drive. This memory is used as a holding place for frequently used bits of data. If the CPU finds the data it needs in the hard drive cache, it saves time because the CPU can load that data directly into memory instead of asking the hard drive to fetch it from the disk. The bigger the hard drive cache, the more data it can hold, so the more likely the CPU is to find the data it needs, and thus the better the overall performance of the hard drive. So, if you're looking at two drives that are more or less the same in other respects (particularly cost/GB), choose the one that has the bigger cache.

- **Seek time**—When I explained the workings of a typical hard drive earlier (refer to section, "How a Hard Drive Works"), you learned that the four measures of hard disk read/write performance are the seek time, latency, write time, and read time. Of these, the seek time is the most important. So, again, if the other factors are about equal, get the drive that has the lower seek time.

Building a hard drive that's fast, solid, reliable, quiet, and cool is a tall order, which might be why there aren't a large number of hard disk manufacturers—and of those manufacturers, only a few produce top-quality drives. In fact, I recommend only the following three hard drive companies:

> Hitachi (www.hgst.com)
>
> Seagate (www.seagate.com)
>
> Western Digital (www.westerndigital.com)

Removing the Old Hard Drive

If the hard drive in your PC has become too small to store your data, or if you're having problems with the drive (or it has failed entirely), you need to remove the old drive and install a new one. Note that in many cases it's not absolutely crucial that you remove the old hard drive. If your current hard drive is working fine and you're just looking to upgrade your PC by adding extra storage, leave the existing hard drive as is and add the new one alongside it. In this case, skip to the next section, "Installing a New Hard Drive."

 NOTE If your existing hard drive still works, but you're replacing it, I highly recommend that you take some time now to create a system image backup, which will make it immeasurably easier to get your PC back on its feet after you've installed the new hard drive. See the section "Creating a System Image Backup," in Chapter 3, "Preparing for Trouble."

Here are the steps to remove a hard drive:

1. Make sure the computer is turned off and the power cable is disconnected.

2. Remove the computer's side panel.

3. Touch something metal to ground yourself.

4. Locate the hard drive. On most PCs, the hard drive is located near the front of the case, usually in the middle or near the bottom.

5. Remove the drive's power cable (see Figure 11.9).

6. Remove the drive's interface cable. Pull straight out. Don't wiggle the cable back and forth, or you risk bending the tiny pins.

FIGURE 11.9

You need to remove the power and interface cables attached to the hard drive.

7. Get the hard drive ready to be removed. How this is done depends on the hard drive enclosure, but two scenarios are the most common:

- **The hard drive is held in place by screws**—Many hard drive enclosures use simple screws (from four to eight in most cases) to hold the hard drive in place, as shown in Figure 11.10. You need to remove these screws.

   NOTE If the screws on the opposite side of the enclosure seem impossible to reach, it's most likely that you have to remove the other side panel to gain access to them.

Hard drive   Enclosure

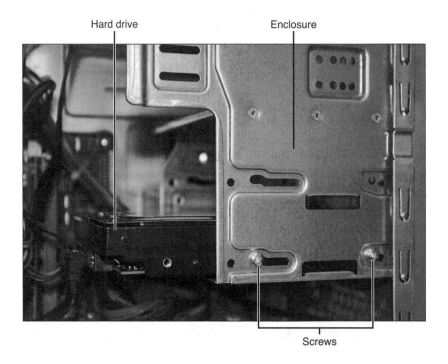

Screws

FIGURE 11.10

Many hard drives are fastened to the enclosure using several screws.

- **The hard drive is held in place by rails**—The next most common system is to attach "rails" on either side of the hard drive and then slide the rails into special slots on the inside walls of the drive enclosure, as shown in Figure 11.11. In most cases, you pinch the rails toward each other slightly to release the hard drive.

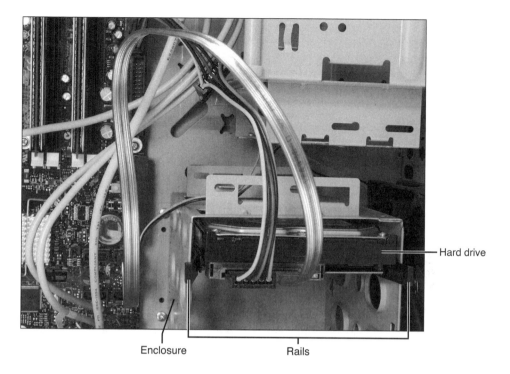

Enclosure   Rails

FIGURE 11.11

Some hard drives are attached to the enclosure using rails that are attached to the sides of the drive.

8. Slide the drive out of the drive bay. If the hard drive has rails attached, remove them for reuse with the new drive, as described in the next section.

Installing a New Hard Drive

With the old hard drive removed from your PC, you're ready to install the new drive. Here are the steps to follow:

1. Touch something metal to ground yourself.

2. If your hard drive enclosure uses rails, orient the hard drive so the connectors are facing you and the drive label is facing up, snap a left rail into the holes on the left side of the hard drive, and snap a right rail into the holes on the right side of the hard drive. Figure 11.12 shows a hard drive fitted with rails.

FIGURE 11.12

A hard drive with left and right rails attached.

3. If you're not replacing your existing hard drive, locate an empty drive bay.

4. With the hard drive connectors facing out, slide the hard drive into the drive bay. If the hard drive is held in place with screws, slide the drive into the bay until the holes on the sides of the drive align with the holes in the enclosure. If the hard drive has rails, slide the drive until the rails click into place.

5. Run an interface cable (such as a SATA cable) from the hard drive's interface connection (such as a SATA port) inside the PC.

6. Connect a power cable from the power supply to the hard drive's power connector.

7. Reattach the side panel and plug the power cord back in.

Finishing Up

With your new hard drive installed, it's time to get your PC back up and running if you replaced your old hard drive. Your first chore is to reinstall Windows, and then you restore your system from a system image backup (if you have one):

1. Insert the Windows installation media.

2. Restart your PC.

3. Boot to the installation media. Note that how you boot to the install media depends on your system. In some cases, you see a message telling you to press a key, whereas other systems ask you to select a boot device from a menu, as shown in Figure 11.13.

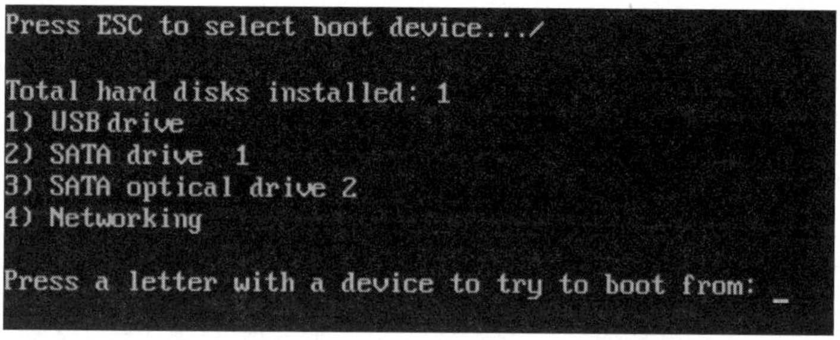

```
Press ESC to select boot device.../

Total hard disks installed: 1
1) USB drive
2) SATA drive   1
3) SATA optical drive 2
4) Networking

Press a letter with a device to try to boot from: _
```

FIGURE 11.13

On some systems, you select the boot device from a menu.

4. When the installation program starts, follow the onscreen prompts to reinstall Windows. If you need help, and if you have access to another PC, here are some online resources to check out:

    - **Windows 8**—http://windows.microsoft.com/en-US/windows/install-upgrade-activate-help

    - **Windows 7**—http://windows.microsoft.com/en-US/windows7/Installing-and-reinstalling-Windows-7

    - **Windows Vista**—http://windows.microsoft.com/en-US/windows-vista/Installing-and-reinstalling-Windows-Vista

    - **Windows XP**—http://windows.microsoft.com/en-US/windows-xp/help/setup/install-windows-xp

5. When Windows is reinstalled, restore your data from a system image backup, as described in Chapter 6, "Recovering from Problems."

THE ABSOLUTE MINIMUM

This chapter gave you some not-too-technical background about how hard drives work and how you go about upgrading your PC's drive. Here are the highlights:

- A hard drive works its electronic magic by using an actuator arm to control a read/write head that floats above the surface of a spinning platter that contains the data.

- The only real choice for your internal hard drive is Serial Advanced Technology Attachment (SATA).

- For an external drive, go with USB 3.0 or eSATA.

- In most cases, you get the best bang for your hard drive buck by buying a capacity in the middle or middle-high range: not too small, not too big.

- To remove a hard drive, open the case, disconnect the power cable and interface cable, and then remove the hard drive either by removing the enclosure screws or by squeezing the rails together.

- To install a hard drive, insert it into an empty drive bay, attach it to the enclosure, and then connect the power and interface cables.

IN THIS CHAPTER

- Some CD, DVD, and Blu-ray drive basics
- A useful and handy CD and DVD drive buying guide
- Taking an existing CD or DVD drive out of your PC
- Outfitting your PC with a shiny, new CD or DVD drive

12

UPGRADING YOUR CD OR DVD DRIVE

You probably use your PC for tasks such as playing audio CDs, showing DVD movies, and perhaps even watching high-definition Blu-ray videos. You might even use CDs or DVDs to install programs and device drivers, store data, and make backups. In each case, just having a CD, DVD, or Blu-ray disc doesn't do you much good. To make the disc do something useful, you have to insert it into a drive that can read the disc's contents. If you find that your PC's existing CD or DVD drive is too slow or just doesn't work at all, you'll be happy to hear that replacing it is not all that hard.

In this chapter, you learn about CD and DVD drives, get information on making your best purchase, and then learn how to replace your existing drive with a new one.

Choosing a CD or DVD Drive

Any PC worth its chips should have an *optical drive*, a catchall term that includes every type of CD and DVD drive, as well as the latest Blu-ray and HD DVD drives. The *optical* part tells you that these drives use light—specifically, a semiconductor laser—to read data from and write data to the disc. (For example, the *Blu* in Blu-ray comes from the fact that it uses laser light with a wavelength in the blue section of the spectrum.)

The next few sections tell you a bit more about optical drives, which will help you decide which kind to buy for the system you're upgrading.

Understanding Disc Capacities

All the discs you use with optical drives have a specific capacity, and that capacity determines the type of content that can go on the disc (for example, most movies can fit on a DVD, but the capacity of a CD is too small). If you have a drive that can write data to a disc, the capacity also tells you the maximum amount of data you can store on the disc. Table 12.1 lists the maximum capacities for the major disc types.

TABLE 12.1   Maximum Capacities for Various Optical Discs

Disc	Capacity
CD	700MB
Single-layer DVD	4.7GB
Double-layer DVD	8.5GB
Single-layer HD DVD	15GB
Dual-layer HD DVD	30GB
Single-layer Blu-ray	25GB
Dual-layer Blu-ray	50GB

 NOTE   The phrase *dual layer* means that the optical drive writes data on both sides of the disc. Note that the drive must support dual-layer recording to do this.

Getting to Know Drive Types

Here's a quick look at the types of optical drives you're likely to come across when shopping for a drive:

- **CD-ROM drive**—This stands for *compact disc read-only memory*. A CD-ROM drive is one in which you insert a CD-ROM disc that might contain data, software, or music. The *ROM* part of the drive name means that your computer can only read the disc's contents; it can't change the contents.

- **CD-R drive**—This stands for *compact disc-recordable*. A CD-R drive allows you to record, or *burn*, data to a CD-R disc. Keep in mind that you can record data to the CD-R disc only once. After that, you can't change the disc's contents. CD-R drives can also read data from previously recorded CD-R discs, as well as from CD-ROM discs.

- **CD-RW drive**—This stands for *compact disc-rewritable*. A CD-RW drive allows you to record data to a CD-RW disc. You can add data to and erase data from a CD-RW disc as often as you want. CD-RW drives can also read data from CD-R and CD-ROM discs.

- **DVD-ROM drive**—This stands for *digital versatile disc–read-only memory*. A DVD-ROM drive allows you to use a DVD-ROM disc, which might contain data or software. The *ROM* part of the drive name means your computer can only read the disc's contents; you cannot change the contents. All DVD drives can also read all CD-ROM, CD-R, and CD-RW discs.

- **DVD-R, DVD+R, or DVD±R drive**—This stands for *digital versatile disc-recordable*. A DVD-R, DVD+R, or DVD±R drive allows you to record data once to a DVD-R, DVD+R, or DVD±R disc. The ± symbol means the drive supports both the DVD-R and DVD+R formats. DVD-R, DVD+R, and DVD±R drives can read data from previously recorded DVD-R, DVD+R, or DVD±R discs, as well as from DVD-ROM discs.

   NOTE   After the DVD-R format was released, a group called the DVD+RW Alliance released the DVD+R format, which is a bit more robust than the earlier format. The two formats aren't compatible, unfortunately, but you shouldn't have to choose between the two. Almost all drives support DVD±R, a hybrid format that supports both DVD-R and DVD+R.

- **DVD-RW, DVD+RW, or DVD±RW drive**—This stands for *digital versatile disc-rewritable*. A DVD-RW, DVD+RW, or DVD±RW drive allows you to record data to a DVD-RW, DVD+RW, or DVD±RW disc. You can add data to and erase data from the disc as often as you want.

- **BD-ROM**—This stands for *Blu-ray disc–read-only memory.* A BD-ROM drive allows you to use a Blue-ray disc, which might contain data or high-definition video. The *ROM* part of the drive name means your computer can only read the disc's contents; you cannot change the contents. All Blu-ray drives can also read all CD and DVD discs.

- **BD-R**—This stands for *Blu-ray disc-recordable.* A BD-R drive allows you to record data once to a BD-R disc. BD-R drives can read data from previously recorded BD-R discs, as well as from Blu-ray discs.

- **BD-RE**—This stands for *Blu-ray disc-recordable erasable.* A BD-RE drive allows you to record data to a BD-RE disc. You can add data to and erase data from the disc as often as you want.

 NOTE If the optical drive supports dual-layer recording, you'll see *DL* added to the supported formats. For example, if a DVD±RW drive supports dual-layer recording, you'll see the format listed as DVD±RW DL.

Understanding Drive Speeds

Besides the supported formats, probably the most important consideration when you are purchasing an optical drive is the speed at which it operates. Optical drive performance is generally measured by how fast it is in three categories:

- **Write speed**—This determines how fast a recordable drive (CD-R, DVD-R, DVD+R, DVD±R, BD-R, or HD DVD-R) records data.

- **Rewrite speed**—This determines how fast a rewritable drive (CD-RW, DVD-RW, DVD+RW, or DVD±RW, BD-RE, or HD DVD-RW) rewrites data.

- **Read speed**—This determines how fast the drive reads a disc's contents.

In all cases, the speed is measured relative to a baseline amount, which is the audio CD rate of 150KBps. This is designated as 1x, and all optical drive speeds are a multiple of this. For example, a read speed of 52x means the drive reads data 52 times faster than a music CD player.

Note that you sometimes see the drive speed shown like this:

```
DVD+RW 16X8X18
```

You interpret the numbers as *writeXrewriteXread,* so in this example the write speed is 16x, the rewrite speed is 8x, and the read speed is 18x.

The following observations are generally true regarding optical drive speeds:

- CD drives are faster than DVD drives, which are faster than Blu-ray drives.

- Read speeds are faster than write speeds, and write speeds are faster than rewrite speeds.

- ROM drive read speeds are faster than burner read speeds.

Buying a CD or DVD Drive

Optical drives are among the least expensive components you'll add to your system. For example, if all you want to do is rip and burn audio CDs, you can buy a super-fast DVD±RW drive (I'm talking about 52x write speed, 32x rewrite speed, and 52x read speed) for under $20!

There's lots of competition in this market, which is why prices are low and features are high. Quite a few manufacturers operate in the optical drive market, but here are the ones I've had good dealings with:

LG Electronics (www.lge.com)

Lite-On (www.liteonit.com)

Pioneer (www.pioneerelectronics.com)

Philips (www.philips.com)

Plextor (www.plextor.com)

Samsung (www.samsung.com)

Sony (www.sony.com)

Here are a few other pointers and notes to consider when buying an optical drive for your custom system:

- **Check the cache size**—All optical drives come with an onboard memory cache for storing bits of frequently used data. This improves performance because it's many times faster for the processor to retrieve the data it needs from the cache than from the disc. The bigger the cache, the better the performance. On burners, the cache also helps to keep the burning process running smoothly by feeding a constant supply of data to the drive. Most drives nowadays come with a 2MB cache, but some drives have a 4MB or even an 8MB cache.

- **Check the access time**—The average time it takes the optical drive to access data on the disc is called the *access time*, and it's measured in milliseconds. The lower the access time, the faster the drive.

- **Check out SATA optical drives**—It used to be that optical drives came with only a PATA interface, but SATA drives started showing up a while back. Unfortunately, those drives were plagued with all kinds of problems, and the interface never took off. I'm happy to report that the manufacturers have fixed the problems, and SATA/150 optical drives are now quite popular. The higher bandwidth improves performance, and the SATA connector and power cables are easier to use than the larger PATA and legacy power cables.

→ To learn about PATA and SATA connections, **see** Chapter 11, "Upgrading the Hard Drive."

- **Consider buying two drives**—Earlier I mentioned that the read speeds of ROM drives are faster than the reader speeds of burners. Given that, a popular system configuration is to add both a ROM drive and a burner, such as a DVD-ROM drive and a DVD±RW drive. This way, you can use the DVD-ROM drive when you need read-only performance (such as when you're installing a program or accessing data on a disc), and you can use the DVD±RW drive when you need to burn data to a disc.

Removing the Existing CD or DVD Drive

If your PC has an existing optical drive that you're going to replace, either because it no longer works or you're upgrading to a better drive, you usually need to remove the old optical before installing the new one. (I say *usually* because many desktop PCs have enough room to hold at least two optical drives, so if your old drive still works, consider leaving it in place.)

Here are the steps to follow to remove an optical drive:

1. Make sure the computer is turned off and the power cable is disconnected.

2. Remove the computer's side panel.

3. Remove the PC's front cover. How you do this depends on the PC, but in most cases there are several plastic tabs holding the cover in place. For example, Figure 12.1 shows a PC that has a front cover held in place by three external tabs and one internal tab.

4. Touch something metal to ground yourself.

5. Locate the optical drive. On most PCs, the optical drive is located at the front of the case, at or near the top.

6. Remove the power cable from the back of the optical drive (see Figure 12.2).

7. Remove the interface cable from the back of the optical drive (see Figure 12.2).

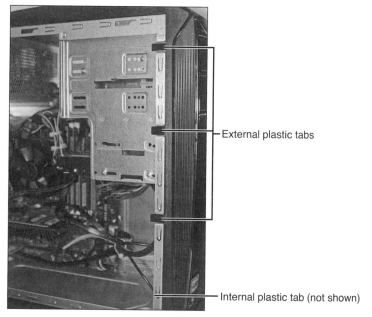

—External plastic tabs

—Internal plastic tab (not shown)

FIGURE 12.1

Most desktop PCs have front covers held in place by several plastic tabs.

Power connection

—Interface connection

FIGURE 12.2

As part of the drive removal process, you need to disconnect both the power cable and the interface cable from the back of the drive.

8. Get the optical drive ready to be removed. How this is done depends on the drive enclosure, but two scenarios are the most common:

- **The optical drive is held in place by screws**—Many optical drive enclosures use simple screws (from four to eight in most cases) to hold the hard drive in place, as shown in Figure 12.3. You need to remove these screws.

 NOTE   If you can't see any way to remove the screws on the opposite side of the enclosure, you most likely need to remove the other side panel to get at them.

Enclosure
Optical drive
Screws

FIGURE 12.3

Many optical drives are fastened to the enclosure using several screws.

- **The optical drive is held in place by rails**—The next most common system is to attach "rails" on either side of the optical drive and then slide the rails into special slots on the inside walls of the drive enclosure. In most cases, you pinch the rails toward each other slightly to release the optical drive.

9. Slide the drive out the front of the drive bay. If the optical drive has rails attached, remove them for reuse with the new drive, as described in the next section.

Installing the New CD or DVD Drive

With the old optical drive removed from your PC, you're ready to install the new drive. Here are the steps to follow:

1. Touch something metal to ground yourself.

2. If your optical drive enclosure uses rails, orient the optical drive so the connectors are facing you and the drive label is facing up, snap a left rail into the holes on the left side of the optical drive, and snap a right rail into the holes on the right side of the optical drive.

3. Open the PC's front cover, if you haven't done so already (as described in the preceding section).

4. With the optical drive's connectors facing the inside of the case, slide the drive into a drive bay. If the optical drive is held in place with screws, slide the drive into the bay until the holes on the sides of the drive align with the holes in the enclosure. If the hard drive has rails, slide the drive until the rails click into place.

5. Run an interface cable from the optical drive's interface connection to a corresponding port inside the PC (see Figure 12.4).

Interface connection

FIGURE 12.4

As part of the drive installation, you need to connect the interface cable to the back of the drive.

6. Connect a power cable from the power supply to the optical drive's power connector.

7. Reattach the front cover.

8. Reattach the side panel, plug in the power cable, and then restart your PC. Windows should recognize and set up the new drive automatically.

THE ABSOLUTE MINIMUM

In this chapter you learned a bit of background about CD and DVD drives and how to replace your current drive with a new one. Here are the highlights:

- CD, DVD, and Blu-ray drives are known in geek circles as *optical* drives because they use light (technically, a laser beam) to read data from and write data to the disc.

- When shopping for a drive, you'll generally see three speeds mentioned: the write speed, rewrite speed, and read speed. Buy the highest speeds that fit within your budget.

- For most people, a DVD-RW, DVD+RW, or DVD±RW drive offers the best combination of price and versatility. Go the Blu-ray drive route only if you need to play Blu-ray movies on your PC.

- To remove a CD or DVD drive, open the case, disconnect the power cable and interface cable, and then remove the drive either by removing the enclosure screws or by squeezing the rails together.

- To install a CD or DVD drive, insert it into an empty drive bay, attach it to the enclosure, and then connect the power and interface cables.

IN THIS CHAPTER

- Getting to know memory specs such as type, speed, and capacity
- Learning how to buy memory for your PC
- Getting those old memory modules out of your PC
- Fitting new memory modules into your PC

13

ADDING MORE MEMORY

If you find that your PC is running slow—we're talking molasses-in-January slow—one of the easiest and cheapest ways to get a significant speed boost is to add more *random access memory (RAM)* to your PC. If you're also finding that your PC crashes every so often, there's a good chance that a lack of memory is the culprit, so adding more memory will help fix that problem, as well. Put simply, the more memory you have, the happier your PC (and the operating system and programs you run on it) will be. This chapter gives you a bit of background about memory and specific recommendations as to how much memory you might want for certain applications; then it shows you how to extract and insert memory modules.

Understanding Memory Specs

Memory comes packaged in a special component called a *memory module* (or sometimes a *memory stick*). Figure 13.1 shows a typical memory module.

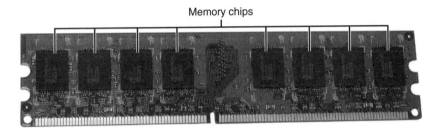

Memory chips

FIGURE 13.1

Modern-day memory comes in the form of a memory module, where the individual memory chips are soldered into place.

If you go online to your favorite computer parts retailer and click the Memory section, you might see a bunch of listings for memory modules that look something like this:

Corsair Vengeance 8GB PC3-12800 DDR3 1600 240-Pin

This description raises computer prose to new heights of unintelligibility, but there's actually quite a bit of useful data packed ever so obscurely into just a few seemingly random characters. You need to understand only a bit of this geekspeak to buy memory modules for your system, but I'll trudge through all the terms anyway, just so you know what you're up against. This description breaks down into a dozen discrete components, some of which I discuss in more detail in the sections that follow:

- **Corsair**—This is the name of the company that manufactures the module.

- **Vengeance**—This is the name of the family of memory products in which the module falls in the company's hierarchy.

- **8GB**—This is the capacity, the amount of RAM contained in the memory module.

- **PC3-12800**—This is a code that specifies the type of memory standard used by the module.

- **DDR3**—This tells you the memory type, which in this case is double data rate (DDR) type 3 memory.

- **1600**—This is the effective speed of the memory chips, in megahertz (MHz).

- **240-Pin**—This is the number of pins the memory module uses.

The Memory Module Standard

All memory modules adhere to a particular standard that specifies certain things such as the speed of the memory chips and the configuration of the module pins. The standard is indicated by a code number that takes one of the following three forms:

- **PC-*nnnn***—The PC part tells you that the module's chips use the DDR memory type (see the next section, "The Memory Type and Speed"), and the *nnnn* part is a number that tells you the theoretical bandwidth of the memory.

- **PC2-*nnnn***—The PC2 part tells you that the module's chips support the DDR2 memory type, and the *nnnn* part tells you the theoretical bandwidth of the memory.

- **PC3-*nnnn***—The PC3 part tells you that the module's chips support the DDR3 memory type, and the *nnnn* part tells you the theoretical bandwidth of the memory.

The theoretical bandwidth of the memory module is a measure of the amount of data that can pass through the module per second under ideal conditions. It's measured in megabytes per second (MBps) and, generally speaking, the higher the value, the better the memory's performance. For example, PC3-12800 implies a theoretical bandwidth of 12800MBps.

The Memory Type and Speed

Modern memory uses *synchronous dynamic RAM (SDRAM)*, which is a type of RAM that contains an internal clock that enables it to run in sync with the motherboard clock. The memory's *clock speed* is the number of ticks (or *cycles*) per second, measured in megahertz (MHz), or millions of cycles per second.

Currently, the most common memory chip type is DDR3 SDRAM, which boasts effective clock speeds ranging from 800MHz (DDR3-800) to 2800MHz (DDR3-2800).

The Memory Module Capacity

The capacity value you see in a memory module description just tells you how much RAM the module contains. If you're not sure of the capacity of a module, most have a sticker on the side that tells you, as shown in Figure 13.2.

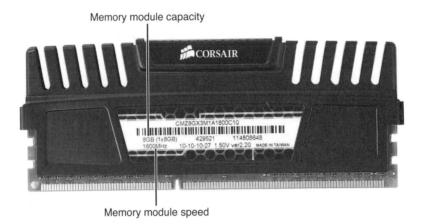

Memory module capacity

Memory module speed

FIGURE 13.2

Most RAM modules come with a sticker that tells you the module's capacity, as well as other data such as the memory type.

Determining How Much Memory Is Installed

Before you get started on your memory upgrade project, it's a good idea to determine how much memory your PC currently has installed. Here are the steps to follow in various versions of Windows:

- **Windows 8**—Press Windows Logo+W to open the Settings search pane, type **system**, and then click System in the search results. In the System window that appears, read the Installed Memory (RAM) value.

- **Windows 7 and Vista**—Select Start and then either right-click Computer and then click Properties, or type **system** in the Search box and then click System in the search results. In the System window, read the Installed Memory (RAM) number.

- **Windows XP**—Select Start, right-click My Computer, and then click Properties. In the System Properties dialog box, look for the RAM value in the General tab.

Determining What Type of Memory Is Installed

When you are adding new memory modules to a PC, by far the most important factor to consider is that the memory you buy should match the memory supported by your system. How are you supposed to find that out?

One way is to go inside the PC to see what you can see:

- Turn off your PC, open the side panel, and then locate the memory sockets on the motherboard (see Figure 13.3). Make a note of how many sockets have a memory module installed and how many sockets are free.

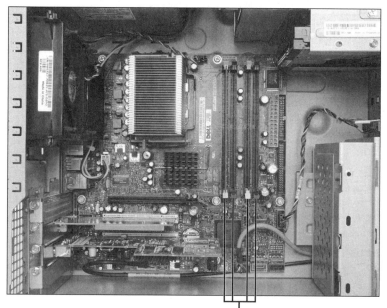

Memory module sockets

FIGURE 13.3

Most PC motherboards come with four memory module sockets.

- Remove a memory module (see the section "Pulling Out the Old Memory Modules," later in this chapter) and look for a sticker on the side of the module (refer to Figure 13.2). It should tell you how much RAM the module contains and either the RAM type or speed.

 TIP Crucial Technology offers a handy Memory Advisor tool that enables you to look up a motherboard or computer (by manufacturer, product line, and model) and find out the exact memory you can use. See www.crucial.com.

Alternatively (or, even better, in addition), if you purchased your PC from a system manufacturer, particularly a larger company such as Dell or HP, chances are you can find the computer's original manual online. (I'm assuming, of course, that the manual that came with the computer is long lost.) Even better, you can sometimes find more in-depth documentation for a machine. Dell, for example, usually offers a "service manual" that shows the motherboard's components, power supply watts (important if you'll be adding more components to your PC), system settings, and instructions for removing and installing parts.

To look for the manual online, you have a couple of ways to proceed:

- Head for the manufacturer's site, find the Support section, look up your old PC's make and model number, and then look for a link named Manual or Documentation.

- Head for Google and run a search on the manufacturer's name, the PC's make and model, and the word *manual*.

Figure 13.4 shows a sample online manual.

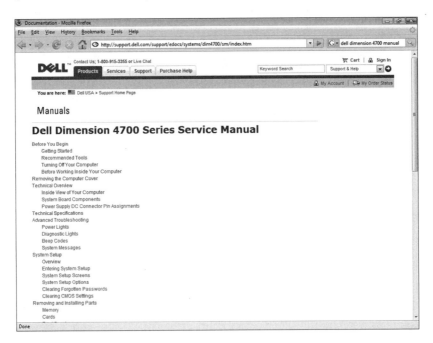

FIGURE 13.4

The service manual for my Dell Dimension 4700.

This service manual is a gold mine of useful information for the upgrader. For example, clicking the System Board Components link takes me to a really useful map of the PC's internal components, as shown in Figure 13.5.

 NOTE The manual is useful only if it applies to the specifications of your computer. Manufacturers often update a model's specs, so they update the manual to reflect those changes. Make sure the manual you find applies to your computer and not some later iteration. If it doesn't, either keep searching for the correct version of the manual, or contact the manufacturer to see whether one is available.

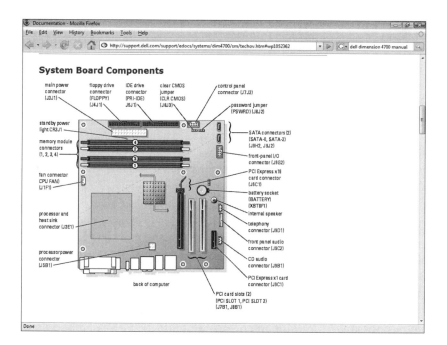

FIGURE 13.5

The service manual includes a useful map of the motherboard's components.

Even better, clicking the Technical Specifications link takes me to a page chock full of great data about the machine and its capabilities, particularly its memory specs (see Figure 13.6).

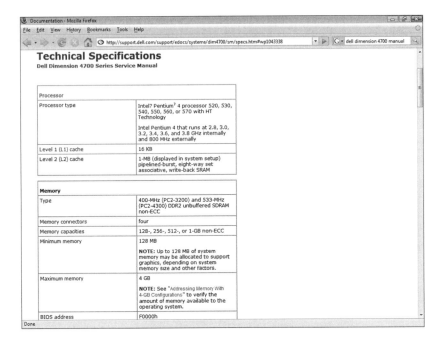

FIGURE 13.6

The service manual's Technical Specifications page contains tons of great information on the machine's components and capabilities.

Determining How Much Memory You Need

Your PC's memory is its work area. When you launch a program or open a document, the data is peeled off the hard drive and loaded into memory so that you can go about your business. So you might think that the answer to the not-so-musical question "How much memory do you need?" would be, simply, "As much as possible!" Unfortunately, you can't just plop an unlimited amount of RAM into a PC since there are maximum RAM constraints to take into account. These maximum RAM values depend on the Windows version you're using, and the reasons these limits exist are too geeky to bother with. Table 13.1 lists the maximum RAM values in the various versions of Windows 8, 7, Vista, and XP.

 NOTE To determine whether your PC uses 32-bit or 64-bit Windows 8, open the Charms menu, select Search, select Settings, type `system`, and then select System in the search results. For Windows 7, Vista, or XP, click Start, right-click Computer, and then click Properties. In the System window that appears, the System Type value says either 32-bit Operating System or 64-bit Operating System.

TABLE 13.1 Maximum Amount of RAM You Can Install in Each Version of Windows.

Windows Version	32-Bit	64-Bit
Windows 8	4GB	128GB
Windows 8 Professional	4GB	512GB
Windows 8 Enterprise	4GB	512GB
Windows 7 Starter	2GB	N/A
Windows 7 Home Basic	4GB	8GB
Windows 7 Home Premium	4GB	16GB
Windows 7 Professional	4GB	192GB
Windows 7 Enterprise	4GB	192GB
Windows 7 Ultimate	4GB	192GB
Windows Vista Starter	1GB	N/A
Windows Vista Home Basic	4GB	8GB
Windows Vista Home Premium	4GB	16GB
Windows Vista Professional	4GB	128GB
Windows Vista Enterprise	4GB	128GB
Windows Vista Ultimate	4GB	128GB
Windows XP Starter	512GB	N/A
Windows XP	4GB	128GB

CAUTION For technical reasons, note that although most 32-bit versions of Windows support up to 4GB of RAM, the maximum amount of usable RAM in those systems is only about 3GB.

So, should you just go with the maximum RAM for your system? Nope. To understand why, think of the restraints you might face in the real world when deciding how big of a work area you need. Clearly, it can't be too small; otherwise, it just wouldn't be practical. On the other hand, if you lease too big of a building, you would overpay for space you don't need.

PC memory works the same way. For starters, you definitely want to avoid getting too little memory. For one thing, all versions of Windows have a minimum amount of memory that they require just to get off the ground. Beyond that, however, this minimum amount (or even an amount slightly more than the minimum) usually means your PC will feel sluggish and slow, and you don't want that, believe me. As a general (but not universal) rule, the more memory your PC has to work with, the faster and more sprightly your programs will feel.

However, like the too-large workspace, there is definitely such a thing as too much memory. Installing, say, 10 or 20 times the minimum memory requirement would probably cost you an extra $1,000 or $2,000 on your purchase price, but the vast majority of the time your PC would only ever use a fraction of that vast memory space.

Okay, so what's the right number? The answer depends on what you're going to be using your PC for and how much you have to spend. Here are five levels to consider:

 TIP Crucial Technology also offers a handy System Scanner tool that scans what's on your PC and then recommends the correct amount of RAM. See www.crucial.com.

- **Bare minimum**—This is the level of the minimum memory requirement for Windows. For most versions of Windows 8, 7, and Vista, the minimum is 1GB of memory (it's 2GB for the 64-bit versions; the XP minimum is 64GB). If your budget is very tight, you can get away with just 1GB in your PC, but don't expect anything to happen quickly on your machine.

- **Real-world minimum**—For real day-to-day work on a PC, you really should have at least 2GB of memory installed. This gives you acceptable performance for most programs, allows you to run several programs at once, and doesn't cost very much money.

- **Sweet spot**—These days, I think the ideal amount of memory for most folks is 4GB. This gives you great performance for almost every program you might want to run, enables you to open many programs at once without slowing things down, and doesn't break the bank. Note, however, that for technical reasons we don't need to go into here, to get the most out of 4GB of memory, you need to get the 64-bit version of Windows (*not* the 32-bit version).

- **Performance**—If you're going to be using your PC for serious pursuits—I'm talking about video editing, big-time photo manipulation, or high-end gaming—you'll be much happier in the long run if you go for 8GB of memory. These activities place maximum demands on a PC and so will be happiest if they have a good chunk of memory to roam around in. Note that this amount of memory requires a 64-bit version of Windows.

- **Over-the-top**—Many PC manufacturers and vendors are only too happy to try to sell you systems that come with 12, 16, or even 24GB of memory, and are also happy to charge you big bucks for the privilege. Just say "Thanks, but no thanks" to these offers because you really do not need this much memory in your PC unless you are a gamer or run powerful graphics apps, such as Photoshop or Illustrator.

NOTE   You can save yourself a lot of money by getting only a small amount of memory when you purchase your PC and then installing more memory yourself. This is particularly true if you're buying from a PC manufacturer, which might charge you $100 to $150 to go from 2GB of memory to 4GB. By contrast, you can purchase 4GB of memory online for $25 to $30.

Buying Memory

Buying RAM isn't nearly as complex as buying many of the other components that make up your PC. Yes, you can obsess on obscure factors such as latency and timings (plus many other memory features I mercifully spared you from in this chapter), but when you're just starting out, you need to worry about only a few things. Before I talk about those things, I should mention that, as with the motherboard and processor, quality counts when it comes to RAM modules, so always buy from a major memory manufacturer. Here are a few I recommend:

Corsair (www.corsair.com)

Crucial Technology (www.crucial.com)

G.SKILL (www.gskill.com)

Kingston Technology (www.kingston.com)

Mushkin (www.mushkin.com)

OCZ Technology (www.ocz.com)

Patriot (www.patriotmem.com)

Here are some pointers to think about before purchasing memory for your system:

- **Match your PC's memory requirements**—As I mentioned earlier, be sure you know what type of memory your PC's motherboard supports.

- **Don't exceed you system's capacity**—All systems have a maximum RAM capacity, so you shouldn't try to install more RAM than the board can handle.

- **Match your RAM to your needs**—Again, you don't want to go with the Windows minimum for RAM, but you don't want to "over-RAM" your PC, either. See my discussion earlier in this chapter (see section, "Determining How Much Memory You Need").

Pulling Out the Old Memory Modules

After you purchase your memory modules, the next step in your memory upgrade is to remove the old modules. First, note that you don't necessarily have to do this.

If your PC has four internal memory slots and you're just filling in the empty slots with the same type of memory that's already in the other slots, feel free to leave the old module in place.

If you're upgrading your memory, however, you should remove the old modules. Here are the steps to remove a memory module:

1. Make sure the computer is turned off and the power cable is disconnected.

2. Remove the computer's side panel.

3. Touch something metal to ground yourself.

4. Locate the memory module you want to remove.

5. Press down on one of the memory socket's ejector tabs to pivot the tab away from the module.

6. Press down on the other memory socket ejector tab to pivot the tab away from the module, as shown in Figure 13.7.

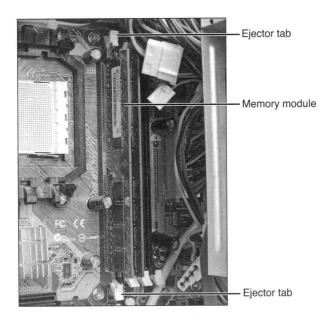

Ejector tab

Memory module

Ejector tab

FIGURE 13.7

Press down on the ejector tabs to pivot the tabs away from the module.

7. Remove the memory module from the socket. Take care not to bump the module against any other component.

8. Repeat steps 4–7 to remove any other module you want to salvage.

Installing the New Memory Modules

The good news about installing memory modules is that they're almost impossible to install incorrectly. To help you understand why, Figure 13.8 shows a memory module hovering above a memory socket. Notice that the memory module has a notch in the pin area. This notch matches a corresponding ridge inside the memory socket, as pointed out in Figure 13.8. The placement of this notch prevents you from installing the module the wrong way around. Also, because the different module configurations have their notches in different places, it also prevents you from installing the wrong type of memory.

The notch on the module...

...matches the ridge inside the memory socket.

FIGURE 13.8

The memory module's notch lines up with the socket ridge to ensure correct installation.

With your new memory module in hand, here are the steps to follow to install it:

1. If the memory socket's ejector tabs are in the vertical position, open them by pivoting them away from the socket.

2. Orient the memory module over the memory socket so that the module's notch lines up with the socket's ridge, as shown in Figure 13.9.

FIGURE 13.9

Line up the module's notch with the socket's ridge.

3. On the ends of the socket, you'll see thin vertical channels. Slide the memory module into these channels, as shown in Figure 13.10.

FIGURE 13.10

Slide the memory module into the channels at both ends of the memory socket.

4. Place your thumbs on the top edge of the module, one thumb on each side.

5. Press the module into the socket. When the module is properly seated, the ejector tabs automatically snap into the vertical position.

6. Put the computer's side panel back on and plug in the power cord.

NOTE Sometimes you need to use a surprising amount of force to get the module fully seated in the socket. Some sockets are just really tight fits, so you have to press really hard to get the module all the way in.

Note that it's very easy to think that you've inserted a memory module fully when in fact it's not quite seated properly. How can you tell? Check out the ejector tabs. If the module isn't fully seated in the socket, the ejector tabs are not perfectly vertical, as shown in Figure 13.11. The ejector tab should look like the one shown in Figure 13.12.

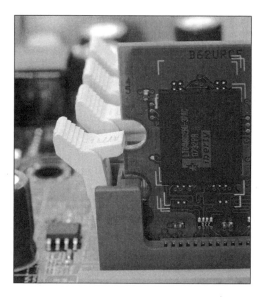

FIGURE 13.11

Wrong: If the ejector tab isn't vertical, the module isn't seated.

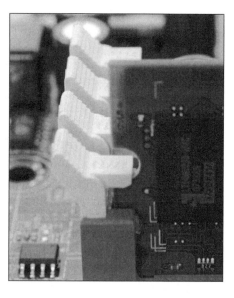

FIGURE 13.12

Right: A vertical ejector tab tells you the module is fully seated in the socket.

THE ABSOLUTE MINIMUM

Memory is one of most crucial components for keeping a PC running smoothly and efficiently, so in this chapter you learned more about what memory is and how to upgrade your PC's store of RAM. Here are some things to think about:

- Memory chips come prepackaged on components called memory modules.

- Your PC's motherboard is designed to use only a specific configuration (or configurations) of memory, which includes the memory module standard (such as DDR3) and the theoretical bandwidth (such as 12800).

- The easiest way to determine the type of memory your PC has installed is to turn off the PC, open the case, and then remove one of the existing memory modules to examine the sticker on the side. Alternatively, look online for the PC's service manual, which should be available from the manufacturer's website.

- You should install 4GB of RAM for most uses, but if you're doing any heavy-duty computing (such as video editing), go with 8GB. Remember you need a 64-bit version of Windows to use these amounts of RAM.

- To remove a memory module from its socket, press down on each of the two ejector tabs to release the module and then lift the module out of the socket.

- To insert a memory module, orient the module's notch over the socket's ridge and then press the module into the socket until the ejector tabs snap into place.

IN THIS CHAPTER

- Learning how video cards work
- Getting the hang of video card specs
- Buying a video card
- Buying a monitor
- Setting up your system to use two (or even three!) monitors

14

UPDATING THE VIDEO CARD AND MONITOR

What goes on inside your PC's processor, memory, and hard drive are essential, but they don't amount to much if you can't *see* what's happening with your machine. The "seeing" side of computing is handled by two components: the video card and monitor. This chapter gives you some necessary background about these PC parts and shows you how to make the best decision when it comes time to buy a video card or monitor. As a special bonus, you also learn how to set up your PC to work with multiple monitors.

Assessing Your Video Card Needs

The *video card* (sometimes called a *video adapter*) is a system component that usually comes in the form of a circuit board that plugs into a slot inside the computer. (Therefore, the video card is also called a *graphics board*, a *graphics card*, and a *graphics adapter*. Note, too, that some video cards are part of the computer's motherboard.) Its job is to enable software to display text or an image on the monitor. The basic process works something like this:

1. The software alerts the processor to let it know the program has something to display on the monitor.

2. The processor contacts the graphics adapter's device driver and passes along the instructions about what to display.

3. The driver contacts the video card and sends along the instructions from the processor.

4. The video card builds the new screen image and stores it in a *frame buffer*: a piece of the adapter's onboard memory.

5. If the video card has an analog connection to the monitor, the card uses a *random access memory digital-to-analog converter (RAMDAC)* to convert the digital data in the frame buffer to analog data the monitor can understand. (Digital monitor connections don't require this conversion.)

6. The monitor displays the screen image by converting the incoming signal into the colors that are displayed using individual screen pixels.

How images appear on your monitor is a function of two measurements: the color depth and resolution.

The *color depth* is a measure of the number of colors available to display images on the screen. In general, the greater the number of colors, the sharper your screen image appears—and the more processing power required to display those colors. Color depth is usually expressed in either bits or total colors. For example, a 4-bit display can handle up to 16 colors (because 2 to the power of 4 equals 16). Table 14.1 lists the bit values for the most common color depths.

TABLE 14.1 Bit Values for Some Standard Color Depths

Bits	Colors
4	16
8	256
15	32,268
16	65,536
24	16,777,216
32	16,777,216

 NOTE The 32-bit color depth yields the same number of colors as the 24-bit depth because the extra 8 bits are used for an alpha channel, which can hold transparency information.

 NOTE On some systems, the color depth value isn't listed as a specific number of bits or colors. Instead, the color depth is listed as either "Medium" or "Thousands," both of which refer to the 16-bit, 65,536-color depth, or as "Highest" or "Millions," both of which refer to the 32-bit, 16,777,216-color depth.

The *resolution* is a measure of the density of the pixels used to display the screen image. The pixels are arranged in a row-and-column format, so the resolution is expressed as *rows × columns*, where *rows* is the number of pixel rows and *columns* is the number of pixel columns. For example, a 1024 × 768 resolution means screen images are displayed using 1,024 rows of pixels and 768 columns of pixels. The higher the resolution, the sharper your images appear. Individual screen items—such as icons and dialog boxes—also get smaller at higher resolutions because these items tend to have a fixed height and width, expressed in pixels. For example, a dialog box that's 320 pixels wide appears half as wide as the screen at 640 × 480. However, it appears to be only one quarter of the screen width at 1280 × 1024 (a common resolution for medium-size monitors).

 NOTE A *pixel* is a tiny element that displays the individual dots that make up the screen image (*pixel* is short for "picture element"). Each pixel consists of three components—red, green, and blue—and they are manipulated to produce a specific color.

The key point to bear in mind about this description is that there's usually a trade-off between color depth and resolution, and that trade-off is based on the memory installed on the video card. That is, depending on how much video memory is installed on the card, you might have to trade off higher color depth with lower resolution, or vice versa.

Why does the amount of video memory matter? Earlier I mentioned that each screen image is stored in a frame buffer. The size of that buffer is a function of the total number of pixels used in the resolution and the number of bits required to "light" each pixel. For example, a resolution of 800 × 600 means there are a total of 480,000 pixels. If each pixel uses a color depth of 16 bits, a total a 7,680,000 bits is required to hold the entire screen image, which is equivalent to about 937KB. If you bump up the resolution to 1280 × 1024 and use a 32-bit color depth, the total number of bits involved leaps to 41,943,040, which is about 5.1MB. However, most video cards support a feature called *triple buffering*, where the card implements two frame buffers for 2D rendering—one for the current screen and one for the next screen image to be displayed—and a third buffer for 3D data (this is called the *Z buffer*). This effectively triples the memory required. In the 1280 × 1024 32-bit example, the total amount of memory needed is 15.3MB. If you have an older video card graphics adapter with just 8MB of video memory, you aren't able to select the 1280 × 1024 resolution unless you drop the color depth down to 16 bits (bringing the memory requirement down to about 7.6MB).

In general, you use the following formula to calculate the number of bytes required to display a screen:

$$rows * columns * bits * 3 / 8$$

rows	The number of rows in the resolution
columns	The number of columns in the resolution
bits	The number of bits in the color depth

Divide the result by 1,048,576 to get the number of megabytes.

Table 14.2 lists the most common resolutions (I also included the name of the corresponding display standard) and color depth values and calculates the amount of memory.

TABLE 14.2 Translating Resolution and Color Depth into Memory Required

Standard	Resolution	Color Depth	Memory
VGA	640 × 480	16 bits	1.8MB
VGA	640 × 480	32 bits	3.6MB
SVGA	800 × 600	16 bits	2.7MB
SVGA	800 × 600	32 bits	5.4B
XGA	1024 × 768	16 bits	4.5MB
XGA	1024 × 768	32 bits	9MB
WXGA	1280 × 800	16 bits	6MB
WXGA	1280 × 800	32 bits	12MB
SXGA	1280 × 1024	16 bits	7.5MB
SXGA	1280 × 1024	32 bits	15MB
WXGA+	1440 × 900	16 bits	7.5MB
WXGA+	1440 × 900	32 bits	15MB
UXGA	1600 × 1200	16 bits	10.8MB
UXGA	1600 × 1200	32 bits	21.6MB
HDTV	1920 × 1080	16 bits	12MB
HDTV	1920 × 1080	32 bits	24MB
QXGA	2048 × 1536	16 bits	18MB
QXGA	2048 × 1536	32 bits	36MB
QSXGA	2560 × 2048	16 bits	30MB
QSXGA	2560 × 2048	32 bits	60MB

Finally, I should mention that the memory requirements shown in Table 14.2 still don't account for all the memory used by a typical video card. For example, all cards require a bit of extra memory to perform *antialiasing* (a rendering technique that smoothes jagged lines and other unwanted artifacts).

Understanding Video Card Specs

Like most PC components, video cards come encrusted with acronyms, jargon, and specs galore. When shopping for a video card, you therefore might come across a description that looks similar to the following:

XFX PVT73EYARG GeForce 7300GT 533MHz 512MB GDDR2,

PCI Express x16, SLI Ready, DVI, VGA, HDTV

The good news is that in this description contains quite a bit of useful information, and not an ounce of marketing fluff. Of course, you need a translator to figure out the useful stuff. Here's a quick summary of what each item in this description represents, and the sections that follow expand on many of them:

- **XFX**—This is the name of the video card manufacturer.

- **PVT73EYARG**—This is the manufacturer's model number for the video card.

- **GeForce 7300GT**—This is the name of the graphics processing unit (GPU) chipset.

- **533MHz**—This is the speed of the memory clock.

- **512MB**—This is the amount of graphics memory on the card.

- **GDDR2**—This is the type of graphics memory on the card.

- **PCI Express x16**—This is the interface slot type used by the card. Refer to Chapter 8, "Basic PC Repair Skills," to learn about motherboard slot types.

→ For a rundown on motherboard slot types, **see** "Understanding Expansion Slot Types," **p. 132**

- **SLI Ready**—This tells you that you can combine this video card with a second video card using the SLI dual-GPU technology (see "Moving Up to Three Monitors," later in this chapter).

- **DVI**—This tells you that the card comes with a DVI connector.

- **VGA**—This tells you that the card comes with a VGA connector.

- **HDTV**—This tells you that the card comes with an HDTV connector.

The GPU Chipset

The heart and soul of any modern video card is the graphics processing unit (GPU). This unit is a dedicated microprocessor that has been optimized to work with graphical operations. This enables the chip to render 2D and 3D graphics at blazing speeds and saves the CPU from having to perform these operations. The GPU is part of a larger graphics chipset that also includes the video memory and bus interface. The GPU and graphics chipset fully determine the capabilities of the video card.

Video Memory

All video cards come with their own set of memory chips, and a big part of the high performance of modern video cards is that they have easy and fast access to onboard memory rather than relying on a slower pipeline to the system memory. When you're examining the specs of video cards, you'll often come across four memory-related numbers:

- **Memory size**—You saw earlier that the amount of video memory on a card is crucial in determining the resolution and color depth. However, modern video cards use memory for many chores other than frame buffering, so the same is true for a video card as it is for a motherboard: the more memory, the better the performance.

- **Memory type**—In Chapter 13, "Adding More Memory," you learned about the various system memory types, and you particularly learned about double data rate (DDR) memory, which transfers data at the beginning and the end of each clock cycle, and DDR2 memory, which offers higher clock speeds than DDR. DDR2 is also a common video memory technology (although it's called GDDR2, where the G stands for graphics), although the need for video RAM speed has caused chipset manufacturers to push the envelope a bit in recent years. These days the most common video memory type is GDDR3, which offers higher clock speeds than GDDR2; GDDR4 cards are also available that offer still higher speeds.

→ For the specifics on DDR system memory, **see** "The Memory Type and Speed," **p. 197**

- **Memory clock speed**—The speed of the memory clock affects performance in that the faster the clock, the more data the card can process. GDDR2 memory usually offers clock speeds in the 350MHz–700MHz range; for GDDR3, the usual range is 500MHz–800MHz; for GDDR4, the range is 800MHz–1GHz.

- **Memory interface width**—This value tells you the width of the data pathway between the GPU and the video memory, in bits. The wider the path, the better the performance. Lower-end cards use a 64-bit path (some even go as low as 32 bits); mid-range video cards use a 128-bit path; and high-end cards use a 256-bit path. Some video cards now even use 320-bit or 384-bit paths.

Video Card Connectors

Your video card has to direct its output to something, and what that something will be is determined by the connectors that appear on the card's bracket. There are a number of different connectors, but four are by far the most common on desktop PCs: VGA, DVI, HDTV, and HDMI.

The VGA connector—also called the D-Sub connector—is a blue, 15-pin port you use to connect to CRT monitors and to the analog input ports on LCD monitors. Figure 14.1 shows a VGA connector.

FIGURE 14.1

You use a VGA port for connections to analog CRT and LCD monitors.

Digital Visual Interface (DVI) is a high-definition video connector available on most LCDs and on most older digital TVs. When you're working with DVI, note that there are three types: DVI-A, DVI-D, and DVI-I. DVI-A works with only analog signals; DVI-D works with only digital signals; and DVI-I works with both analog and digital and is shown in Figure 14.2. Unfortunately, each type of DVI uses a slightly different pin arrangement (see Figure 14.3), so when you're matching your monitor, DVI cable, and video card, you need to ensure that they all use the same DVI connectors. Just to confuse matters, DVI-D and DVI-I connectors also come in *single-link* and *dual-link* configurations. In this case, make sure you get dual-link; it also works with single-link, though. Here's a summary of the five available connection types:

- **DVI-A**—This connector consists of one 4-pin grouping, one 8-pin grouping, and a single flat pin.

- **DVI-D Single-Link**—This connector consists of two 9-pin groupings and a single flat pin.

- **DVI-D Dual-Link**—This connector consists of one 24-pin grouping (three rows of 8 pins) and a single flat pin.

- **DVI-I Single-Link**—This connector consists of two 9-pin groupings and a single flat pin surrounded by 4 pins.

- **DVI-I Dual-Link**—This connector consists of one 24-pin grouping (three rows of 8 pins) and a single flat pin surrounded by 4 pins.

 NOTE DVI uses a transmitter to send information along the cable. A single-link cable uses one transmitter, whereas a dual-link cable uses two transmitters. This means that dual-link connections are faster and offer a better signal quality than single-click connections.

 TIP A dual-link DVI connector can plug into a single-link DVI port. Unfortunately, the reverse isn't true; that is, you can't plug a single-link DVI connector into a dual-link DVI port. Note, too, that a DVI-D connector can plug into a DVI-I port, but a DVI-I connector doesn't fit into a DVI-D port.

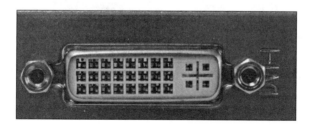

FIGURE 14.2

You use a DVI port for digital connections to LCD monitors and some TVs.

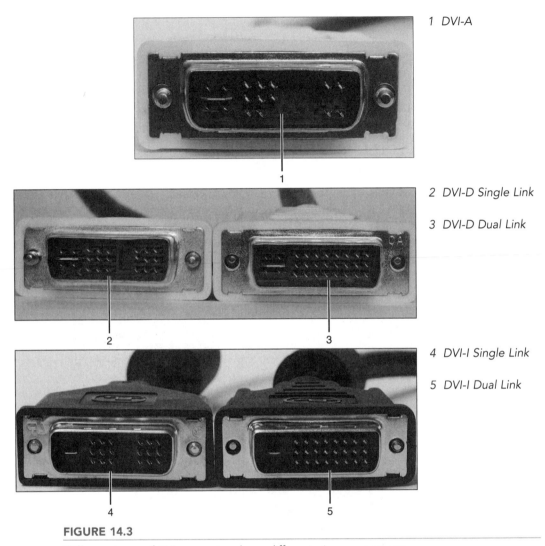

1 DVI-A

2 DVI-D Single Link

3 DVI-D Dual Link

4 DVI-I Single Link

5 DVI-I Dual Link

FIGURE 14.3

Different types of DVI connectors have different pin arrangements.

Many modern video cards come with adapters that enable you to make higher-quality connections to an HDTV. For example, some cards come with a separate HDTV adapter or cable that plugs into the S-Video port and offers component video ports (red, green, and blue connectors) for connection to your HDTV's component input ports (see Figure 14.4). Similarly, some cards offer a DVI-to-HDMI adapter. High-Definition Multimedia Interface (HDMI) is currently the gold standard for displaying digital video signals, and it's now relatively common to find an HDMI connector on a digital TV.

FIGURE 14.4

Many video cards come with an HDTV adapter that plugs into the S-Video connector and offers component video ports for connecting to a TV.

If you want to watch or record TV on your PC, you need a separate TV tuner card, which comes with a cable TV connector, as shown in Figure 14.5.

FIGURE 14.5

To watch or record TV, you need a TV tuner card with a cable TV connector.

Buying a Video Card

Current GPU chipsets are excellent products, so it's hard to go wrong when choosing a card manufacturer. In general, it's better to stick with larger companies because you're more likely to get better technical support and better driver support. Here are my recommended video card manufacturers:

ASUS (www.asus.com)

AMD (www.amd.com)

EVGA (www.evga.com)

Gigabyte (www.giga-byte.com)

HIS (www.hisdigital.com)

MSI (www.msicomputer.com)

PNY (www.pny.com)

Sapphire (www.sapphiretech.com)

XFX (www.xfxforce.com)

Here are a few other points to think about when making your video card purchase:

- **Decide whether you need a separate video card**—If you don't have any extra cash or motherboard slots, and your video needs aren't extravagant, you can probably get away with using a motherboard that has an integrated video adapter. Today's built-in video cards are much higher quality than they used to be, so most offer decent-looking screen images. The only major downside to using integrated video is that the adapter doesn't have its own memory supply, so it must use some of the PC's system memory instead. This can slow down overall system performance, unless you put a lot of memory into your PC.

- **Go with PCI Express**—Unless your motherboard either doesn't have any PCI Express slots (unlikely, these days) or has no free PCI Express slots available, be sure to get a video card that uses PCI Express because this bus type is much faster than AGP and PCI.

- **Buy as much memory as you can afford**—Today's graphical systems require lots of video memory, and they'll use any memory your video card carries. Therefore, load up your video card with as much memory as you can afford. The minimum these days should be 128MB, but you won't regret getting 256MB, 512MB, or even more.

- **Decide whether you need multiple-monitor support**—Even if you're using a nice 20- or even 22-inch LCD monitor, if you use your computer a lot, you probably find yourself constantly Alt+Tabbing from one of your many open windows to another. A single monitor—even a big one—just doesn't have the necessary real estate to show more than a couple of windows at once. The solution to this problem that also happens to be a sure-fire way to boost productivity is to add a second monitor to your setup. Doubling your monitors effectively doubles your desktop (at least horizontally) and enables you to keep more windows in view. To do the dual-monitor thing, you either need to install two video cards or, much better, install a single video card that has two output ports: either one VGA and one DVI or two DVI (as shown in Figure 14.6). For more on this issue, see "Setting Up a Multimonitor System," later in this chapter.

 CAUTION   Some video cards offer two connectors but support only one monitor connection at a time. Check the video card specs to ensure that the card supports multiple monitors.

FIGURE 14.6

To extend your desktop onto another monitor, you need a video card with dual output ports and support for connecting two monitors simultaneously.

- **Get a separate TV tuner card**—If you want to watch and capture TV via the digital media hub, you need a TV tuner device. Some video cards have TV tuners built in, but you can also purchase standalone TV tuners either as internal adapter cards or external boxes. In general, standalone TV tuners give you a better signal and are less flaky overall than all-in-one cards that try to do both graphics and TV, so I recommend getting a separate device. Be sure to match the TV tuner device to the type of signal you receive. For example, if your signal arrives via a digital or an analog TV cable, you need a digital or an analog cable connector; similarly, *over-the-air (OTA)* broadcast signals require the appropriate type of antenna to capture the signal.

Choosing a Monitor

Because you look at the monitor all day long, you should get a good monitor/video card combination that is easy on your eyes and doesn't break your budget. Of course, this advice applies only if you're buying a desktop PC because all-in-ones, laptops, and tablets come with the monitor built in. (That's not to say that you should ignore the monitor component of a laptop or all-in-one. Screen sizes vary, so you need to choose a screen that suits your needs. Also, larger screens add weight to a laptop, so bear that in mind when you're selecting a screen size.)

The good news about choosing a monitor is that there is only one type to consider: a *liquid crystal display* (LCD, also called a *flat panel*). *Light-emitting diode* (LED) monitors also are available, but they're too expensive.

 NOTE Although full LED monitors are too expensive, many LCD monitors use LEDs as backlights (because LCDs need some source of illumination to produce an image). These backlights use much less power than regular LCD light sources, so look for "LED backlight" in the monitor specifications if you want to get an energy-efficient display.

The most important consideration for a monitor is the size of the screen. Put simply, a large monitor allows you to display more elements on the screen than a small monitor. You can determine the size of a monitor by measuring diagonally from corner to corner. Keep in mind that if you see a computer ad that says "19-inch monitor (18.5-inch *viewable image size,* or v.i.s.)," this means that although the monitor has a full 19 inches of glass, only 18.5 inches of that glass are actually used to display the image.

When choosing a monitor, you really don't need to delve much deeper than that. However, if you want to get into it, or if you're just wondering what those weird monitor specs are all about, here's a quick summary:

- **Resolution**—As I mentioned earlier, the higher the resolution, the more items you can fit on the screen and the sharper those objects will appear.

- **Connections**—This term refers to the ports that appear on the back or bottom of the monitor, and they determine how it connects to your PC. The three most common connection types are VGA, DVI, and HDMI. The only real concern here is to make sure your get a monitor that has at least one connection port that matches the monitor connection port on your PC.

- **Dot pitch**—The distance between each pixel is called the *dot pitch* (or *pixel pitch*). This is a measure of the clarity of the monitor's image: the smaller the dot pitch, the sharper the image. Look for a monitor with a dot pitch of 0.26 millimeters (mm) or less.

- **Brightness**—This tells you how bright the screen appears, and it's measured in candelas per square meter (cd/m^2). For most uses, 200–250 cd/m^2 is fine.

- **Contrast ratio**—This is a measure of the difference between the light intensity of the brightest white and the darkest black. Most monitors offer a contrast ratio of around 1,000:1. However, you might see monitors advertising "dynamic" contrast ratios on the order of 10,000,000:1. This is hype and should be ignored.

- **Other features**—Some monitors come with built-in speakers, which is handy because it means you don't have to put separate speakers somewhere on your desk, although the sound quality tends to be a tad low. Many newer monitors also come with several USB ports, which is useful for plugging in desktop devices such as your keyboard, mouse, smartphone, or digital camera.

Setting Up a Multimonitor System

Over the past few years, many studies have shown that you can greatly improve your productivity by doing one thing: adding a second monitor to your system. This setup enables you to have whatever program you are currently working with displayed on one monitor, and your reference materials, email program, or some other secondary program on the second monitor. Using two monitors is more efficient because you no longer have to switch back and forth between the two programs.

To work with two monitors on a single computer, one solution is to install a second video card and attach the second monitor to it. However, most video cards now available come with multiple output ports, which can be any combination of VGA, DVI, HDTV, and HDMI (refer to Figure 14.6). Also, almost all notebook PCs have at least one video output port that you can use to connect to a second monitor.

Setting Up Multiple Monitors on Windows 8

For most people, the extra expense of a second monitor is justified if it increases productivity, and you can do that by extending the Windows 8 interface across a second monitor. In this case, Windows 8 leaves the Start screen displayed on the original monitor, and it opens the Desktop app on the second monitor. Here are the steps to follow to extend the Windows 8 screen to the second monitor:

1. Connect the second monitor to your Windows 8 PC.

2. Press Windows Logo+K. Windows 8 displays the Devices pane.

3. Click Second Screen. The Second Screen pane appears, as shown in Figure 14.7.

 TIP You can jump directly to the Second Screen pane by pressing Windows Logo+P.

4. Click Extend. Windows 8 connects to the second monitor and uses it to display the Desktop app.

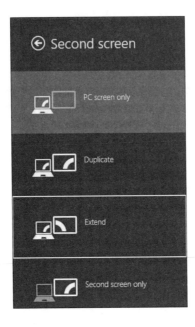

FIGURE 14.7

Use the Second Screen pane to extend your Start screen and desktop onto your second monitor.

Now you need to choose which monitor is the main display that shows the taskbar's notification area. This is also the display that Windows 8 uses to open desktop apps when you launch them from the Start screen. Follow these steps:

1. Press Windows Logo+W. The Settings search pane appears.

2. Type **resolution**.

3. Click Adjust Screen Resolution. The Screen Resolution window appears on the desktop, as shown in Figure 14.8.

4. Click the monitor you want to set as the main display.

5. Activate the Make This My Main Display check box.

6. Click OK.

 TIP Ideally, you should be able to move your mouse continuously from the left monitor to the right monitor. If you find that the mouse stops at the right edge of your left monitor, it means you need to exchange the icons of the left and right monitors. To do that, click and drag the left monitor icon to the right of the other monitor icon (or vice versa).

Windows 8 displays an icon for each of your monitors

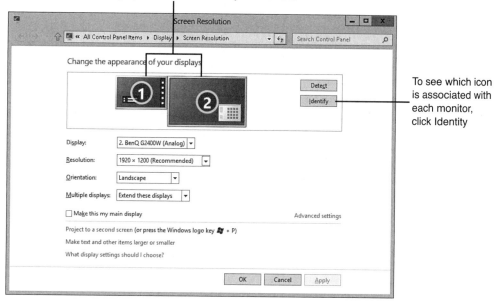

To see which icon is associated with each monitor, click Identity

FIGURE 14.8

Use the Screen Resolution window to set the main display.

Setting Up Multiple Monitors in Windows 7

After you have installed the new video card (if needed) and attached the monitors, you then need to configure Windows 7 to extend the desktop across both monitors and choose which monitor is the main display that shows the Windows 7 taskbar and Start menu. Follow these steps:

1. Connect the second monitor to your Windows 7 PC.

2. Select Start, Control Panel, Appearance and Personalization.

3. Under Personalization, click the Adjust Screen Resolution link to get the Screen Resolution dialog box onscreen, as shown in Figure 14.9.

4. In the Multiple Displays list, select Extend These Displays.

5. Click Apply. Windows 7 asks if you want to keep the changes.

6. Click Keep Changes.

7. To change the main monitor, click the monitor you want to set as the main and then select the Make This My Main Display check box.

Windows 7 displays an icon for each of your monitors

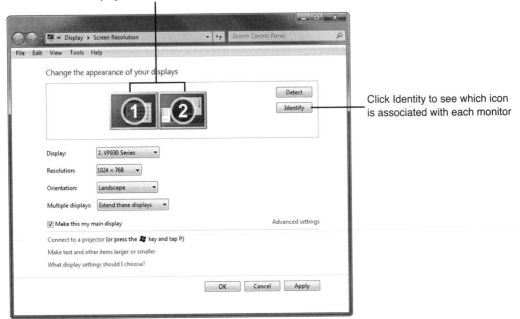

Click Identity to see which icon is associated with each monitor

FIGURE 14.9

Use the Screen Resolution dialog box to set the screen resolution and color quality.

8. Click OK. Windows 7 performs the adjustment and then displays a dialog box asking if you want to keep the new setting.

9. Click Yes.

Setting Up Multiple Monitors in Windows Vista or XP

Here are the steps to follow to set up Windows Vista or Windows XP to recognize your second monitor and choose which monitor is the main monitor that displays the Start button and taskbar:

1. Connect the second monitor to your Windows Vista or XP PC.

2. Select Start, Control Panel, Appearance and Personalization.

3. Under Personalization, click the Adjust Screen Resolution link to get the Display Settings dialog box onscreen, as shown in Figure 14.10.

Windows displays an icon for each of your monitors

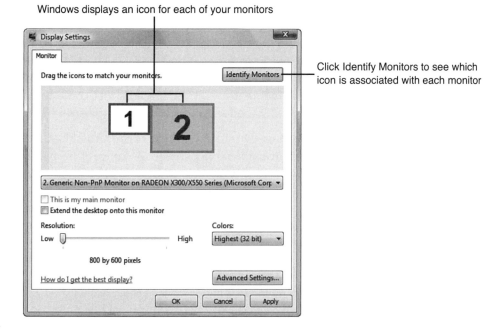

Click Identify Monitors to see which icon is associated with each monitor

FIGURE 14.10

Use the Display Settings dialog box to set the screen resolution and color quality.

4. Click the monitor icon labeled 2 and then select the Extend the Desktop onto This Monitor check box.

5. Click Apply. Windows Vista asks if you want to keep the changes.

6. Click Keep Changes.

7. To change the main monitor, click the monitor you want to set as the main and then select the This Is My Main Monitor check box.

8. Click OK. Windows performs the adjustment and then displays a dialog box asking if you want to keep the new setting.

9. Click Yes.

Moving Up to Three Monitors

Rocking with two monitors is great, but let's crank things up a notch and go for not two, but *three* monitors! You could have Word on one monitor, reference materials or whatever on a second monitor, and Outlook on the third. It's almost scary how productive this setup will make you.

How does this arrangement work? The secret is that you need three output ports on your PC. Many new PCs ship with three or even four output ports—usually VGA, DVI, or HDMI—so you just need to match them with your monitor input ports. If your PC has only two output ports, you have to install a second video card on your system. However, you can't just plop any old video card in there and hope things will work. Instead, you need to use video cards that come with dual-GPU support. Both AMD and NVIDIA offer dual-GPU technologies:

- **AMD CrossFireX**—AMD's dual-GPU technology is called CrossFireX (or CFX). To use it, you need a motherboard with a CrossFireX-compatible chipset and two free PCI Express slots that are designed for CrossFireX, as well as two CrossFireX-capable video cards from the same chipset family. Figure 14.11 shows two video cards connected with a CrossFireX bridge. To learn more about CrossFireX-compatible equipment, see http://sites.amd.com/us/game/technology/Pages/crossfirex.aspx.

 NOTE Both AMD and NVIDIA now offer both *triple*-GPU and *quadruple*-GPU video cards, just in case you feel like running Windows with six or even eight monitors!

CrossFireX bridge

FIGURE 14.11

Two video cards connected with a CrossFireX bridge.

- **NVIDIA SLI**—NVIDIA's dual-GPU technology is called *scalable link interface (SLI)*. To use it, you need a motherboard with an SLI-compatible chipset and two free PCI Express slots designed for SLI, as well as two SLI-capable video cards that use the same NVIDIA chipset. To learn more about SLI-compatible equipment, see http://www.geforce.com/hardware/technology/sli.

 CAUTION Running two high-powered graphics cards in your system can burn up the watts in a hurry, so make sure your power supply unit (PSU) is up to the challenge. Some PSUs are certified to work with SLI or CrossFire setups, which means they have enough watts to handle two video cards and have two power connectors for video cards that require direct connections to the PSU.

Each of these video cards has two output ports, so you have a total of four ports to use. After you get the cards installed, you run VGA, DVI, or HDMI cables from three of those ports (or four, if you want to go all the way and use four monitors) to the corresponding ports on your monitors. When you next start Windows, install the video card drivers.

Now you're ready to configure Windows to extend the desktop across all your monitors. Here are the steps to follow in Windows 8 (the steps for earlier versions of Windows are similar to those I showed you earlier for dual monitors):

1. Make sure all your monitors are connected and turned on.

2. Press Windows Logo+W. The Settings search pane appears.

3. Type **resolution**.

4. Click Adjust Screen Resolution. The Screen Resolution window appears on the desktop. You now see icons for four monitors, which represent the four output ports of the video cards.

 TIP If you're not sure which three of the four icons represent your actual monitors, click Identify. Windows 8 displays large numbers—1, 2, and 3—on each monitor, and the numbers correspond to the numbered icons in the Screen Resolution window.

5. In the Multiple Displays list, select Extend These Displays.

6. Click the monitor you want to set as the main display.

7. Activate the Make This My Main Display check box.

8. Click and drag the monitor icons to the orientation you prefer. For example, you might want your main monitor (the monitor that holds the taskbar) in the middle and the other two monitors on either side.

9. Click OK.

THE ABSOLUTE MINIMUM

This chapter showed you how to get your graphics game on by upgrading your video card and monitor (or monitors). Here's the takeaway:

- A *video card* is either circuit board that plugs into a motherboard slot or a chip embedded in the motherboard itself. The video card enables software to display text or images on the monitor.

- The most common video card connection types are VGA, DVI, and HDTV.

- When buying a video card, get as much graphics memory as you can afford and be sure to get a card with multiple output ports, just in case you want to use multiple monitors in the future.

- To set up your PC with dual monitors, you need either a video card that offers two output ports or a second video card.

- To set up your PC with three monitors, you need either a video card that offers three output ports or two multiport video cards that support dual-GPU configurations.

IN THIS CHAPTER

- Learning how digital audio gets the job done
- Getting a handle on sound card specs
- Buying a sound card for your PC
- Connecting the speakers to your PC

15

IMPROVING THE SOUND SYSTEM

The ear is a fine and sensitive instrument, attuned to nuance on the one hand, but shamelessly craving novelty on the other. How else do you explain, in a society supposedly in love with the visual image, the relentless popularity of radio after all these years? So when you're upgrading your PC, keep your ears in mind and treat them to improved sound by upgrading the sound card and speakers.

Understanding Audio

One reason audio is such an important part of PC multimedia is that most people are used to their computers being, if not voiceless, at least monotonic. Most mainstream applications are content to utter simple beeps and boops to alert you to an error or otherwise get your attention. Multimedia, however, with its music and unusual sound bites, can provide quite a jolt to people who aren't used to such things.

In other words, there's no reason to think of the *sound card*—the internal component that processes your PC's audio and delivers it to the speakers—as the poor cousin of the flashier video card. Before getting to some sound card specifics, let's begin our look at audio with a primer of digital audio concepts and formats. This will help you understand exactly what you're dealing with when you're examining sound card specs later.

Analog-to-Digital Sound Conversion

Sound cards work by converting analog sound waves into digital signals that can be sent to your computer's speakers. To help you evaluate sound cards, you should know a bit (but, fortunately, just a bit) about how the analog-to-digital conversion takes place.

The Nature of Sound

When an object such as a violin string or speaker diaphragm vibrates or moves back and forth, it alternately compresses and decompresses the air molecules around it. This alternating compression and decompression sets up a vibration in the air molecules that propagates outward from the source as a wave. This is called a *sound wave*. When the sound wave reaches your ear, it sets up a corresponding vibration in your eardrum, and you hear the sound created by the object.

Each sound wave has two basic properties:

- **Frequency**—This property determines the pitch of the sound. It's a measure of the rate at which the sound wave's vibrations are produced. The higher the frequency, the higher the pitch. Frequency is measured in cycles per second, or *hertz (Hz)*, where one cycle is a vibration back and forth.

- **Intensity**—This property is a measure of the loudness of the sound (that is, the strength of the vibration). It's determined by the *amplitude* (roughly, the height) of the sound wave. The greater the amplitude, the greater the motion of the sound wave's molecules and the greater the impact on your eardrum. Amplitude is measured in *decibels (db)*.

Figure 15.1 shows part of a waveform for a typical sound. The amplitude is found by taking the midpoint of the wave (which is set to 0) and measuring the distance to a positive or negative peak. Because the period from one peak to the next is defined as a cycle, the frequency is given by the number of peaks that occur per second.

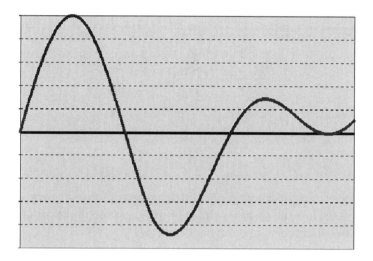

FIGURE 15.1

An analog waveform for a sound.

How an Analog Sound Wave Gets Digitized

Sound waves are inherently analog, so if you want to work with them on a computer, you must convert them to a digital audio format. A sound card has a small chip called an *analog-to-digital converter (ADC)*, whose sole purpose is to convert analog sound waves into the digital 1s and 0s that computers know and love. (Sound cards also have a *digital-to-analog converter [DAC]* chip that performs the reverse process: converting digitized audio back into an analog wave so that you can hear it.) This is done through a technique called *Pulse Code Modulation (PCM)*: taking "snapshots" of the analog wave at discrete intervals and noting the wave's amplitude. These amplitude values form the basis of the digital representation of the wave. Because each snapshot is really a sample of the current state of the wave, this process is called *sampling*. I discuss this in more detail in the next section when I describe sample frequency and sample depth.

Understanding Sound Card Specs

The first thing you need to know about a sound card is that there's a really good chance you don't need one! Actually, to be more accurate, I should say that there's probably a good chance you don't need a *separate* sound card. All modern motherboards have some kind of integrated sound capability, and many come with high-end sound features that are good enough for all but professional audio jockeys and the most rabid gamers. So when I describe sound cards specs in this section, bear in mind that these specs apply both to standalone sound cards and to motherboard integrated sound chips.

If you're shopping for a sound card, you might come across an ad or a description that looks something like this:

Creative Labs Sound Blaster Audigy 2 ZS 192KHz

24-bit 7.1 DTS Dolby Digital S/PDIF

A motherboard description might show a subset of these specs. In any case, here's a quick look at what each part of this description means (and the sections that follow expand on the most important of them):

- **Creative Labs**—This is the name of the sound card manufacturer.

- **Sound Blaster**—This is the name of the overall family to which the sound card belongs.

- **Audigy 2 ZS**—This is the name of the sound card.

- **192KHz**—This is the maximum sample frequency supported by the sound card.

- **24-bit**—This is the maximum sample depth supported by the sound card.

- **7.1**—This is the maximum number of channels supported by the sound card.

- **DTS**—This tells you that the sound card supports DTS surround sound.

- **Dolby Digital**—This tells you that the sound card supports Dolby Digital surround sound.

- **S/PDIF**—This tells you that the sound card includes a *Sony/Philips Digital Interface Format (S/PDIF)* digital audio connector.

The Sampling Frequency

One of the major determinants of digital audio quality is the rate at which the sound card samples the analog data. The more samples taken per second—that is, the higher the *sampling frequency*—the more accurately the digitized data will represent the original sound waveform.

To see how this works, consider the chart shown in Figure 15.2. This is a graph of digitized data sampled from the analog waveform shown earlier in Figure 15.1. Each column represents an amplitude value sampled from the analog wave at a given moment. In this case, the sampling frequency is very low, so the "shape" of the digitized waveform only approximates the analog wave, and much data is lost.

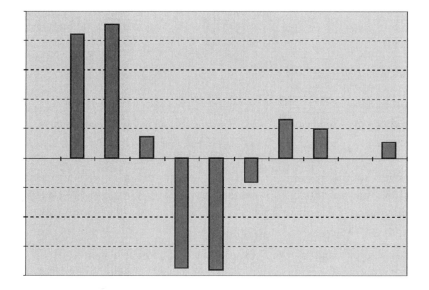

FIGURE 15.2

A digitized waveform generated by a low sampling frequency.

To improve the quality and fidelity of the digitized waveform, you need to use a higher sampling frequency. For example, the chart shown in Figure 15.3 shows the resulting digital waveform with a sampling frequency four times greater than the one shown in Figure 15.2. As you can see, the waveform is a much more accurate representation of the original analog wave.

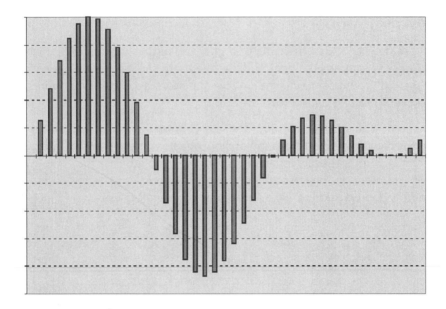

FIGURE 15.3

To improve the sound quality of the digitized waveform, you need to increase the sampling frequency.

So, which sampling frequency is best? The general rule of thumb is that, for the most faithful reproduction of analog sound, your sampling frequency should be roughly twice the highest sound frequency you want to reproduce, plus another 10% for good measure.

Human hearing ranges from a low of 20Hz to a high of about 20KHz (20,000Hz). So, for an accurate reproduction of anything within the human audible range, you'd sample at a frequency of about 44KHz (two times 20KHz plus 10%). CD-quality digital audio samples at 44.1KHz, and DVD-quality audio samples at 48KHz, which is the minimum frequency supported by most modern sound cards. Many good sound cards support 96KHz sampling, which is used with some high-resolution DVD movies. For the DVD-Audio format used with high-definition movies, the sample frequency is either 96KHz or 192KHz, and a few high-end sound cards sample at up to 192KHz.

The Sample Depth

Another major determinant of digital audio quality is the number of bits used to digitize each sample. This is sometimes called the *sample depth*. To see why sample depth makes a difference, consider a simplified example. Suppose you're sampling a wave with amplitudes between 0db and 100db. If you had only a 2-bit sample depth, you'd have only four discrete levels with which to assign amplitudes.

If you used, say, 25db, 50db, 75db, and 100db, all the sampled values would have to be adjusted (by rounding up, for example) to one of these values. Figure 15.4 shows the result. The smooth line shows the original amplitudes, and the columns show the assigned sample values, given a 2-bit sample depth. As you can see, much data is lost by having to adjust to the discrete levels.

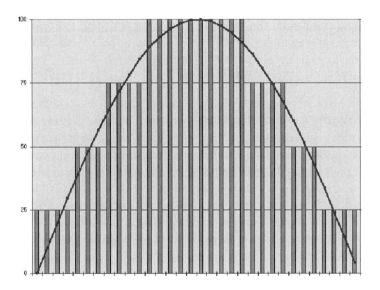

FIGURE 15.4

The lower the sample depth, the more information that gets lost during sampling.

Fortunately, there is no such thing as 2-bit sampling. Instead, older sound cards supported two levels of sample depth—8-bit and 16-bit—while almost all newer sound cards support 24-bit sampling. The 8-bit sample depth might sound like a lot, but it means that the digitized amplitude values must be shoehorned into just 256 possible levels, which is a far cry from the infinite number of levels in the original analog waveform. With 16-bit sampling, 65,536 discrete levels are available, but when you jump to 24-bit samples, the number of discrete levels rises to a whopping 16,777,216, which makes a huge difference in sound quality.

 NOTE   Another way to look at sample depth is to consider a ruler. The accuracy with which you can measure something with a ruler depends on the number of divisions. A ruler with only quarter-inch divisions won't provide as exact a measurement as a ruler with sixteenth-inch divisions. In audio, an 8-bit sample depth is like a ruler with 256 divisions per sample; a 16-bit sample depth is like a ruler with 65,536 divisions per sample; and a 24-bit sample depth is like a ruler with 16,777,216 divisions per sample.

The Number of Channels

The final consideration for digital audio quality is the number of channels you want to store. In the old days you only had a choice of mono (one channel) or stereo (two channels), where the latter required a sound card that supported two channels as well as a PC with two speakers attached to the card.

Nowadays, mono-only sound cards are nonexistent and stereo-only cards are almost obsolete. In their place, most modern sound cards support some form of *surround sound* using either Dolby Digital or Digital Theater Systems (DTS), and some cards support both technologies.

The number of surround-sound channels is shown in sound card specs using the *n*.1 format, where *n* is the number of speakers and the 1 represents a subwoofer. (A *subwoofer* is a separate amplifier that helps play low-frequency [bass] sounds, giving the audio a deeper, richer sound.) The most common configurations are 5.1 (sometimes called 6-channel) and 7.1 (sometimes called 8-channel).

 NOTE In the discussion that follows, I assume your system will connect to two or more analog speakers. If you have digital speakers, you use different connections, as described in the next section, "Sound Card Connectors."

A 5.1 surround-sound configuration consists of five speakers and a subwoofer, arranged as follows:

- **Front speakers**—These are two speakers positioned to the left and right of the monitor (or TV). You connect these speakers using the Line Out or Front Speaker port on the sound card, which is usually a lime green color.

- **Rear speakers**—These are two speakers positioned behind and to the left and right of the listener. You connect these speakers using the Rear Speaker port on the sound card, which is usually black.

- **Center/subwoofer**—The center speaker is positioned in the middle behind the display, and the subwoofer is positioned on the ground, usually in the closest corner. You use the Center/Subwoofer port on the sound card, which is usually orange.

A 7.1 surround-sound configuration uses the same setup as the 5.1 configuration but adds two more speakers:

- **Side speakers**—These are two speakers positioned to the left and right of the listener. You connect these speakers using the Side Speaker port on the sound card, which is usually gray.

NOTE   Some sound cards support 7.1 surround sound but come with only three analog output ports. How does that work? On such cards, the Rear Speaker and Center/Subwoofer ports usually do double-duty. For example, the Rear Speaker port might also supply the side left channel, and the Center/Subwoofer port might also supply the side right channel.

Sound Card Connectors

Although I touched on some sound card ports in the preceding section, here's a summary of the various types of ports you're likely to come across in your sound card travels (I'm ignoring peripheral ports such as joystick connectors and IEEE-1394 connectors that appear on some cards):

- **Line Out**—This is the main output port on all sound cards. It's a stereo mini jack connector usually colored lime green. You use it to connect headphones, 2-channel analog speakers, or the front analog speakers in a surround-sound 5.1-channel or 7.1-channel audio setup.

- **Rear Speaker**—This is a secondary output port on some sound cards. It's a stereo mini jack connector usually colored black. You use it to connect the rear analog speakers in a surround-sound 5.1-channel or 7.1-channel audio configuration.

- **Center/Subwoofer**—This is a secondary output port on some sound cards. It's a stereo mini jack connector usually colored orange. You use it to connect the center analog speaker and subwoofer in a surround-sound 5.1-channel or 7.1-channel audio setup.

- **Side Speaker**—This is a secondary output port on some sound cards. It's a stereo mini jack connector usually colored gray. You use it to connect the side analog speakers in a surround-sound 7.1-channel audio configuration.

- **Optical S/PDIF Out**—This is a digital output port on some sound cards. It's an optical connector that uses the S/PDIF; the sound card connector is labeled S/PDIF Out or Digital Out. You use it to output audio to a digital audio device that has a digital optical (also called TOSLink) audio input port.

- **Optical S/PDIF In**—This is a digital input port on some sound cards. It's an optical connector that uses S/PDIF; the sound card connector is labeled S/PDIF In or Digital In. You use it to input audio from a digital audio device that has a digital optical audio output port.

- **Coaxial S/PDIF**—This is a digital output port on some sound cards. It's an RCA jack that uses S/PDIF; the sound card connector is labeled S/PDIF Out or Coaxial Out. You use it to output audio to a digital audio device that supports digital coaxial audio.

 NOTE   You can purchase adapters that convert one type of audio output to another type of audio input. For example, you can get an adapter that enables you to connect a single-channel stereo mini jack on the sound card with a digital (coaxial or optical) input on the audio device.

- **Line In**—This is an input port on some sound cards. It's a stereo mini jack connector usually colored blue. You use it to connect an audio device such as a digital audio tape player or CD player.

- **Mic In**—This is an input port on some sound cards. It's a stereo mini jack connector usually colored pink. You use it to connect a microphone.

Figure 15.5 points out these ports on a typical (albeit high-end) sound card.

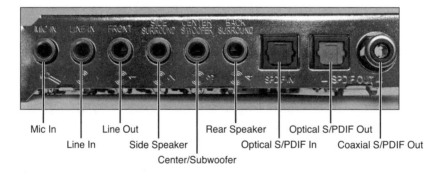

FIGURE 15.5

The ports on a high-end sound card.

Buying a Sound Card

The sound card market is thoroughly dominated by Creative Labs and its highly regarded Sound Blaster family of audio products. That isn't to say you should only consider Creative Lab's products, however. Many other sound card companies are out there, but they tend to offer only a limited number of cards. Still, the biggest issue with all sound cards is driver support, so it pays to stick with the major players. Here are my recommendations:

> Auzentech (www.auzentech.com)
>
> Creative Labs (www.creative.com)
>
> HT Omega (www.htomega.com)
>
> M_AUDIO (www.m-audio.com)
>
> Turtle Beach (www.turtlebeach.com)

Here are some pointers to think about when deciding on a sound card for your homebuilt system:

- **Decide whether you need a separate sound card**—I mentioned earlier that's it's becoming more common to see decent video integrated into modern motherboards. However, decent audio has been a motherboard feature for a while now. Even low-end boards often come with audio chipsets that boast 5.1-channel (usually called 6-channel in motherboard specs) sound, and mid-range motherboards routinely come with 7.1 (8-channel) analog audio and connectors for digital audio output. Either way, this audio support is more than good enough for almost all PC applications, including most games. You really need a separate sound card only if your motherboard doesn't have the audio connectors you require (such as S/PDIF) or if you need a sound card's advanced features to get the most out of high-end gaming or audio applications. The downside to using integrated audio is that the chip offloads much of the sound processing to the CPU, which can slow down overall system performance if you do a lot of audio work.

- **Determine whether your motherboard comes with a sound card**—Some higher-end motherboards come with a separate sound card rather than integrated audio. For example, in the motherboard shown in Figure 15.6, digital S/PDIF audio is integrated, but analog 7.1 audio is handled through a separate sound card.

- **Choose playback features**—To play sounds on your system, check out the card's specs. It should support at least the highest levels of digitized sound you plan to use. For example, if all you want to do is play CDs, the card's DAC should support CD-quality audio: sampling frequencies up to 44.1KHz, 16-bit sample depth, and stereo. If you want to play DVDs, you might need 48KHz sampling, or possibly even 96KHz sampling. For high-definition audio, you might need a card that supports 192KHz sampling.

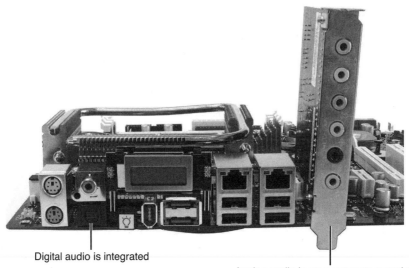

Digital audio is integrated

Analog audio is on a separate sound card

FIGURE 15.6

Some motherboards come with a separate sound card.

- **Decide whether you need 3D audio**—If you're a hardcore gamer, you might want to invest in a sound card that offers *3D audio* (also called *3D spatial imaging* or *positional audio*). This feature means that sounds are located in 3D space. For example, if you're playing a game and an explosion happens in front of you, 3D audio ensures that the sound comes through the center speaker (the one directly in front of you in a 5.1 or 7.1 surround-sound configuration). Similarly, the sound of a car passing on the left would start in the left rear speaker, travel to the left side speaker (in a 7.1 setup), and continue to the left front speaker. Although 3D audio costs a bit more, it can add a lot to a high-end game. Note that Creative Labs' 3D audio technology Environmental Audio Extensions (EAX) is currently the gold standard.

- **Get a breakout box for easier access**—If you plan on attaching many devices to your PC's sound system, the sound card (or motherboard) connectors are hard to get at, and most cases have only rudimentary connectors (usually just for headphones and a microphone). In that case, consider purchasing a sound card that has a separate *breakout box* (also called an *audio bay*), which is a device that slips into a front drive bay and gives you easier access to a wide variety of connectors. Figure 15.7 shows the breakout box that comes with the Sound Blaster X-FI Platinum FATAL1TY card.

FIGURE 15.7

Some sound cards come with a breakout box that offers front-of-the-case access to a large collection of audio connectors.

- **Check device driver support**—Make sure the card comes with drivers for whatever operating system you plan on installing on your custom PC. Although the OS might comes with its own sound card drivers, you're usually better off with the latest drivers from the manufacturer.

Connecting Speakers or Headphones

PCs are not quiet machines, not by a long shot. The Windows operating system makes all kinds of sounds that let you know when things are happening on the screen and within your PC. Similarly, programs such as music players and video players make plenty of noise. To get sound from your PC to your ears, you need some kind of sound output device, which means one of the following:

- **Speakers**—These speakers are much like the ones you use with your stereo system or TV. Many laptops and tablet PCs have built-in speakers (although the sound quality tends to be a bit low). Some monitors even come with speakers on the sides. For all other systems, however, you need to connect external speakers.

- **Headphones**—These are either standard headphones that fit over your ears or earbuds that fit inside your ears.

Although many headphones and even some speakers connect through USB, the more common connection is a stereo mini jack like the one shown in Figure 15.8. For speakers and headphones, this jack is green, and the corresponding port on your PC is also green and is usually labeled Line Out, as shown in Figure 15.9.

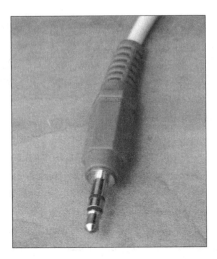

FIGURE 15.8

A stereo mini jack used for connecting most types of speakers or headphones.

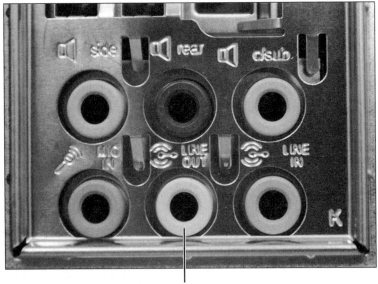

Line Out

FIGURE 15.9

Connect the jack shown in Figure 15.8 to the Line Out port on your PC.

 NOTE Many desktop PCs also include a Line Out port on the front for easier access.

THE ABSOLUTE MINIMUM

This chapter gave you some sound advice on upgrading your PC with new audio hardware. Highlights? There were a few:

- A sound card is an internal component that processes your PC's audio and delivers it to the speakers or headphones.

- A sound card's basic task is to convert analog sound waves to digital signals by sampling the sound at discrete intervals. The higher the sampling frequency, the greater the sound fidelity compared to the original sound.

- The two basic properties of any sound wave are the frequency, measured in hertz (Hz), which determines the pitch; and the intensity, measured in decibels (db), which determines the loudness.

- Each sound card supports a number of channels, which usually include one subwoofer and either five speakers (5.1- or 6-channel sound) or seven speakers (7.1- or 8-channel sound).

- Before buying a sound card, check your PC's motherboard specs to see if the integrated audio is good enough for your needs.

- You connect speakers or headphones to your PC either through a USB port or through a stereo mini jack plugged into the sound card's Line Out port.

UPGRADING THE CPU

So far, you've learned about upgrading PC parts such as the power supply, hard drive, CD or DVD drive, memory, and video card. Those seem like (and are) reasonable things to upgrade but, if you're like most people, the idea of upgrading your PC's CPU seems daunting, to say the least. Isn't the CPU, you know, *important*? Why would anyone mess around with that? It's true that a CPU upgrade isn't for everyone. It's a much more involved task than the other upgrades, and you can turn your PC into a large and expensive boat anchor if the upgrade doesn't go well. That said, although it takes a bit more research, time, and effort to upgrade the CPU, it's not brain surgery. With care and patience, anyone can upgrade his PC's CPU, and that includes you. This chapter tells you everything you need to know.

Understanding What the CPU Does

Anthropomorphic metaphors that compare computers to the human body have an unfortunate tendency to be stretched beyond the breaking point. For example, the computer case is like the body's skin and skeleton because it holds everything, and the motherboard is like the spinal cord because most things are attached to it either directly or indirectly.

That brings us to this chapter and its topic, the *central processing unit*, also known as the *CPU*, the *microprocessor*, or simply the *processor*. What body part extends our metaphor to the CPU? I know you know the answer already, but bear with me a second as I justify taking the metaphor this far. As you might know, the spinal cord acts as a conduit for signals that other body parts send to the brain and for signals the brain sends to other body parts. The spinal cord itself doesn't process these signals in any way; all the processing goes on inside the brain. The motherboard, too, doesn't process any of the electrical signals that ride along its data buses, which is yet another reason the spinal cord is a good motherboard metaphor. But just as the spinal cord relays signals to and from the brain, so too does the motherboard relay signals to and from the processor. So it will come as no surprise by now that the brain forms the third part of our metaphor because (at least at the level we're dealing with here) it's a good analogue to the processor.

With a few exceptions, no matter what happens on your computer, the CPU has a hand in it somehow. Press a key on your keyboard, for example, and the signal goes through the motherboard's keyboard port to the processor, which then passes along the keypress to the operating system. Similarly, if a program you're using needs to send data to a network location, it hands off that data to the operating system, which sends it to the CPU, which then routes the data to the motherboard for transmission via the network card. The only major exception to the CPU's micromanaging is with most of today's graphics cards, which usually have a dedicated graphics processing unit (GPU) that handles much of the graphics chores so the CPU can work on other things.

Intel or AMD?

From the point of view of a first-time system upgrader, the CPU world is a duopoly, with just two colossi bestriding the market: Intel and AMD. So, which one should you choose when picking out a processor for your PC? The short answer is that it really doesn't matter even a tiny bit. Both Intel and AMD are world-class CPU designers and manufacturers, and almost any CPU you choose from either company will be a high-quality product and will serve you well whatever you do with your computer.

Having said all that, it's possible to differentiate the two CPU giants a little bit by resorting to some gross generalizations (one of my favorite things to do):

- AMD generally competes on price, so for processors that offer low- and mid-range performance and features, an AMD processor will be cheaper than an equivalent Intel processor.

- Intel generally competes on performance, so if you want to get the most out of your computer, Intel processors that offer higher-end performance and features are the way to go.

Of course, all this might have changed by the time you read this. For example, the next generation of AMD processors (not yet available as I write this) are said to have features that will enable AMD to once again compete with Intel on the high end. Similarly, AMD's competitive pricing has forced Intel to reduce its own prices, and further reductions could mean that Intel's low- and mid-range processors could become just as good a bargain as AMD's generally are.

Okay, have I hedged enough bets for you? The bottom line is that choosing a CPU really comes down to two things:

- Buy a processor that matches your motherboard. All motherboards are designed to work with a limited set of CPUs. In particular, every motherboard accepts only either an Intel CPU or an AMD CPU. So first and foremost, get a CPU that's compatible with your motherboard.

- Buy the processor that matches your needs or, if you want to go the power-user route, that has the best features you can afford. What features am I talking about? Ah, that's the subject of the next section, so read on....

Understanding CPU Specs

If you're shopping around for a CPU, you might come across a description similar to this:

> Intel Core i5-3570 3.4GHz Quad Core LGA1155
>
> 6MB L3 cache Ivy Bridge 22nm

This shockingly unintelligible bit of prose is actually jam-packed with information about the processor, but it's couched in a form of "CPU speak" that could warm the cockles of only the geekiest of hearts. Fortunately, you need to understand only some of this when buying a CPU. However, I'm going to explain all of it just so you have an idea of what the retailers or the online reviewers are nattering on about when they talk this way. The preceding description can be broken down into nine discrete components, most of which I discuss in more detail in the sections that follow:

- **Intel**—This, clearly, is the company name.

- **Core i5**—This is the broad brand name under which the processor exists within Intel. This is usually called the processor's *family* (see the next section, "The Processor Family").

- **3570**—This is the name of the processor (see "The Processor Name" later in this chapter).

- **3.4GHz**—This is the processor's clock speed (see "The Processor Clock Speed" later in this chapter).

- **Quad Core**—This tells you that the CPU has four *cores*, a term I explain a bit later (see "The Processor Cores" later in this chapter).

- **LGA1155**—This is the motherboard socket the processor fits into (see "The Processor Socket" later in this chapter).

- **6MB L3 cache**—This is the size of the CPU's L3 cache (see "The Processor Cache Size" later in this chapter).

- **Ivy Bridge**—This is the type of core the processor uses (see "The Processor Core Type" later in this chapter).

- **22nm**—This is the CPU manufacturing process (see "The Processor Manufacturing Process" later in this chapter).

The Processor Family

The processor's family name is kind of an umbrella term that encompasses a series of related processors that use the same underlying architecture. The features in each processor architecture redefine the word *arcane*, but fortunately, you don't need to understand even word one about any of it. All you need to know is that both Intel and AMD have a set of processor families from which you can choose, and that generally speaking these families can be divided (very roughly) into low-, mid-, and high-end ranges, as shown in Table 16.1.

TABLE 16.1 The Low-, Mid-, and High-Range Processor Families

Range	Families	Description
Low	Intel Celeron; AMD Athlon II	These are inexpensive CPUs (generally around $50–$60) that offer fewer features and lower performance than other processor families.
Mid	Intel Pentium, Core i3; AMD Phenom II, A	These are mid-priced CPUs (generally around $70–$160) that offer extra features and better performance than the low-range processor families.
High	Intel Core i5, i7; AMD FX	These are expensive CPUs (generally $180–$1,000) that offer more features and better performance than other processor families.

The Processor Cores

The processor *core* (short for *execution core*) refers to the actual processing unit that performs all the tasks a CPU is asked to handle. Previously, the terms *core* and *processor* were equivalent because all CPUs contained just one core. In early 2005, however, Intel changed everything by introducing the Pentium D and the Pentium Extreme Edition, both of which somehow managed to shoehorn *two* cores into a single chip. Older CPUs were now described as *single core*, and these newfangled processors were described as *dual core*.

Does dual core mean twice the performance? Well, yes and no:

- Yes, because the processor can now divide tasks *between applications* among the cores (a process Intel calls HyperThreading). So if you're, say, compressing a large file, the processor can hand off that task to one core, and the other core is free to handle tasks from other programs.

- No, because the processor usually can't divide tasks *within an application* among the cores. For example, if you're compressing a large file, you aren't able to do anything else with that program until that task is complete. Note that it *is* possible to program individual applications to take advantage of two cores, and we're starting to see more of this as dual-core processors become mainstream.

In early 2007, Intel introduced the first *quad-core* processor: yup, *four* cores stuffed into a single chip. This gives you even better performance than a dual-core CPU, although not twice the performance. Again, because most systems and programs aren't optimized to take advantage of quad core, performance gains over dual core are only on the order of 10%–20%, depending on the task. Still not good enough? Okay, several members of AMD's FX-series come with *eight* cores!

The Processor Name

Each CPU is given a name (sometimes called the *model number*), and that name tells you a bit about the processor's features.

Let's start with Intel's processor names, which take the form of four digits followed by a letter or two. The six general names you'll see most often are

- *gnnn*M—This name refers to the Core family's dual-core mobile processors (for example, 2520M).

- *gnnn*QM—This name refers to the Core family's quad-core mobile processors (for example, 3840QM).

- *gnnn*S—This name refers to the Core family's performance-optimized processors (for example, 3470S).

- *gnnn*T—This name refers to the Core family's power-optimized processors (for example 2120T).

- *gnnn*K—This name refers to the Core family's *unlocked* processors, which enable hardware experts to change the clock speed (for example, 2600K).

- *gnnn*X—This name refers to the Core Extreme Edition family's processors (for example, 3970X).

The numbers themselves don't meaning anything per se, except as follows:

- The first number (*g* in the preceding list) refers to the Core family generation. The first-generation used no number, and the second- and third-generations use 2 and 3, respectively. So an i7-2600K processor is second-generation, while an i5-3770K is third-generation.

- The next three numbers (*nnn* in the preceding list) get higher as better features are added to each chip.

For example, consider the i5-3000 series processors that use the Ivy Bridge CPU core and come with the same L3 cache size. What's different is the clock speed:

CPU Name	Clock Speed
i5-3330	3.0GHz
i5-3450	3.1GHz
i5-3570	3.4GHz

In other cases, a higher number might mean a bigger L3 cache.

For AMD, the model numbers are a mixed bag. For the FX-series, the general model number looks like this:

FX-cgnn

Here, *c* is the number of cores (4, 6, or 8); *g* is the architecture generation (1, 2, or 3), and *nn* is a two-digit number that denotes the relative clock speed (for example, 50 is faster than 20, which is faster than 00). So an FX-8320 processor is an eight-core, third-generation CPU with a clock speed (3.5GHz) between that of an FX-8350 (4.0GHz) and an FX-8300 (3.3GHz).

For the A-series, the general model number looks like this:

As-nnnn

Here, *s* is an even number that denotes the series (4, 6, 8, or 10), with a higher number implying greater performance; *nnnn* is a four-digit number where, again, the higher the value, the greater the performance of the processor. So an A8 processor is generally more powerful than an A6 processor, while an A8-5550 gives greater performance than an A8-3850.

For the Phenom II processors, the general model number looks like so:

Xc-nnnn

Here, *c* is the number of cores (2, 4, or 6); and *nnnn* is a three- or four-digit number that denotes the relative performance of the processor (the higher the number, the better the performance). So a Phenom II X6 1035 is a six-core processor that's not quite as powerful as a Phenom II X6 1100.

The Processor Clock Speed

The *clock speed* is a measure of how fast the process operates internally. With each "tick" (which is called a *cycle*) on the clock, the processor performs an operation; therefore, the more ticks per second, the faster the processor, and the better performance your computer will have. Note that clock speeds are now measured in gigahertz (GHz), where 1GHz is one billion cycles per second. That's fast! Current processor clock speeds range from 2.0GHz in low-end CPUs to 4.0GHz in some high-end chips. Note, too, that many CPUs now also offer *turbo mode*, which offers a speed boost of anywhere from 0.2GHz to 0.8GHz.

 CAUTION Don't read *too* much into CPU clock speeds. Yes, if everything else is the same, a 3.2GHz processor is a bit faster than a 3.0GHz processor. However, other factors are at play when it comes to CPU performance, including the size of the cache (see "The Processor Cache Size," later in this chapter).

The Processor Socket

The processor *socket* refers to the type of motherboard connector required by the processor:

- Almost all mainstream Intel processors use a socket named LGA 1155, while a few use a socket named LGA 2011.

- Almost all mainstream AMD processors use one of the following sockets: AM3, AM3+, FM1, or FM2.

The good news is that you don't need to know anything about the inner workings of sockets. However, there's one absolutely crucial bit of information you must tape to your cat's forehead so you don't forget:

> The socket on your motherboard *must* match the socket type supported by the CPU.

Each socket has a particular number of connection points arranged in a particular pattern, and this combination produces a unique connector. That uniqueness means you simply can't plug in a CPU designed for a different socket, or you could damage the processor, the motherboard, or both.

How the processor connects to the motherboard depends on the socket. For example, a socket 1155 CPU has copper pads on the bottom that match up with pins on the motherboard socket, as shown in Figure 16.1. A socket AM3 processor is the opposite, with pins on the bottom of the chip and corresponding holes in the motherboard socket, as shown in Figure 16.2.

Copper pads on the CPU match...

...the pins on the motherboard socket

FIGURE 16.1

The copper pads on the bottom of a socket 1155 CPU match the pins on the motherboard socket.

The tiny pins on the CPU match...

...the holes on the motherboard socket

FIGURE 16.2

The pins on the bottom of a socket AM3 CPU match the holes on the motherboard socket.

The Processor Cache Size

One of the main jobs a CPU performs is to transfer data to and from storage areas such as the hard drive and system memory. The time it takes for the processor to retrieve data from either area isn't significant for data that's required only every now and then. However, processors are constantly dealing with the same data over and over. In that case, having to request that data from memory or the hard drive every time is inefficient.

To get a sense of what I mean, imagine that when you're preparing a meal and using a knife to chop vegetables, you put the knife away after every cut and then grab it again for the next cut. You'd be lucky to eat one meal a week! The solution is to hang onto the knife until you've finished chopping one vegetable, put the knife off to the side while you bring the next veggie onto the cutting board, grab the handy knife, and off you go again.

The processor does something similar, although with less tasty results. All processors have a couple of on-chip memory areas they use to store frequently accessed bits of data. These are called *memory caches*, and all CPUs have at least three: L1, L2, and L3. The L1 cache is tiny and doesn't affect CPU performance significantly, so you can ignore it. The bigger deals are the L2 cache, which is larger and each core has its own L2 cache, and the L3 cache, which is on-chip memory shared by all the cores. Generally speaking (and as usual, assuming the other CPU features are equal), the bigger the L2 and L3 cache, the better the performance.

The Processor Manufacturing Process

The earliest PC processors (such as Intel's 4004) contained just 1,000 transistors. Today's Intel Core 2 processors pack a whopping 291 *million* transistors into a much smaller space, and forthcoming Intel CPUs will up the number of transistors to an amazing 820 million. How does Intel (and AMD) cram more transistors into its chips? It does it by improving the chip *manufacturing process* (also called the *fabrication process*). This refers not only to how the transistors themselves are built, but also to the on-chip pathways that connect the transistors. By making these components smaller, the manufacturer can squeeze more transistors onto the chip.

 NOTE A *transistor* is a semiconductor device that's the most basic component in the integrated circuits that make up most electronic devices. Transistors amplify and control the current running through the circuit.

The CPU process is known by the width of the pathways that connect the transistors, and these widths are becoming vanishingly small. For example, most modern Intel processors use pathways that are either 32 nanometers (nm) or 22nm wide. You could put several thousand of these paths side-by-side and the resulting bundle would be only as thick as a human hair!

NOTE Processors are following the seemingly inevitable trend known as *Moore's Law*, which tells us that the number of transistors on an integrated circuit will double every two years. The Moore behind this law is Gordon E. Moore, a cofounder of Intel, and he first formulated his idea back in 1965, although in his original formulation, he thought the number of chip components would double every year:

"The complexity for minimum component costs has increased at a rate of roughly a factor of two per year."

The Processor Core Type

The final processor spec is the core type, which is a codename that refers to a combination of CPU process and CPU family. So, for example, the Intel Core chips that use the 32nm process go by the code name *Sandy Bridge*, and the Intel Core chips that use the 22nm process go by the code name *Ivy Bridge*.

These names are essentially meaningless for PC upgraders like you and me, so feel free to ignore them. However, you might want to bear in mind the codenames of Intel's future processors:

- **Haswell**—This is the codename for Intel's next-generation 22nm process.

- **Broadwell**—This is the codename for Intel's 14nm process.

- **Skylake**—This is the codename for Intel's 14nm follow-up to Broadwell.

- **Skymont**—This is the codename for Intel's 10nm process.

Keeping It Cool: Fans and Heatsinks

Processors consume a *ton* of electricity, more than any other component in the system (with the possible exception of some high-end video expansion cards, which have their own processors built in). Processor manufacturers speak of a CPU's *thermal design power (TDP)*, which is, roughly speaking, the amount of power (measured in watts) a processor requires under maximum load. Some mobile CPUs designed for notebooks might have a TDP of only about 10 watts

(W). Desktop CPUs typically require several times that. For example, most Intel Core processors require between 65W and 95W, with a few high-end CPUs require a whopping 130W. (AMD's numbers are similar, with most FX-series processors requiring either 95W or 125W; A-series processors requiring 65W or 100W; and Phenom II processors requiring 65W, 95W, or 125W.)

 TIP For a complete list of CPUs and their respective TDP values, see the Processor Electrical Specifications page at http://pclinks.xtreemhost.com/elec.htm.

Intel and AMD take these numbers seriously and have taken steps in recent years to reduce power consumption in their CPUs. For example, the typical Core i3/i5/i7 TDP of 65W is a far sight better than the 95W–130W TDPs that were typical of the previous generation CPUs.

No matter how much power a CPU requires, some of that power is converted to heat—*lots* of heat. For example, each time a transistor handles a pulse of electric current, the transistor gives off a tiny amount of heat. One transistor's heat output is insignificant, but put hundreds of millions or even *billions* of transistors together (as in any modern CPU) and heat becomes a problem. In fact, we've reached the point now that it's impossible to operate a modern CPU without some kind of cooling equipment attached because it would simply overheat and either shut itself down or destroy itself.

To prevent overheating, most processors now require some form of *forced-air cooling*, which is a system that consists of two parts:

- **Heatsink**—This metal component (made of copper, aluminum, or some other highly conductive material) literally sits on top of the processor. Technically, it sits on top of the processor's *integrated heat spreader (IHS)*, a piece of copper glued on top of the processor to help dissipate heat away from the cores. The heat generated by the processor conducts into the heatsink, which keeps the processor relatively cool.

- **Fan**—The heat transferred to the heatsink has to go somewhere, and that's the job of the fan attached to the heatsink. The fan pulls air up from the heatsink into a collection of fins attached to the heatsink, and from there the heat dissipates into the computer case. The case's natural airflow created by the intake and exhaust fans moves the hot air away from the heatsink and eventually out of the case.

Heatsinks come in many styles and shapes, as you can see in Figure 16.3.

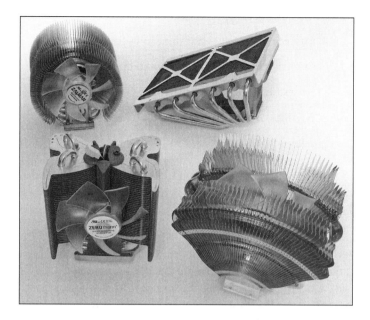

FIGURE 16.3

All modern CPUs require a heatsink and fan to keep cool.

Here are a few notes to bear in mind when deciding on which heatsink to buy for your CPU:

- **Decide whether you need a third-party heatsink**—Many CPUs either come with their own heatsink (and fan) or offer a heatsink as an option. These stock coolers do the job, but they don't tend to be as good as third-party coolers (that is, they don't keep the processor as cool), and the fans tend to be loud. If you're working on a strict budget, stick with the stock heatsink/fan. Otherwise, you're almost always better off with a third-party cooling system, although note that you're voiding your CPU warranty if you do so.

- **Buy from a reputable heatsink manufacturer**—A few companies specialize in PC cooling products, and you're better off dealing with these companies to ensure quality products that do the job. Here's a list of heatsink manufacturers I recommend:

AeroCool (www.aerocool.us)

Coolermaster (www.coolermaster.com)

Thermalright (www.thermalright.com)

Thermaltake (www.thermaltake.com)

SilverStone (www.silverstonetek.com)

Scythe (www.scythe.com)

Zalman (www.zalman.com)

- **Make sure the heatsink fits your CPU socket**—Most heatsinks work with a variety of processor sockets, such as AM3 and LGA1155. However, some of them work with only a particular socket, so check compatibility with your motherboard.

- **Watch the heatsink height**—Some heatsinks are incredibly tall (140mm [5.6 inches] or more). The height helps dissipate heat, but it can also make the heatsink a tight, or impossible, fit for some cases. Many case manufacturers list the maximum heatsink height, so check the website.

- **Check the noise level**—The better heatsinks come with quiet fans that don't add much to the overall noise level of your system. Check the heatsink's fan specs and make sure the noise level doesn't exceed 30dBA (and is, ideally, much less than that) at maximum RPMs.

- **Buy some thermal compound**—Earlier I said that the heatsink sits directly on top of the processor (or, really, the IHS). To improve the conduction from the processor to the heatsink, you need to apply a little *thermal compound* to one of the surfaces. Thermal compound is a thick substance with a glue-like consistency that contains metal particles to enhance its conductivity. Most new processors come with the thermal compound already applied to the stock heatsink; third-party CPU coolers usually come with enough thermal compound for a one-time installation. However, if you think you might need to reuse a processor in a different project later, having your own tube of thermal compound is a necessity (see Figure 16.4).

 CAUTION When applying thermal compound, be sure not to overdo it. Otherwise, when you install the cooler on the processor, the extra compound squeezes out onto the motherboard, causing who knows how many problems. You just need to apply a thin, even layer to either the processor's IHS or to the cooler's heatsink.

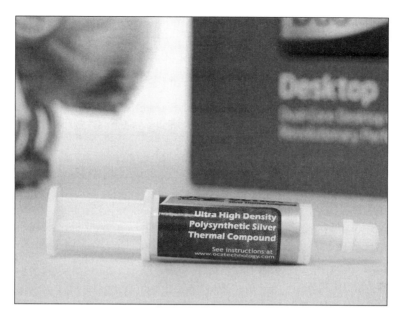

FIGURE 16.4

You improve conductivity between the CPU's heat spreader and the heatsink by applying thermal compound to one of the surfaces.

Buying a CPU

I mentioned earlier that on most levels, particularly when you're just getting started with the PC-upgrading business, there really isn't much to choose from between Intel and AMD. Both are world-class companies that make uniformly excellent products, so you really can't go wrong whichever you choose. So your choice of a processor comes down to other considerations, the most important of which I've listed here:

- **Match your motherboard**—Your motherboard includes a particular socket type, and that socket fits only a limited collection of CPUs. So first and foremost, your choice of processor must be one that fits your motherboard socket. Here are some ways to figure this out:
  - Turn off the computer, open the case, and then examine the motherboard itself to look for a model name and/or number.

- Restart the PC and access the motherboard system configuration program, which you usually do by pressing a key soon after turning on the power (usually Delete or F2; look for a message onscreen that tells you what to press). Once you're in, look for specific information about either the motherboard itself or the chipset that it uses. If you just get the latter, Google it to see whether you can find the manufacturer's information page, which should tell you which processors it supports.

- Download Intel's Chipset Identification Utility (see www.intel.com/support/chipsets/sb/CS-009266.htm). To run it, right-click the downloaded `chiputil.exe` file and then click Run As Administrator.

- If your PC uses non-Intel hardware, you need to turn to one of the other available hardware detection tools. One utility I like is HWiNFO32, a Freeware product that's available from www.hwinfo.com.

- **Assess your needs**—Everyone's talking about quad-core (and even 6- and 8-core) processors, but you don't need that many cores if all you'll be doing is surfing the Web and sending and receiving email. You can get dual-core processors for around $40–$45, and they'll do you just fine. Of course, you need spend only another $30–$40 to move up to quad-core, so consider an entry-level quad-core CPU unless your budget's particularly tight. On the other side of the spectrum, if you're into high-end 3D gaming, you have no choice but to head for 6- or 8-core territory and get the best processor you can afford.

- **Shop around**—The processor is a relatively expensive component, and in the mid-range and high-range, you'll often find that one online retailer is selling the same CPU for $100 more than another. Don't assume that prices are the same wherever you shop.

- **Pass on the stock heatsink**—Unless you're on a strict budget, buy the CPU without the stock heatsink and fan (most online retailers offer CPUs with and without heatsinks). You can save a bit of money this way, and you can put that cash toward buying a quality heatsink, as described in the preceding section.

Removing the Old CPU

It seems only a short while ago that the insertion or removal of a processor was a task fraught with all kinds of danger. Back in the day (I'm talking here about the early 1990s, so please forgive this mercifully brief detour into ancient history), you needed to exert up to 100 pounds of force to insert a CPU properly in its socket! Later so-called *low insertion force* sockets required a mere 60 pounds of force! As you can imagine, any processor that required so much force to seat properly wasn't going to come out very easily and, indeed, all those old processors required special extraction tools.

You can be very thankful that those old socket types are long gone. Since at least the mid-90s, all motherboard processor sockets have used a technology called *zero insertion force (ZIF)*, which makes installing a processor almost as easy as dropping a battery into a flashlight.

This is good news, indeed, because it also means that taking out any CPU is just as easy, as the following steps show:

1. Make sure the computer is turned off and the power cable is disconnected.

2. Remove the computer's side panel.

3. Touch something metal to ground yourself.

4. Locate the CPU cooler's fan, trace its power cable to its motherboard connection, and then disconnect the power cable.

5. Remove the CPU cooler:

    -   Many Intel stock coolers are attached to the motherboard using four plastic snap-in standoffs. In most cases, you loosen these standoffs by using a flat-head screwdriver to turn each standoff 90° counterclockwise.

    -   Most AMD stock coolers are attached to the motherboard using a metal clip. You loosen the clip by turning a lever on the side of the cooler counterclockwise (see Figure 16.5).

    -   Third-party coolers use a variety of attachment methods, but they're almost always a variation on the preceding two themes. That is, the cooler either attaches to the motherboard directly using screws of some type or sits on the motherboard using some type of metal clip you release using a lever.

FIGURE 16.5

Remove the CPU cooler.

6. Clean the thermal grease from the bottom of the cooler and from the processor's heatsink. A soft cloth and a bit of isopropyl alcohol should do the trick.

7. Find the ZIF lever on the side of the motherboard's processor socket.

8. Press the lever down and away from the socket to release the lever, as shown in Figure 16.6; then slowly raise the lever to the upright position.

 CAUTION On some sockets, there is quite a bit of pressure on the lever, so don't just let it go after it's loose.

FIGURE 16.6

Release the ZIF lever that's holding the processor in place.

9. If the processor socket has a cover, raise the cover.

10. Using your thumb and forefinger, grasp the processor's heatsink and lift the processor out of the socket.

Installing the New CPU

Installing a processor into a motherboard's CPU socket is a relatively delicate operation, but it doesn't require any extraordinary skills. Almost all processor installations take one of the following forms:

- Inserting an Intel processor in a socket 1155 motherboard.

- Inserting an AMD processor in a socket AM3 motherboard.

The next two sections take you through the steps required to install both types of processors.

Installing an Intel CPU in a Socket 1155 Board

Almost all Intel processors fit in motherboards that come with an LGA1155 CPU socket, and the following steps show you how it's done:

1. Make sure the computer is turned off and the power cable is disconnected.

2. Remove the computer's side panel.

3. Touch something metal to ground yourself.

4. Take the processor out of the packaging and remove the plastic cover.

 CAUTION Handle the processor only by its side edges. Don't touch the pads on the bottom of the processor.

5. On the top of the processor, locate the gold triangle that appears in one corner.

6. Holding the processor on the edges with your thumb and forefinger, orient the processor so the gold triangle is on the bottom left.

7. Orient the processor over the CPU socket, as shown in Figure 16.7.

FIGURE 16.7

Orient the processor over the socket so that the gold triangle is on the bottom left.

8. When you're sure the processor is lined up exactly with the edge of the socket, carefully place the processor into the socket.

TIP To help you align the processor, the socket includes two small protrusions: one on the top wall of the socket (near the upper-left corner) and one on the bottom wall (near the bottom-left corner). These protrusions correspond to notches on the top and bottom edges of the processor, so make sure they line up exactly before placing the processor into the socket.

9. Close the metal plate.

10. Press the socket lever down and then under the metal hook at the side of the socket, as shown in Figure 16.8. (Note that it's not unusual to have to apply a lot of force to get the lever under the hook.)

FIGURE 16.8

Press the socket lever down and under the metal hook to secure the processor in place.

Installing an AMD CPU in a Socket AM3 Board

Many AMD processors fit in motherboards that come with an AM3 CPU socket, and the following steps show you how it's done:

1. Make sure the computer is turned off and the power cable is disconnected.

2. Remove the computer's side panel.

3. Touch something metal to ground yourself.

4. Take the processor out of the packaging.

 CAUTION Handle the processor only by its side edges. Don't touch the pins on the bottom of the processor.

5. On the top of the processor, locate the gold triangle that appears in one corner.

6. Holding the processor on the edges with your thumb and forefinger, orient the processor so that the gold triangle is on the upper right.

7. Orient the processor over the CPU socket, as shown in Figure 16.9.

FIGURE 16.9

Orient the processor over the socket so that the gold triangle is on the upper right.

8. When you're sure the processor is lined up exactly with the edge of the socket, carefully place the processor into the socket.

9. Press the socket lever down and then under the plastic hook at the side of the socket, as shown in Figure 16.10. (Note that it's not unusual to have to apply quite a bit of force to get the lever under the hook.)

FIGURE 16.10

Press the socket lever down and under the metal hook to secure the processor in place.

Installing the CPU Cooler

Your last chore is to add the CPU cooler to the processor. The actual steps involved vary quite widely depending on the cooler, so see the instructions that came with the device. Here are the general steps to follow to install the CPU cooler:

1. Touch something metal to ground yourself.

2. Remove the cooler from the box.

3. Spread a thin but even coating of thermal compound over the cooler's heatsink.

4. With the cooler's fan facing up, attach the cooler to the motherboard. In most cases, you position the cooler's four fasteners over the four holes that surround the motherboard's CPU socket, as shown in Figure 16.11. As you hold the cooler in place, push down on each fastener until it clicks into place. For the smoothest installation, follow a diagonal pattern. For example, if you start with the bottom-right fastener, next do the upper-left fastener.

CPU cooler fasteners

FIGURE 16.11

In most cases, you attach the cooler's fasteners to four holes that surround the CPU socket.

5. Connect the cooler's power cable to the motherboard's CPU fan connector, as shown in Figure 16.12.

FIGURE 16.12

Connect the CPU cooler's power cable to the motherboard's CPU fan connector.

THE ABSOLUTE MINIMUM

This chapter gave you some background about the processor, offered some buying advice, and then showed you how to swap out an old CPU for a new one. Here are a few things to think about in your spare time:

- If the computer case is analogous to the body's skin and skeleton, and the motherboard is akin to the spinal cord, the central processing unit (CPU) is like the brain.

- Both Intel and AMD make high-quality, reliable processors.

- The main specs to look for when deciding on a CPU are the number of cores, the size of the L3 cache, and the clock speed.

- The processor *core* refers to the actual processing unit that performs all the tasks a CPU is asked to handle. All modern CPUs come with multiple cores.

- The *clock speed* is a measure of how fast the processor operates internally, where the processor performs an operation with each "tick" (or *cycle*) on the clock.

- When buying a CPU, be sure to match it to your PC's motherboard and buy as many features (cores, clock speed, and so on) as fit your needs and your budget.

17

CHANGING THE LAPTOP BATTERY

A desktop PC requires a nearby power outlet, but a laptop is capable of running off its internal battery for those times when AC is nowhere in sight. Consequently, you can use your laptop almost anywhere, including at a coffee shop, in a taxi, on an airplane, and even at the park. However, to make the most out of this portability, you need to take good care of the laptop battery. This includes saving as much energy as possible when you're on battery power, periodically reconditioning the battery, and replacing the battery at the end of its life cycle. This chapter shows you how to perform all these battery-related chores.

Understanding Laptop Batteries

A laptop PC has an internal battery that enables you to operate the computer without the use of an electrical outlet. The battery also serves as a backup source of power should the electricity fail. All laptop batteries are *rechargeable*, meaning that once the battery runs out of juice, you plug the laptop into an AC outlet and the battery automatically stocks up on a fresh supply of power. How long the battery lasts depends on the type of battery and what tasks you perform with your laptop (for example, simple emailing uses hardly any battery power, while watching a video uses lots of power).

Laptops use various types of battery technology, but the following three are the most common:

- **Nickel Metal Hydride Battery**—Older portable computers use rechargeable nickel metal hydride (NiMH) batteries. The NiMH type is being phased out because they can suffer from a problem called the *memory effect,* in which the battery loses capacity if you repeatedly recharge it without first fully discharging it.

- **Lithium-ion Battery**—Almost all new notebooks have rechargeable lithium-ion (Li-ion) batteries. Li-ion batteries are lighter and last longer than NiMH batteries, and Li-ion batteries do not suffer from the memory effect.

- **Lithium Polymer Battery**—The rechargeable lithium polymer (LiPo or Li-Poly) battery is a variation on the lithium-ion battery. LiPo batteries are generally smaller and lighter than Li-ion batteries and have about the same capacity. However, LiPo batteries are also more expensive, so they have only recently starting appearing in notebook computers.

Getting More Out of Your Battery

This chapter's main topic is replacing your laptop battery, but that doesn't mean you shouldn't first try to get as much as you can out of your *current* laptop battery. After all, batteries aren't cheap—replacements generally cost between $50 and $100, but can go as high as $175—so you might as well max out your current battery. This means two things: extending your battery's overall lifetime and extending the time you get with each charge.

Extending Your Battery's Life

Although all laptop batteries eventually fail, you can do a few things to extend a battery's productive lifetime for as long as possible:

- **Avoid temperature extremes**—Laptop batteries don't like it to be too hot or too cold, so avoid things like leaving your laptop in your car or trunk on very hot or very cold days, or letting the computer sit for a long time in direct sunlight. In fact, your laptop may not power up at all (assuming it's not on AC power) if it detects that the battery's current temperature is out of its safety zone. In particular, try to avoid letting your laptop get too hot too often because this will really shorten your battery's life.

- **Don't let the battery go unused**—Laptop batteries are happiest when they're used, so from time to time (at least every two weeks; preferably more often) be sure to unplug the power cord and let your laptop run on battery power. Note, too, that an idle battery will simply die after a while, so don't leave your laptop turned off for long periods.

- **Remove an idle battery**—If you won't be using your laptop for a long time— say, a month or more—remove the battery (see "Installing the Battery," later in this chapter) and store it in a spot that's dry and relatively cool.

 CAUTION Before removing the battery for storage, make sure it has some charge on it because the battery requires a small amount of charge to maintain its integrity while being stored. A charge of 40%–60% should be plenty.

- **Cycle the battery every now and then**—*Cycling* the laptop battery means switching to battery power, letting the battery drain completely, switching to AC power, and then letting the battery fully recharge. You should do this every few months or so, or every 20 to 30 times you perform a partial discharge. You should also cycle the battery if you haven't used your laptop on battery power for more than two weeks.

- **Don't cycle the battery *too* often**—Cycling the laptop battery is a good idea, but only if you don't do it too often. This is particularly true of lithium-based batteries, which dislike frequent full discharges.

Extending Your Battery's Charge

If you find yourself on a long plane trip, train or bus ride, or similar situation where you won't have access to electrical power for a while, and you don't have a backup battery with you, it's crucial to maximize battery life. Generally, this means turning off or closing anything you don't need while running on battery power. Here are some suggestions:

- **Let Windows do the work for you**—Windows offers various *power plans* that enable it to control various aspects of your laptop's power consumption (such as the monitor and hard disk). For maximum battery time, switch to the Power Saver plan. To do this, right-click the notification area's Power icon, click Power Options, and then click the Power Saver option. You can also click Change Plan Settings to display the Edit Plan Settings window, shown in Figure 17.1. In the On Battery column, select intervals for when Windows should dim the display, turn off the display, and put the computer to sleep. You can also turn down the screen brightness to save even more power.

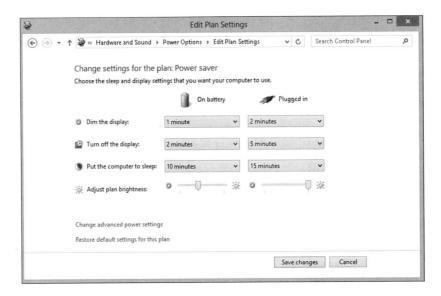

FIGURE 17.1

Use the Edit Plan Settings window to adjust the settings for the Power Saver plan.

- **Quit any unneeded applications**—Running programs may still use up some processor cycles, even when you're not actively using them. For example, your email program may check for new messages every so often. To avoid these power drains, you should shut down any application unnecessary for your work.

- **Avoid media**—Media tasks such as watching videos and listening to music are huge power drains, so forgo movies and tunes while on battery power.

- **Minimize your tasks**—Avoid secondary chores, such as checking for software updates and organizing your Media Player library. If your only goal is to finish your presentation, stick to that until it's done (given that you don't know how much time you'll have).

- **Sleep your laptop by hand, if necessary**—If you get interrupted—for example, the in-flight meal arrives—don't wait for Windows to put your laptop to sleep because those few minutes will use up precious battery time. Instead, put your laptop to sleep manually right away by closing the lid. If that doesn't work, tell Windows to sleep the laptop: In Windows 8, display the Charms menu, select Settings, select Power, and then select Sleep. In earlier versions of Windows, click Start, display the shutdown menu, and then click Sleep.

- **Disconnect any devices you don't need**—Even an unused device can drain battery power, so if you have anything connected to a USB port, disconnect it.

- **If you have a disc in the CD or DVD drive, eject the disc**—Even if you don't use the disc, the drive still occasionally spins up to read something from it, which drains battery power. Eject the disc if you don't need it.

- **Turn off Wi-Fi if you don't need it**—When Wi-Fi is on, it regularly checks for available wireless networks, which drains the battery. If you don't need to connect to a wireless network, turn off Wi-Fi to conserve energy. In Windows 8, display the Charms menu, click Settings, click the Network icon, and then click the Airplane Mode switch to On. In earlier versions of Windows, click Start, type **connections**, click View Network Connections, click Wireless Network Connection, and then click Disable This Network Device.

   TIP Many laptops come with an external button that turns the Wi-Fi antenna on and off, so it's often easiest just to toggle that button.

- **Use simple applications to accomplish simple tasks**—For example, if you're just typing a to-do list, you don't need to fire up Microsoft Word; use Notepad instead.

When Should You Replace the Battery?

It's an unfortunate fact of life that laptop batteries don't last forever. No matter which type of battery technology your laptop uses, the constant discharging and recharging eventually take their toll on the battery itself. In most cases, a Li-ion battery is good for anywhere from 200 to 400 discharge/recharge cycles (or about two or three years), which will keep your laptop powered for quite a while. However, eventually you'll start to notice one or both of the following:

- The battery runs down very quickly when your laptop is running without the benefit of AC. If you originally got four or five hours of typical use on battery power, eventually you'll get only two or even just one hour.

- The battery won't recharge at all.

If your battery life is down to an hour or less, or if you can't get it to charge at all, it's time to consider swapping that worn-out battery for a fresh one.

Buying a Battery

Of all the PC parts we've explored in this book, the purchase options for a laptop battery are by far the simplest. Unlike other components where you have to compare various features to get a part that is not only compatible with your system but also offers performance within your budget, a laptop battery has only one criteria: it must be an exact replacement for the current battery.

The easiest way to ensure you have the correct replacement is to purchase the new battery from the laptop manufacturer. The battery itself often provides you with a part number to use when ordering, as shown in Figure 17.2.

FIGURE 17.2

Some manufacturers helpfully provide you with a battery part number for easy ordering.

Ordering from the manufacturer ensures you get an exact replacement, but it will almost certainly cost you more because the manufacturer will charge you list price. A cheaper way to go is to look for the same battery online either at a major retailer such as Amazon, or one of the many third-party battery retailers, including the following:

Batteries.com (www.batteries.com)

eBatts (www.ebatts.com)

Laptop Battery Depot (www.laptopbatterydepot.com)

Laptops for Less (www.laptopbattery.net)

Installing the Battery

The good news about replacing your laptop battery is that it's almost always an easy job. The reason is that the vast majority of laptop batteries reside not inside the laptop itself, but as a detachable module that you can detach and reattach without having to access the laptop's innards.

How can you tell for sure that this is the case with your laptop? Turn your laptop over so that you can examine the bottom. Look for a slab that is longer than it is wide, something like the examples shown in Figure 17.3. Most batteries also come with several raised ridges along the exposed flat surface to help slide the battery out of its slot or socket.

FIGURE 17.3

Some examples of laptop batteries.

NOTE What if you *don't* see anything that looks like the sample batteries shown in Figure 17.3? That likely means the battery is inside the laptop, so you need to remove the bottom panel to access it. At this point I highly recommend you check out the laptop's user manual (you can usually find it online, if you don't know where your original copy is). The steps for removing the cover and locating and disconnecting internal batteries vary widely between manufacturers and even between models with the same manufacturer.

After you've located the battery, follow these steps to remove it and install the replacement:

1. Turn off and then unplug the laptop's AC adapter.

2. Open (usually by sliding or pressing) the latch, switch, or release button that unlocks the battery, as pointed out in Figure 17.4. Here are two things to note:

   • Some laptops come with *two* release buttons (as is the case in Figure 17.4).

   • In some cases you must hold the release button (or buttons) in place while you remove the battery.

Battery release buttons

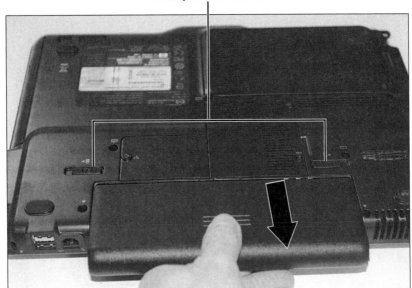

FIGURE 17.4

Begin by opening the release button (or buttons, as shown here) to unlock the battery.

3. Slide the battery out of its slot or socket.

4. Remove the new battery from its packaging, being careful not to touch any exposed metal contacts.

5. Slide the new battery into the laptop's slot or socket.

6. Close the latch, switch, or release button to lock the new battery into place.

7. Connect the AC adapter.

8. Restart the laptop and allow the battery to fully charge.

CAUTION Be sure to recycle your old battery. Do *not* just throw it in the garbage! Check with your local municipality to see if it offers a battery-recycling program. Also, many major retailers (such as Best Buy, Office Depot, and Staples) offer battery-recycling programs.

THE ABSOLUTE MINIMUM

This chapter showed you how to get the most out of your current laptop battery and how to replace the battery once it's reached the end of its useful life. Here are a few of the highlights:

- Most modern laptop batteries are either lithium-ion (Li-ion) or lithium polymer (Li-poly). Neither type suffers from the memory effect associated with older nickel metal hydride (NiMH) batteries.

- To maximize your laptop battery's usable lifetime, avoid extreme heat and cold, use the battery regularly, and cycle the battery every so often.

- To maximize your laptop battery's usable charge, switch to Windows' Power Saver plan, use applications sparingly, avoid media, disconnect unused devices, turn off Wi-Fi, and sleep the laptop whenever you don't need it for a while.

- You need to replace the battery if you find that it runs down very quickly after a full recharge, or if it doesn't recharge at all.

- Most laptop batteries are removable modules that you can disconnect by opening the release button (or buttons) and then sliding the battery out of its slot or socket.

18

UPGRADING YOUR NETWORK

Your PC needs some networking hardware to connect to the Internet, assuming you have a broadband connection. Moreover, you probably have at least one other computer, and it would be handy if all your machines could see each other and share resources such as folders, printers, and Internet connections. That's what networking is all about, but to get that far requires a hardware investment. This chapter gives you the information you need to make good networking investments. I describe the network devices you can add to your PC, but I also expand things a bit and discuss some external devices that you'll need to get your network up and running.

Understanding Wireless Networks

If you did any networked computing in the previous century, your PC was connected to your network using a special attachment called an ethernet cable, which ran from your PC to a box called a router or switch. Ethernet technology is still alive and well nearly a decade and a half into *this* century, but it's exceedingly rare for a small network (such as one you might want in your home or small office) to use wired connections. Instead, wireless is the way to go, so that's what I talk about in this chapter.

Wireless devices transmit data and communicate with other devices using *radio frequency (RF)* signals that are beamed from one device to another. Although these radio signals are similar to those used in commercial radio broadcasts, they operate on a different frequency. For example, if you use a wireless keyboard and mouse, you have an RF receiver device plugged into a USB port on your computer (usually). The keyboard and mouse have built-in RF transmitters. When you press a key or move or click the mouse, the transmitter sends the appropriate RF signal, that signal is picked up by the receiver, and the corresponding keystroke or mouse action is passed along to Windows just as though the original device had been connected to the computer directly.

A *radio transceiver* is a device that can act as both a transmitter and a receiver of radio signals. All wireless devices that require two-way communications use a transceiver. In wireless networking—also called *wireless local area network* (WLAN)—your PC requires a network interface card (NIC) that comes with a built-in transceiver that enables the NIC to send and receive RF signals. (For more information, see "Learning About Wireless NICs," later in this chapter.) The resulting beam takes the place of the network cable. The wireless NIC communicates with a nearby *wireless router*, a device that contains a transceiver that enables the device to pass along network signals. (For more details, see "Putting It All Together with a Wireless Router," later in this chapter.)

The most common wireless networking technology is *wireless fidelity*, which is almost always shortened to *Wi-Fi* (which rhymes with *hi-fi*); the generic Institute of Electrical and Electronics Engineers (IEEE) designation for this wireless networking standard is *802.11*. The five main types are 802.11a, 802.11b, 802.11g, 802.11n, and 802.11ac—each of which has its own range and speed limits, as you see in the next few sections.

 CAUTION All wireless speeds are theoretical because interference and bandwidth limitations almost always mean that real-world speeds are slower than the optimum speeds.

802.11b

The original 802.11 standard was published by the IEEE in 1997, but few people took it seriously because it was hobbled by a maximum transmission rate of just 2Mbps. By 1999, the IEEE had worked out not one but *two* new standards: 802.11a and 802.11b. The 802.11b standard became the more popular of the two, so I discuss it first.

The 802.11b standard upped the Wi-Fi data transmission rate to 11Mbps, which is just a bit faster than 10BASE-T, the original ethernet standard, which has a maximum rate of 10Mbps. The indoor range of 802.11b is about 115 feet.

The 802.11b standard operates on the 2.4GHz radio frequency, which is an unregulated frequency often used by other consumer products such as microwave ovens, cordless telephones, and baby monitors. This keeps the price of 802.11b hardware low, but it can also cause interference problems when you attempt to access the network near another device that's using the 2.4GHz frequency.

802.11a

The 802.11a standard was released at around the same time as the 802.11b standard. There are two key differences between these standards: 802.11a has a maximum transmission rate of 54Mbps, and it operates using the regulated 5.0GHz radio frequency band. This higher frequency band means 802.11a devices don't have the same interference problems as 802.11b devices, but it also means 802.11a hardware is more expensive, offers a shorter range (about 75 feet), and has trouble penetrating solid surfaces such as walls. So, despite its impressive transmission speed, 802.11a just had too many negative factors against it, and 802.11b won the hearts of consumers and became the first true wireless networking standard.

802.11g

During the battle between 802.11a and 802.11b, it became clear that consumers and small businesses really wanted the best of both worlds. That is, they wanted a WLAN technology that was as fast and as interference free as 802.11a but that had the longer range and cheaper cost of 802.11b. Alas, "the best of both worlds" is a state rarely achieved in the real world. However, the IEEE came close when it introduced the next version of the wireless networking standard in 2003: 802.11g. Like its 802.11a predecessor, 802.11g has a theoretical maximum transmission rate of 54Mbps, and like 802.11b, 802.11g boasts an indoor range of about 115 feet and is cheap to manufacture. That cheapness comes from its use of the 2.4GHz RF band, which means 802.11g devices can suffer from interference from other nearby consumer devices that use the same frequency.

Despite the possibility of interference, 802.11g quickly became the most popular of the Wi-Fi standards, and almost all WLAN devices sold today support 802.11g.

 NOTE Most WLAN devices support multiple Wi-Fi standards. Older devices often offer *a/b* support, meaning you can use the device with both 802.11a and 802.11b devices. Newer WLAN devices now often offer *b/g/n* support, meaning you can use the device with 802.11b, 802.11g, and 802.11n devices.

802.11n

The 802.11n standard implements a technology called *multiple-input multiple-output (MIMO)* that uses multiple transmitters and receivers in each device. This enables multiple data streams on a single device, which greatly improves WLAN performance. For example, using three transmitters and two receivers (the standard configuration), 802.11n promises a theoretical transmission speed of up to 600Mbps. The 802.11n standard also doubles the wireless range to about 230 feet.

802.11ac

The IEEE is working on a new wireless standard called 802.11ac as this book goes to press, and this amendment is expected to be finalized sometime in 2014. The 802.11ac standard extends the MIMO technology of 802.11n and adds other new features that theoretically promise speeds up to three times faster than 802.11n. In fact, so-called Draft 5.0 devices now available promise transmission speeds of 1.75Gbps (1,750Mbps). "Draft 5.0" refers to the fifth draft of the 802.11ac standard, which was approved by the IEEE in February 2013. The word on the street is that there are unlikely to be substantive changes to the standard between the Draft 5.0 version and the final version.

Does this mean it's safe to purchase Draft 5.0 devices now? The answer is a resounding *maybe*. Most WLAN manufacturers are saying that their current Draft 5.0 products will be upgradeable; so, if there are changes between now and the final draft, you'll be able to apply a patch to the device to make it conform to the new standard. Trusting that this will be so means taking a bit of a chance on your part, so *caveat emptor*.

 NOTE What does it mean to say that a device is "upgradeable"? Most devices are controlled by *firmware*, programming code embedded in the device, often stored in a special memory chip called an *EPROM*, which is short for erasable programmable read-only memory. The *erasable* part means the firmware can be replaced by a newer version; hence, the device's firmware is upgradeable.

Learning About Wireless NICs

A wireless network interface card is a transceiver that can both transmit data to the network and receive signals from the network. The rate at which the NIC processes this data and the distance from the network that you can roam depend on the 802.11 standard implemented by the NIC. Almost all wireless NICs sold today (or that come preinstalled in new computers) are 802.11n compliant, and most implement b/g/n support, meaning the NIC also works seamlessly with 802.11b and 802.11g NICs and devices.

There are three main types of wireless NICs:

- **Expansion card**—One common wireless NIC type is an expansion card you insert into a free slot inside your PC. Most computers today use a PCI bus, so you need to get a PCI network adapter. The NIC's backplate usually includes a small post onto which you screw the antenna, either directly or via a longish wire that enables you to position the antenna to avoid interference. Figure 18.1 shows both types.

FIGURE 18.1

You insert an internal wireless NIC into a free slot on the system bus inside your computer.

- **USB**—If your motherboard doesn't have any free slots, you can still go wireless by attaching an external wireless NIC to an open USB port. As with all USB devices, get a USB 2.0 wireless NIC for optimum performance. USB wireless NICs either attach directly to the USB port or come with a USB cable, as shown in Figure 18.2.

FIGURE 18.2

A USB wireless NIC attaches to a free USB slot on your computer.

- **Motherboard NIC**—A few manufacturers are now offering a wireless NIC built directly in to the motherboard, and the post onto which you screw the antenna appears flush with the rest of the back panel connectors, as shown in Figure 18.3.

Antenna post

FIGURE 18.3

A wireless NIC built in to a motherboard.

Putting It All Together with a Wireless Router

If you just want to exchange a bit of data with one or more nearby computers, Windows enables you to set up and connect to an ad-hoc wireless network where the computers themselves manage the connection. A longer-term solution is to set up and connect to an *infrastructure* wireless network, which requires an extra device called a *wireless router*. A wireless router (Figure 18.4 shows a couple of examples) is a device that receives and transmits signals from wireless computers to form a wireless network, as shown in Figure 18.5.

FIGURE 18.4

Examples of wireless routers.

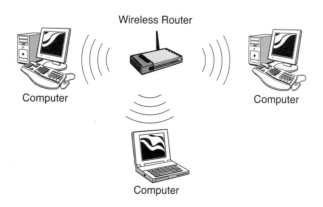

FIGURE 18.5

Add a wireless router to create a wireless network.

For a wireless router to work properly, it must support an 802.11 standard that's compatible with all your wireless NICs. For example, if all your wireless NICs use 802.11n, your wireless router must also support 802.11n. Similarly, if your wireless NICs are a mixture of 802.11g and 802.11n, your wireless router must implement 802.11g/n.

A wireless router is really two devices in one: a wireless *access point* that enables the sending and receiving of wireless signals, and a *router* that enables you to give your wireless network users access to the Internet (see Figure 18.6) by connecting a broadband modem to the WAN port in the back of the wireless router.

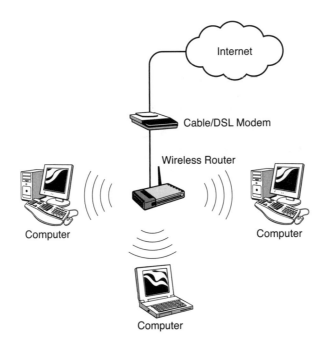

FIGURE 18.6

With a combination wireless router and broadband modem, you can give wireless network users access to the Internet.

A Buyer's Guide to Wireless Networking Hardware

Purchasing wireless hardware is, unfortunately, no easier than buying other types of PC hardware because the acronyms and jargon are just as prevalent. If there's an advantage to outfitting a wireless network, it's that to get started you really need just two types of equipment: wireless NICs for each PC that needs one and a wireless router to manage the network. The next two sections offer you a few tips and suggestions on what to look for and what to avoid when purchasing devices in these two wireless hardware categories.

Before getting to those tips, I want to emphasize the idea of quality versus price when it comes to wireless networking devices. There is an inherently finicky quality to Wi-Fi networking because of interference from other devices, humidity, and even the phase of the moon (or so it seems on occasion). Quality wireless devices minimize this flakiness, so on that point alone they're worth the extra few dollars. Of course, wireless devices manufactured by reputable companies are also reliable, conform to the 802.11 standard, come with a wide selection of device drivers, and offer decent support. Here are some companies that manufacture quality wireless networking devices:

> ASUS (asus.com)
>
> Belkin (belkin.com)
>
> D-Link (dlink.com)
>
> Linksys (linksys.com)
>
> NETGEAR (netgear.com)
>
> TP-Link (tp-link.com)
>
> TRENDnet (trendnet.com)

Purchasing a Wireless NIC

When you need to purchase a wireless NIC or two, here are some issues to think about in advance:

- **Choose internal or external**—The fastest wireless NICs—those that support 802.11n or even 802.11ac Draft 5.0 if you want to take the plunge (more on this later)—are available both as internal cards and as external USB devices. The choice really comes down to whether you have a free USB port. Most computers come with a decent collection of USB ports these days, but more and more devices are coming out in USB form, so it's not unusual for USB ports to fill up.

NOTE If your computer's USB ports are full, consider purchasing a *USB hub*, a device that offers multiple USB ports (usually three, four, or seven).

- **Get only USB 2.0 NICs**—If you want to purchase a USB wireless NIC, make sure it uses the faster USB 2.0 technology, and not USB 1.1. Wireless USB 1.1 NICs are actually hard to find nowadays, but it pays to read the fine print in the specifications, just to be sure.

- **Get wireless security**—Wireless security is a crucial topic, and it's important not only that all your wireless devices use the same type of security, but also the strongest possible security. Right now, that means the NIC must support the *Wi-Fi Protected Access (WPA)* security standard, ideally the latest iteration, which is WPA2. At all costs, avoid any wireless NIC that supports only *Wired Equivalent Privacy (WEP)*, an older security scheme that is easily compromised.

- **Choose 802.11g or 802.11n**—This one's a no-brainer: Go with 802.11n, no matter what. If you can even find 802.11g devices (perhaps at a geek's garage sale), they'll be temptingly cheap. However, remember that you get up to 12 times the speed with 802.11n, and that extra speed is worth it, believe me.

- **To 802.11ac or not to 802.11ac**—As I write this, 802.11ac devices are still relatively rare, but they should be thick on the ground by the time you read this. Should you take a chance on these products, even though they'll be more expensive than their 802.11n counterparts? My own feeling is that if you have a real need for more wireless speed—for example, if you're itching to stream video over a wireless connection—you should probably jump in. One strategy to consider is purchasing all your 802.11ac devices from the same manufacturer, the theory being that devices from the same company should work well together. So, for example, if you want to purchase 802.11ac NICs from, say, Linksys, you should also purchase your 802.11ac wireless router from Linksys.

- **Check the claims**—Lots of wireless NICs claim they use fancy new technology to, say, double the data transmission rate or triple the range of standard 802.11g. In some cases, these claims are true. For example, I mentioned earlier that 802.11n uses MIMO technology to improve speed and range, but some companies are incorporating MIMO into 802.11g NICs, too, and those NICs show genuine improvements in speed and range. Other claims might or might not be true. It's best in these cases to do some homework by reading reviews of the NICs to see whether the claims hold up under real-world conditions. Most online retailers solicit reviews from purchasers, online networking sites review the latest NICs, and you can use sites such as Epinions (epinions.com) and ConsumerReview (consumerreview.com) to search for reviews of devices you're considering.

Purchasing a Wireless Router

The wireless router is the most complicated of the wireless products, so not surprisingly the ads and specifications for these devices are riddled with $10 technical terms, acronyms and abbreviations, and a fair dose of marketing hype. Fortunately, you can ignore most of what you read and just concentrate on the following points:

- **Purchase wireless security**—I mentioned in the preceding section that you should get only wireless NICs that support WPA security, ideally WPA2. It's important that your wireless router supports the same security standard. To see why, understand that most new wireless NICs support multiple security standards, usually WEP, WPA, and WPA2. If you purchase an older wireless router that supports only, say, WEP, *all* your wireless activity will use WEP because the NICs will lower their security to work with the router. So, again, you should ideally purchase only a wireless router that supports the WPA2 standard.

- **Make sure it's a router, not an access point**—A device that's very similar to a wireless router is a wireless access point. However, the latter is designed only to offer wireless networking; it doesn't enable you to share an Internet connection.

- **Check the 802.11 support**—Because it's the router's job to manage your network's wireless connections, you must ensure that the router supports the same 802.11 standards as your wireless devices. For example, if all your wireless devices use 802.11n, you can get a wireless router that supports only 802.11n. However, if your wireless devices use a mixture of 802.11g and 802.11n, your router must support both standards. If you get an 802.11ac wireless router, make sure it also supports 802.11g and 802.11n because you'll certainly have other devices on your network that use those standards.

- **Make sure it has a firewall**—All wireless routers that have built-in routing technology support network address translation (NAT) for security, but for maximum safety ensure that the router comes with a dedicated firewall you can configure.

THE ABSOLUTE MINIMUM

Upgrading your network is a matter of upgrading your wireless technology to the highest standard you can afford. Here are the details:

- Wi-Fi is by far the most common wireless networking technology, and the generic designation for the Wi-Fi standard is *802.11*. The five main types are 802.11a, 802.11b, 802.11g, 802.11n, and 802.11ac.

- The current Wi-Fi standard is 802.11n, which offers a maximum theoretical transmission speed of 600Mbps.

- The next wireless standard is called 802.11ac, which is expected to be finalized sometime in 2014. The 802.11ac standard offers transmission speeds of up to 1.75Gbps.

- A wireless network interface card (NIC) is a transceiver that can both transmit data to the network and receive signals from the network.

- A wireless router is a device that receives and transmits signals from wireless computers to form a wireless network and to share a broadband modem's Internet access.

- When purchasing wireless networking equipment, make sure you get the WPA2 security standard for maximum protection.

Index

E

Q

R

S

W

X – Z

Fixing Your Computer

ABSOLUTE BEGINNER'S GUIDE

No experience necessary!

Paul McFedries

que

FREE
Online Edition

Your purchase of *Fixing Your Computer Absolute Beginner's Guide* includes access to a free online edition for 45 days through the **Safari Books Online** subscription service. Nearly every Que book is available online through **Safari Books Online**, along with thousands of books and videos from publishers such as Addison-Wesley Professional, Cisco Press, Exam Cram, IBM Press, O'Reilly Media, Prentice Hall, Sams, and VMware Press.

Safari Books Online is a digital library providing searchable, on-demand access to thousands of technology, digital media, and professional development books and videos from leading publishers. With one monthly or yearly subscription price, you get unlimited access to learning tools and information on topics including mobile app and software development, tips and tricks on using your favorite gadgets, networking, project management, graphic design, and much more.

Activate your FREE Online Edition at
informit.com/safarifree

STEP 1: Enter the coupon code: CGVCUWA.

STEP 2: New Safari users, complete the brief registration form.
Safari subscribers, just log in.

If you have difficulty registering on Safari or accessing the online edition,
please e-mail customer-service@safaribooksonline.com